Transforming Education With AI-Powered Personalized Learning

Houssem Chemingui
Brest Business School, France

Munir Ahmad
Survey of Pakistan, Pakistan

Suela Bylykbashi
Brest Business School, France

IGI Global
Scientific Publishing
Publishing Tomorrow's Research Today

Vice President of Editorial	Melissa Wagner
Director of Acquisitions	Mikaela Felty
Director of Book Development	Jocelynn Hessler
Production Manager	Mike Brehm
Cover Design	Jose Rosado

Published in the United States of America by
IGI Global Scientific Publishing
701 East Chocolate Avenue
Hershey, PA, 17033, USA
Tel: 717-533-8845
Fax: 717-533-7115
Website: https://www.igi-global.com E-mail: cust@igi-global.com

Library of Congress Cataloging-in-Publication Data

Names: Chemingui, Houssem, 1990- editor. | Ahmad, Munir, 1978- editor.
Title: Transforming education with AI-powered personalized learning / edited by: Houssem Chemingui, Munir Ahmad.
Description: Hershey PA : IGI Global Scientific Publishing, [2025] | Includes bibliographical references. | Summary: "This book provides a comprehensive examination of the transformative impact of AI on the educational landscape"-- Provided by publisher.
Identifiers: LCCN 2024054479 (print) | LCCN 2024054480 (ebook) | ISBN 9798369383827 (hardcover) | ISBN 9798369383834 (paperback) | ISBN 9798369383841 (ebook)
Subjects: LCSH: Artificial intelligence--Educational applications.
Classification: LCC LB1028.43 .T737 2025 (print) | LCC LB1028.43 (ebook) | DDC 370.285/63--dc23/eng/20250312
LC record available at https://lccn.loc.gov/2024054479
LC ebook record available at https://lccn.loc.gov/2024054480
British Cataloguing in Publication Data
A Cataloguing in Publication record for this book is available from the British Library.

Table of Contents

Detailed Table of Contents

AI in education has evolved from rule-based systems to generative AI, enabling personalized learning and adaptive instruction. While AI enhances education through intelligent tutoring and automated feedback, challenges remain, including ethical concerns, data privacy, and accessibility gaps. This chapter traces AI's historical development, examines key milestones, and explores solutions for equitable integration. Balancing innovation with ethical responsibility is crucial for AI's future in education.

This study explores the impact of AI-driven tutoring systems on personalized learning, aiming to identify best practices for their integration in diverse educational contexts. Utilizing a mixed-methods approach, the research combines qualitative narratives from educators with quantitative data on student engagement and performance. Key findings reveal that tools like ChatGPT and Canva significantly enhance personalization, engagement, and collaboration among students, while also providing actionable insights for educators. However, challenges such as equity, accessibility, and the need for professional development are highlighted, emphasizing the importance of addressing these issues for effective implementation. The study concludes that while AI tools hold great potential for transforming education, careful consideration of ethical implications and long-term impacts is essential for maximizing their benefits.

AI is revolutionizing education with personalized learning, real-time feedback, and better instruction. To improve learning and efficiency, teachers are using AI-powered tutoring and grading technologies. Schools are unprepared to deploy AI tools for data privacy, algorithmic bias, and equitable access. Many teachers are unprepared for AI's technological and ethical problems in education. To assist teachers incorporate AI, this chapter covers professional development, hands-on training, and ethics. Our research shows that concentrated AI training can considerably increase instructors' AI tool use and responsibility. Results suggest that AI in education can create more customized and egalitarian learning environments with proper management and professional growth. These repercussions highlight the need for educators, governments, and institutions to collaborate to use AI's potential while preserving student privacy and promoting justice in education.

This chapter investigates the transformative impact of artificial intelligence (AI) on student learning outcomes, concentrating on the possibilities and constraints of AI-powered personalized learning systems. AI offers a dynamic approach to education by enabling tailored learning paths that respond to individual student needs, enhancing both interest and accomplishment. Through a detailed study of important success measures, this chapter illustrates how AI-driven technologies boost student performance and outlines the primary issues associated with their adoption, including data protection, teacher adaptability, and the digital divide. Case examples of successful AI integration highlight the effectiveness of these technologies, while future recommendations underline the need for equal access and continuing growth in the field. Ultimately, this chapter contends that AI has the potential to improve education, but success requires careful monitoring and addressing inherent obstacles.

Student outcomes in enhanced learning environments can be effectively predicted using advanced machine learning techniques. This study proposes an integrated approach combining Random Forest and XGBoost models to predict student performance accurately. Random Forest provides stability and robustness in handling noisy and imbalanced data, while XGBoost refines predictions by iteratively correcting errors. By integrating these models through ensemble techniques such as stacking, the method capitalizes on their complementary strengths to achieve superior prediction accuracy. The approach is validated using a comprehensive dataset that includes demographic, academic, behavioral, and interactional attributes. The integrated model demonstrates improved predictive performance, enabling early identification of at-risk students and supporting personalized educational interventions. This work underscores the potential of machine learning in enhancing education outcomes through data-driven insights.

This chapter delves into the performance evaluation of blockchain-integrated Artificial Intelligence (AI) and Machine Learning (ML) in Cognitive Internet of Things (CIoT) systems, focusing on data analytics. We examine metrics for assessing the precision and accuracy of CIoT systems enhanced by blockchain technology. The chapter outlines experimental designs for evaluating these systems, comparing their performance with traditional AI/ML data analytics that do not use blockchain. Benchmarking methods are discussed to measure and contrast the effectiveness of blockchain-enabled data analytics. Through these evaluations, we provide insights into the practical advantages of incorporating blockchain with AI/ML to improve data analytics in CIoT applications.

The Book Review Application is a comprehensive web platform developed using React.js for the front end and Spring Boot for the back end. The application offers features such as personalized book lists, and the ability to write and rate reviews. React.js ensures a fast, interactive, and responsive user interface. Spring Boot provides a robust back end with RESTful APIs to handle book data, user information, and review submissions. MongoDB is used to store book details, user profiles, and reviews, offering flexibility for managing large and unstructured data sets. Administrators have access to manage book entries, approve or delete reviews, and monitor the platform's activity. Security is integrated through user authentication and role-based access control, ensuring that only authorized users can modify sensitive data. The application also supports real-time updates, enabling dynamic interaction between users and the system without page reloads, handles high traffic, provides scalable user-friendly environment for book enthusiasts to connect, discover, and engage in literary world.

This chapter, discuss how AI technologies can be applied in curriculum design, especially in promoting individualized learning and equity in education. The need for personalized learning has been emphasized, as educational settings are becoming more complex and AI has the ability to process students' information and modify the educational content in accordance with the learners' tastes and interests. With the use of adaptive learning devices, educators assist in developing adaptive curricula which fit learners with diverse educational and cultural backgrounds. This chapter in addition touches on the issues of biasness in AI systems and the potential of such

Preface

Education has always been at the heart of societal progress, serving as the foundation upon which individuals build knowledge, skills, and critical thinking. Yet, for centuries, the structure of education has remained relatively unchanged, rooted in standardized models that often fail to accommodate the rich diversity of student backgrounds, abilities, and learning styles. Today, we are witnessing a profound shift, a transformation driven by the integration of artificial intelligence (AI) into the fabric of educational systems.

Transforming Education With AI-Powered Personalized Learning emerges at this crucial juncture. This book seeks to explore how AI, particularly advanced techniques such as generative models, neural networks, and natural language processing, is revolutionizing the way we design, deliver, and experience education. AI no longer belongs solely to the realm of science fiction or high-tech laboratories, it is actively reshaping classrooms, influencing pedagogical strategies, and enabling personalized learning at an unprecedented scale.

The promise of AI lies in its ability to tailor learning experiences to individual students, adjusting content, pace, and delivery methods in real time based on continuous analysis of learner data. Such personalized approaches not only enhance academic outcomes and student engagement but also promote equity by providing customized support to those who need it most. From automated content creation to intelligent tutoring systems and adaptive assessments, AI offers tools that make learning more dynamic, inclusive, and responsive.

This book is designed to serve multiple audiences. For educators and academic leaders, it offers insights into how AI can be leveraged to support innovative teaching practices. For computer scientists and engineers, it provides context and examples of how their technologies are being applied to real-world educational challenges. For researchers and policy-makers, it highlights critical themes such as ethics, privacy, digital literacy, and the implications of AI for the future of learning.

Special attention is also given to emerging intersections between AI and other technological domains, such as blockchain, which offers new models of credentialing and academic record-keeping, and data analytics, which powers evidence-based decision-making in education systems.

In writing this book, the goal has been to bridge the gap between theory and practice, between visionary thinking and actionable insight. Whether you are a teacher experimenting with AI tools in the classroom, a researcher studying the pedagogical impacts of adaptive learning, or a technologist developing the next generation of educational software, this book offers perspectives and resources to guide your journey.

The transformation of education through AI is not a distant possibility, it is happening now. And as we move forward, we are collectively tasked with shaping a future where technology enhances, rather than replaces, the human connections and creativity that lie at the heart of meaningful learning.

by Houssem Chemingui, Phd

Chapter 1
Foundations of AI-Driven Education

Houssem Chemingui
https://orcid.org/0000-0002-3351-250X
Brest Business School, France

Suela Bylykbashi
Brest Business School, France

ABSTRACT

AI in education has evolved from rule-based systems to generative AI, enabling personalized learning and adaptive instruction. While AI enhances education through intelligent tutoring and automated feedback, challenges remain, including ethical concerns, data privacy, and accessibility gaps. This chapter traces AI's historical development, examines key milestones, and explores solutions for equitable integration. Balancing innovation with ethical responsibility is crucial for AI's future in education.

DOI: 10.4018/979-8-3693-8382-7.ch001

1. INTRODUCTION TO AI IN EDUCATION

Context

The integration of technology into education has undergone a remarkable transformation over the past six decades (Harry, 2023; Holmes et al., 2022, Zhai et al., 2021), evolving from rudimentary computer-assisted instruction systems (Blok et al., 2002) to advanced generative AI tools (Baidoo-Anu et al., 2023). This evolution reflects broader technological advancements and shifting educational paradigms, as educators and technologists have sought to harness the potential of AI to enhance learning experiences. From the early days of static, rule-based systems to the dynamic, adaptive, and generative AI tools of today, the journey of AI in education has been marked by both breakthroughs and challenges. Understanding this historical progression is essential for appreciating the current state of AI in education and envisioning its future trajectory.

Problem Statement

Despite the significant advancements in AI technologies, their integration into educational settings has not been without challenges (Pedro et al., 2019). Early AI systems, such as expert systems (Khanna et al., 2010) and rule-based models (Aleven, 2010), were limited in their ability to adapt to individual learners' needs, while modern AI tools, including generative AI, face ethical, practical, and accessibility concerns (Al-kfairy et al., 2024). Key questions arise:

- How has the role of AI in education evolved from its inception to the present day?
- What are the key technological milestones that have shaped the development of AI in education?
- What challenges have hindered the widespread adoption of AI in educational contexts, and how can they be addressed?

Objectives and Contributions

This chapter aims to:

- Trace the historical evolution of AI in education, highlighting key technological milestones and their impact on teaching and learning.
- Examine the transition from early AI systems, such as expert systems, to modern generative AI tools, emphasizing their capabilities and limitations.
- Identify the challenges associated with integrating AI into education, including ethical concerns, data privacy issues, and the digital divide.
- Provide a foundation for understanding how AI technologies can be leveraged to create more personalized, inclusive, and effective learning experiences.

This chapter contributes to the broader discourse on AI in education by:

- Offering a comprehensive historical overview of AI's role in education, contextualizing its evolution within technological and pedagogical advancements.
- Highlighting the transformative potential of generative AI in creating dynamic, interactive, and personalized learning experiences.
- Addressing critical challenges and ethical considerations that must be resolved to ensure equitable and responsible AI integration in education.
- Providing a framework for understanding how AI technologies, such as machine learning (ML), natural language processing (NLP), and reinforcement learning (RL), can be applied to enhance educational outcomes.

Structure of the Chapter

The remainder of this chapter is structured to provide a comprehensive understanding of AI in education. It begins with a discussion on the Historical Context and Evolution, exploring how educational technologies have developed over time and led to the current integration of AI in education. The chapter then delves into the key concepts in AI for Learning, examining fundamental AI technologies and their specific applications within educational settings. It also highlights the gap between theory and practice in bridging research and practice, drawing on case studies and real-world examples. The vision for the chapter outlines the objectives of the chapter, emphasizing both the opportunities and challenges AI presents for educators and institutions. Finally, the conclusion provides a summary of the chapter's key takeaways, looking ahead to the future potential of AI in education and areas requiring further exploration and development.

2. HISTORICAL CONTEXT AND EVOLUTION

The integration of technology into education began in the 1960s with the advent of computer-assisted instruction (CAI) (Fletcher et al., 1995). Early milestones such as IBM's PLATO system[1] and MIT's LOGO programming language[2] focused on enhancing the learning experience by providing interactive content, albeit in a limited, static format. These systems were designed to offer structured learning paths, but the technology available at the time constrained their scope and flexibility.

In the 1980s and 1990s, the rise of expert systems (Ana, 2020) aimed to replicate the knowledge and behavior of human tutors, but these systems lacked the ability to adapt dynamically to individual students' needs. These early AI systems were rule-based and largely dependent on static inputs, which limited their scalability and applicability in diverse educational contexts. Despite these challenges, expert systems offered valuable insights into the potential of AI in education, which would shape future innovations.

The turn of the millennium marked a significant shift, as improvements in computational power and the advent of ML (Kučak et al., 2018), NLP (Alhawiti, 2014), and big data analytics (Murumba et Micheni, 2017) led to more sophisticated AI applications. This period saw the rise of AI-driven recommendation systems, virtual learning assistants, and predictive analytics used to assess and predict student performance. These advancements allowed educational technologies to move from simple automation of tasks to dynamic, personalized learning experiences.

A key aspect of this evolution has been the role of generative AI. Initially, AI systems in education were focused on automation and adaptation, but with the introduction of generative AI, new capabilities emerged. Generative AI models, such as GPT (Fuchs, 2023), have the ability to create original content, simulate real-world scenarios, and provide personalized feedback in real time. These systems are now able to generate learning materials, solve complex problems interactively, and even provide tutoring in various subjects. This shift from AI as a passive tool to an active, generative agent represents the latest phase in the evolution of AI in education. Today, AI tools in education include everything from personalized learning platforms, AI-driven chatbots, and virtual assistants, to AI-based systems that provide tailored feedback and automate administrative tasks. Despite the promising progress, challenges related to data privacy, the digital divide, algorithmic bias, and ethical concerns still hinder the full potential of AI in educational contexts. These concerns must be addressed as AI becomes more pervasive in classrooms and learning environments.

Generative AI has marked a new era in education by shifting from tools that assist with tasks (e.g., grading, scheduling) to creating entirely new learning experiences. This includes generating educational content like quizzes, reading material, and problem-solving scenarios, offering students the chance to interact with dynamic content that is tailored to their needs. Unlike traditional AI applications, which were limited to pre-programmed responses or rule-based actions, generative AI can create novel responses, explanations, and solutions, enhancing the learning experience by providing personalized feedback and assistance on demand. For instance, generative AI systems are capable of producing detailed answers to complex questions, simulating real-world problems, and even writing essays or reports based on a set of instructions. These capabilities not only make learning more interactive but also bridge gaps where access to personalized teaching may be limited, such as in large classrooms or underfunded educational institutions. Moreover, these systems can support educators by automating content generation and offering real-time feedback on students' progress.

Table 1 outlines the key milestones in the development and integration of AI technologies in education, highlighting the transition from early, limited systems to the advanced generative AI tools.

Table 1. Evolution of AI in Education: From Expert Systems to Generative AI

Aspect	Early AI Systems (1980s-1990s)	Modern AI Systems (2000s-Present)	Generative AI in Education (2020s-Present)
Technology	Expert systems, rule-based learning	ML, NLP, big data	Generative AI (e.g., GPT-3), ML, deep learning
Adaptability	Limited dynamic adaptability	Personalized learning, dynamic feedback	High adaptability; generates real-time content and personalized feedback
Data Utilization	Basic student data for diagnostics	Big data analytics for student performance and engagement	Uses large datasets to generate content, answer questions, simulate scenarios
Interactivity	Simple user interfaces with predefined responses	Interactive, dynamic, and responsive to student inputs	Generates real-time, interactive learning experiences and content
Purpose	Mimicking human tutoring	Automating administrative tasks, recommending learning paths	Generating new content, real-time problem solving, and personalized tutoring

While the integration of AI, especially generative AI, holds tremendous potential for revolutionizing education, its adoption is not without challenges. One of the key barriers is data privacy and security concerns (Haldar, 2024). AI systems rely heavily on collecting and analyzing student data, which can raise ethical issues if not properly safeguarded. There are also concerns about the digital divide, where access to advanced AI tools may be uneven, particularly in lower-income or rural areas. Furthermore, biases embedded in AI algorithms could perpetuate inequalities in education if not properly addressed.

Despite these challenges, AI's potential to reshape education remains undeniable. As technology continues to evolve, it is crucial for educational stakeholders, policymakers, educators, and technology developers, to work together to create frameworks that address these concerns while leveraging AI to improve educational outcomes.

3. KEY CONCEPTS IN AI FOR LEARNING

AI in education harnesses a variety of core technologies that enable more personalized, interactive, and efficient learning experiences. Below is an exploration of the most prominent AI technologies and their applications within educational settings:

ML

ML is one of the most pivotal AI technologies in education. ML algorithms are used to create adaptive learning platforms that can tailor content and assessments to individual students based on their performance (Kotsiantis et al., 2004). By analyzing vast amounts of student interaction data, ML models can predict learning trajectories, identifying areas where students excel or struggle. This allows for the delivery of personalized recommendations, such as supplementary resources or customized learning paths, enhancing the learning experience for each student. For example, platforms like Khan Academy and Duolingo utilize ML to adjust lesson difficulty and content presentation in real-time, ensuring that students receive challenges aligned with their proficiency levels. These systems continually learn from student behavior, adapting content dynamically to provide optimal learning opportunities. This personalized approach is proven to improve student engagement and retention rates.

NLP

NLP enables AI systems to understand, interpret, and generate human language. This technology powers a range of tools in educational environments, including chatbots, automated feedback systems, and virtual tutors (Admane et al., 2024). NLP allows AI-driven applications to process and respond to student queries in real time, making learning more interactive and responsive. For instance, AI-powered chatbots like those used in platforms such as Coursera or Edmodo can answer student questions, offer explanations, and even provide additional learning material, creating a more interactive and engaging experience. In language learning, NLP helps students practice pronunciation, grammar, and vocabulary by analyzing their speech or writing and providing instant feedback. This can make the learning process more accessible, especially for students who may need additional support outside traditional classroom hours. Moreover, NLP is essential in automated feedback systems, which help educators by quickly processing large volumes of student submissions and providing detailed, personalized feedback without delay. This frees up time for educators to focus on other aspects of teaching while ensuring timely responses for students.

Computer Vision

Computer vision is a branch of AI that enables computers to interpret and understand visual information from the world. In education, computer vision is increasingly being used in proctoring solutions to monitor student behavior during exams, ensuring academic integrity (Bayraktar et al., 2017). For example, AI-powered proctoring systems use facial recognition and eye-tracking technologies to confirm the identity of a student and detect any suspicious activity during online exams. Additionally, computer vision is employed in interactive educational content. For example, some virtual reality (VR) or augmented reality (AR) platforms use computer vision to create immersive learning experiences that respond to a student's actions or environment. This can be particularly beneficial in science and engineering education, where students can engage with 3D models of molecules, mechanical systems, or historical artifacts. Another application is in assessing student engagement and participation. AI systems that utilize computer vision can analyze facial expressions and eye movements to gauge a student's level of attention during lessons, offering educators insights into how engaged their students are, and allowing them to adjust teaching methods accordingly.

RL

RL is a type of ML where an AI agent learns to make decisions by interacting with an environment and receiving feedback in the form of rewards or penalties (Fahad Mon et al., 2024). This technology is often used to power intelligent tutoring systems, which dynamically adjust the learning paths and strategies based on the student's responses and behaviors. For instance, a personalized math tutor powered by RL would not only provide feedback on correct or incorrect answers but would also assess the student's overall learning progress. By continuously optimizing the learning experience, RL systems ensure that students are always challenged at an appropriate level, neither bored with too easy content nor overwhelmed by difficult material. This type of system promotes an iterative learning cycle, where the tutor adapts to the student's pace, building knowledge gradually and efficiently. RL is also widely used in gaming-based learning environments, where students can learn by trial and error in simulated scenarios. This not only makes learning fun but also highly effective by simulating real-world problem-solving tasks.

Neural Networks

Neural networks are computational models inspired by the structure of the human brain. These networks are used in deep learning to analyze complex patterns in large datasets, such as student behavior, performance, and engagement. Deep learning models powered by neural networks can automatically detect hidden patterns in student data, which may not be immediately obvious to human educators (Kanchon et al., 2024). For example, neural networks can identify at-risk students by recognizing patterns in their interaction with digital learning platforms, such as frequent skipping of lessons, incomplete assignments, or poor test performance. This early detection allows educators to intervene proactively, offering additional support before students fall too far behind. Neural networks also power more sophisticated AI-driven content generation systems. By analyzing educational materials and understanding the relationships between concepts, neural networks can generate practice problems, quizzes, and even explanations tailored to the student's current understanding and learning style.

Table 2 breaks down AI technologies, providing a brief description and highlighting its specific educational applications.

Table 2. AI Technologies and Their Applications in Education

AI Technology	Description	Applications in Education
ML	Algorithms that allow systems to learn and improve from data without explicit programming.	Adaptive learning platforms, personalized content recommendations, student performance prediction, and intervention systems.
NLP	A branch of AI focused on enabling machines to understand and respond to human language.	AI tutors, chatbots, automated feedback, language learning apps, and real-time student query processing.
Computer Vision	Uses AI to interpret and understand visual information from the world, often through image or video processing.	Proctoring solutions, student engagement tracking, interactive learning materials, facial recognition, and eye-tracking.
RL	A type of ML where agents learn by interacting with an environment and receiving feedback based on their actions.	Intelligent tutoring systems, adaptive learning paths, personalized learning experiences, and gamified learning.
Neural Networks	Computing systems inspired by the human brain's structure, capable of learning complex patterns from large datasets.	Data analysis, student behavior predictions, personalized feedback, and content generation in deep learning models.

4. BRIDGING RESEARCH AND PRACTICE

The transition from AI research to practical application in educational settings has been an ongoing challenge. While advancements in AI technologies, such as ML, NLP, and RL, have demonstrated their potential in educational research, their real-world implementation has faced several hurdles. One significant challenge is the gap between theoretical AI models and the complexity of real-world educational environments (Admane et al., 2024). Many AI-driven tools, despite their promise, struggle to overcome issues like ethical considerations, data privacy concerns, and institutional resistance.

In research labs, AI models often work well in controlled environments where data is plentiful and clean, but in the real world, education systems are diverse and complex (Nguyen-Duc et Abrahamsson, 2020). Variations in student populations, teaching methods, and institutional structures require AI tools to be flexible and adaptive. Moreover, educators may resist adopting AI due to concerns about the technology replacing their roles, lack of trust in machine-generated feedback, or the technical challenges associated with AI integration. Several universities and ed-tech companies have made strides in successfully deploying AI-driven educational tools. For example, Carnegie Learning[3] has developed AI-based tutoring systems that personalize math instruction, adapting to each student's learning pace and providing real-time feedback. This approach has shown promise in enhancing student engagement and improving learning outcomes. Knewton[4], another prominent company, offers adaptive learning solutions that adjust content delivery based on real-time assessments of a student's progress, ensuring that each learner receives content suited to their individual needs. Platforms like Coursera[5] and edX[6] have integrated AI to personalize learning experiences by recommending courses based on student preferences, predicting performance, and tailoring learning pathways to enhance user engagement.

Despite these successes, the widespread adoption of AI in education still faces significant challenges. One of the main concerns is bias in AI models. AI algorithms, particularly those using ML, can inherit biases from the data they are trained on (Gianfrancesco et al., 2018). If historical data reflects inequities or biases, the AI system may inadvertently reinforce these patterns, leading to unfair or discriminatory outcomes. This risk is especially critical in education, where AI could perpetuate or even exacerbate existing disparities in access, resources, or opportunities. Additionally, accessibility concerns remain a barrier to AI integration in education (Nair et al., 2024). Not all students have equal access to technology, and AI tools may inadvertently widen the gap for those in under-resourced schools. This issue emphasizes the need for AI tools to be designed with accessibility in mind, ensuring that they can be effectively used by all students, regardless of their socio-economic status or technological access. Another challenge is the lack of educator training in AI integration. Teachers are pivotal in the successful implementation of AI tools in classrooms, but many educators may not have the necessary technical expertise or support to use these tools effectively. Professional development and training programs are essential to ensure that educators understand how AI can support teaching and learning and how to integrate it into their existing curricula without replacing their instructional roles.

To ensure that AI in education is equitable and inclusive, developers must address these challenges. This includes designing AI tools that are transparent, free from bias, and accessible to all learners. Collaboration between technologists and educators is crucial for developing AI solutions that align with pedagogical best practices. Educational stakeholders, schools, universities, policymakers, and tech companies, must work together to ensure that AI tools enhance, rather than hinder, educational equity.

5. VISION FOR THE BOOK

The future of education lies in the ability to offer personalized learning experiences that cater to the diverse needs of students. Traditional one-size-fits-all teaching methods are no longer sufficient to meet the demands of modern learners, and personalized learning has emerged as a critical solution. AI offers the potential to revolutionize the way education is delivered, enabling the creation of adaptive learning environments that respond to the individual needs, preferences, and progress of each student. Through AI-powered tutorial systems, students can experience a one-to-one tutoring environment, which can provide real-time, tailored feedback, guidance, and explanations that are unique to their learning journey. This personalized approach ensures that students are not left behind, regardless of their academic background or learning pace.

AI has the capability to deliver individualized training, rapidly providing feedback and automating routine administrative tasks that traditionally occupy much of educators' time. For instance, AI can handle grading, generate personalized learning pathways, and provide immediate responses to student queries. This automation of routine chores frees up valuable time for teachers to engage in more meaningful interactions with their students, focusing on building relationships, fostering creativity, and encouraging critical thinking (Van den Berg et Du Plessis, 2023). While AI systems are powerful tools that can enhance learning experiences, it is important to recognize that they cannot replace teachers. Teachers remain central to the educational process, as they provide the emotional intelligence, mentorship, and human connection that AI cannot replicate. AI serves to complement traditional teaching practices by augmenting teachers' abilities to address the varying needs of each student, allowing them to focus on teaching the 'whole' student, academically, emotionally, and socially. In this context, the integration of AI into learning spaces must also consider students' emotional states, as emotions play a significant role in the learning process. Emotional well-being is linked to student engagement, motivation, and overall academic success. However, traditional AI systems have predominantly focused on cognitive and academic aspects, often neglecting the emotional dimension of learning. To address this gap, the concept of *Emotionally Intelligent AI (EI-AI)* (Bilquise et al., 2022) tutors is emerging. EI-AI tutors integrate emotional recognition and adaptive response capabilities into personalized learning systems, allowing them to detect, interpret, and respond to a wide range of emotional cues that students exhibit during their learning process.

These emotional cues can include facial expressions, variations in voice tone, and physiological signals such as heart rate and galvanic skin response. By analyzing these signals, EI-AI tutors are able to determine whether a student is frustrated, excited, bored, or confused. Based on this emotional data, the system can adapt the learning experience accordingly, offering encouragement when a student is feeling discouraged, adjusting the difficulty of tasks if a student is struggling, or providing more challenging content if a student is becoming disengaged due to boredom. This dynamic response helps maintain student motivation and engagement, creating a more holistic and effective learning experience. An example of EI-AI in action is an intelligent tutoring system designed for mathematics learning. Suppose a student is working on algebra problems, and the system detects through facial recognition and voice analysis that the student is showing signs of frustration—furrowed brows, a tense voice, and increased pauses between answers. Additionally, a wearable device measures an elevated heart rate, confirming heightened stress levels. In response, the EI-AI tutor dynamically adjusts the learning environment. It provides a step-by-step breakdown of the problem, offers a simpler example to build confidence, and delivers encouraging feedback such as, "You're on the right track! Let's try breaking this down together." If frustration persists, the system might suggest a short break or a gamified exercise to re-engage the student.

Conversely, if the AI detects excitement and quick, accurate responses, it might introduce more complex challenges to sustain engagement.

In addition to emotional intelligence, the integration of *gamification and interactive features* into AI systems further enhances student motivation and involvement (Orlovskyi, 2023). Gamification, through elements such as rewards, progress tracking, and competitive features, turns learning into an enjoyable and immersive experience. Interactive simulations, role-playing games, and adaptive learning scenarios make education feel less like a traditional classroom and more like a real-world, interactive adventure. These gamified elements are particularly effective in maintaining student engagement, especially in subjects that may otherwise feel dry or challenging. By integrating these features, AI can transform learning into an interactive experience that students actively participate in, rather than a passive, one-way flow of information. An example of EI-AI combined with gamification can be seen in a language learning application. Suppose a student is practicing vocabulary through an AI-powered quiz. The system detects, via facial expression analysis and voice tone, that the student is becoming frustrated after several incorrect answers. At the same time, eye-tracking data shows reduced focus, indicating disengagement. To re-engage the student, the AI tutor dynamically adapts the experience by introducing a gamified challenge: a role-playing scenario where the student must use the learned vocabulary to navigate a virtual conversation with an AI character. The system also introduces a reward mechanism—completing the challenge earns points and unlocks new interactive levels. Additionally, the AI provides encouraging feedback, saying, "You're improving! Let's try a different approach and win some bonus points!"

While conventional AI systems focus on cognitive learning aspects, EI-AI tutors go a step further by addressing emotional and social factors. EI-AI tutors provide a more comprehensive approach to personalized learning by not only considering the academic performance of students but also their emotional and psychological states. This makes the learning experience more balanced, as it supports both cognitive and emotional growth. In addition to recognizing emotional cues, EI-AI tutors can respond empathetically, tailoring their feedback to soothe, motivate, or challenge students based on their emotional needs.

Furthermore, AI's ability to process vast amounts of data allows for the forecasting of student performance (Bressane et al., 2022). By utilizing historical data, such as past academic performance, behavioral trends, and engagement levels, AI can predict which students may be at risk of underperforming. This predictive capability allows educators to intervene early and provide targeted support to help students who may need additional assistance. Early identification of struggling students ensures that interventions can be proactive rather than reactive, improving the chances of academic success and preventing students from falling behind.

The role of AI in promoting equity in education cannot be overstated. Personalized learning powered by AI ensures that every student, regardless of background or ability, has access to an education tailored to their individual needs. AI can bridge educational gaps by providing additional support for underprivileged students, helping them to overcome challenges that may have previously hindered their academic progress. By ensuring that all students have access to the same high-quality, personalized learning experiences, AI can level the playing field and promote greater inclusivity in education.

The responsible integration of AI in education requires careful regulation and collaboration among key stakeholders. Educators, policymakers, and technology developers must work together to ensure that AI-driven tools are ethical, fair, and effective. For instance, educators play a vital role in shaping AI systems to align with pedagogical objectives and meet diverse student needs. In adaptive learning platforms like Smart Sparrow, teachers contribute by customizing AI-driven lesson plans to ensure they support individual learning styles. Policymakers must establish clear regulatory frameworks to ensure responsible AI use, with a focus on data privacy, security, and inclusiveness. The General Data Protection Regulation (GDPR)[7] in Europe sets strict guidelines on student data protection, while the Family Educational Rights and Privacy Act (FERPA)[8] in the U.S. safeguards student records from unauthorized access. These regulations help prevent misuse of personal data in AI-powered learning tools. Technology developers must also prioritize transparency and fairness when designing AI systems. For example, OpenAI's ChatGPT for Education includes safeguards against biased responses, ensuring that content remains neutral and reliable. Additionally, UNESCO's Recommendation on the Ethics of AI [9] provides guidelines for creating AI systems that uphold ethical standards in education.

As we look to the future, this book will delve deeper into how AI-driven educational innovations are transforming the learning landscape. It will examine the role of AI in personalized learning, the promotion of equity, the use of AI-driven tutoring systems, and the integration of technologies like blockchain and gamification into education. By providing educators, researchers, and policymakers with insights into the potential of AI in education, this book aims to help shape the future of learning, ensuring that AI serves as a powerful tool for creating more personalized, inclusive, and effective educational experiences for all students.

6. CONCLUSION

The integration of AI into education represents a transformative shift in how learning is delivered, experienced, and assessed. This chapter has explored the foundational aspects of AI-driven education, highlighting its potential to revolutionize traditional teaching methods through personalized learning, adaptive systems, and automated administrative tasks. From intelligent tutoring systems that cater to individual learning needs to generative AI tools that create dynamic, interactive content, AI is poised to enhance both student engagement and educational outcomes. However, the journey toward fully realizing AI's potential in education is not without challenges. Ethical concerns, such as data privacy, algorithmic bias, and the digital divide, must be addressed to ensure equitable access and fair implementation. Additionally, the readiness of educational institutions and educators to adopt and adapt to these technologies remains a critical factor. Effective integration of AI requires collaboration among educators, policymakers, and technology developers to create frameworks that prioritize inclusivity, transparency, and pedagogical alignment.

The historical evolution of AI in education, from early computer-assisted instruction to modern generative AI systems, underscores the rapid advancements in technology and its growing impact on learning environments. Key AI technologies, such as ML, NLP, and RL, have already demonstrated their ability to personalize learning experiences, automate routine tasks, and provide actionable insights into student performance. Yet, the transition from research to practice reveals gaps that must be bridged to ensure AI tools are both effective and equitable.

Looking ahead, the future of AI in education lies in its ability to create emotionally intelligent, inclusive, and adaptive learning environments. EI-AI tutors, which recognize and respond to students' emotional states, represent a promising direction for fostering holistic learning experiences. Furthermore, the integration of gamification and interactive features can enhance student motivation and engagement, making learning more enjoyable and effective.

AI-driven education holds immense promise for transforming the educational landscape, but its success depends on addressing the challenges of implementation, ensuring ethical practices, and fostering collaboration among all stakeholders. By leveraging AI responsibly and inclusively, we can create a future where every student has access to personalized, high-quality education that meets their unique needs and prepares them for the challenges of tomorrow. This chapter and subsequent chapters set the stage for further exploration into how AI can be optimized to overcome existing barriers and unlock its full potential in shaping the future of education.

REFERENCES

Admane, R., Sawale, P. S., Jayasree, R., Kurup, S. J., & Thomas, S. A. (2024). Artificial Intelligence in Education: Tailoring Curriculum to Individual Student Needs through AI-Based Systems. Library of Progress-Library Science, Information Technology & Computer, 44(3).

Al-kfairy, M., Mustafa, D., Kshetri, N., Insiew, M., & Alfandi, O. (2024, September). Ethical challenges and solutions of generative AI: An interdisciplinary perspective. In Informatics (Vol. 11, No. 3, p. 58). Multidisciplinary Digital Publishing Institute.

Aleven, V. (2010). Rule-based cognitive modeling for intelligent tutoring systems. In *Advances in intelligent tutoring systems* (pp. 33–62). Springer Berlin Heidelberg. DOI: 10.1007/978-3-642-14363-2_3

Alhawiti, K. M. (2014). Natural language processing and its use in education. *International Journal of Advanced Computer Science and Applications*, *5*(12).

Ana, A. (2020). Trends in expert system development: A practicum content analysis in vocational education for over grow pandemic learning problems. *Indonesian Journal of Science and Technology*, *5*(2), 246–260. DOI: 10.17509/ijost.v5i2.24616

Baidoo-Anu, D., & Ansah, L. O. (2023). Education in the era of generative artificial intelligence (AI): Understanding the potential benefits of ChatGPT in promoting teaching and learning. *Journal of AI*, *7*(1), 52–62. DOI: 10.61969/jai.1337500

Bayraktar, E., Yigit, C. B., & Boyraz, P. (2017, February). Tailoring the AI for Robotics: Fine-tuning Predefined Deep Convolutional Neural Network Model for a Narrower Class of Objects. In *Proceedings of the 2017 International Conference on Mechatronics Systems and Control Engineering* (pp. 10-14). DOI: 10.1145/3045714.3045716

Bilquise, G., Ibrahim, S., & Shaalan, K. (2022). Emotionally intelligent chatbots: A systematic literature review. *Human Behavior and Emerging Technologies*, *2022*(1), 9601630. DOI: 10.1155/2022/9601630

Blok, H., Oostdam, R., Otter, M. E., & Overmaat, M. (2002). Computer-assisted instruction in support of beginning reading instruction: A review. *Review of Educational Research*, *72*(1), 101–130. DOI: 10.3102/00346543072001101

Bressane, A., Spalding, M., Zwirn, D., Loureiro, A. I. S., Bankole, A. O., Negri, R. G., de Brito Junior, I., Formiga, J. K. S., Medeiros, L. C. C., Pampuch Bortolozo, L. A., & Moruzzi, R. (2022). Fuzzy artificial intelligence—Based model proposal to forecast student performance and retention risk in engineering education: An alternative for handling with small data. *Sustainability (Basel)*, *14*(21), 14071. DOI: 10.3390/su142114071

Fahad Mon, B., Wasfi, A., Hayajneh, M., Slim, A., & Abu Ali, N. (2023, September). Reinforcement Learning in Education: A Literature Review. In Informatics (Vol. 10, No. 3, p. 74). MDPI. DOI: 10.3390/informatics10030074

Fletcher-Flinn, C. M., & Gravatt, B. (1995). The efficacy of computer assisted instruction (CAI): A meta-analysis. *Journal of Educational Computing Research*, *12*(3), 219–241. DOI: 10.2190/51D4-F6L3-JQHU-9M31

Fuchs, K. (2023, May). Exploring the opportunities and challenges of NLP models in higher education: Is Chat GPT a blessing or a curse? *Frontiers in Education*, *8*, 1166682. DOI: 10.3389/feduc.2023.1166682

Gianfrancesco, M. A., Tamang, S., Yazdany, J., & Schmajuk, G. (2018). Potential biases in machine learning algorithms using electronic health record data. *JAMA Internal Medicine*, *178*(11), 1544–1547. DOI: 10.1001/jamainternmed.2018.3763 PMID: 30128552

Haldar, S. K. (2024, August). Privacy and security in AI education for gender studies. In Artificial Intelligence in Education (p. 39).

Harry, A. (2023). Role of AI in Education. *Interdiciplinary Journal and Hummanity*, *2*(3), 260–268.

Holmes, W., & Tuomi, I. (2022). State of the art and practice in AI in education. *European Journal of Education*, *57*(4), 542–570. DOI: 10.1111/ejed.12533

Kanchon, M. K. H., Sadman, M., Nabila, K. F., Tarannum, R., & Khan, R. (2024). Enhancing personalized learning: AI-driven identification of learning styles and content modification strategies. *International Journal of Cognitive Computing in Engineering*, *5*, 269–278. DOI: 10.1016/j.ijcce.2024.06.002

Khanna, S., Kaushik, A., & Barnela, M. (2010, March). Expert systems advances in education. In Proceedings of the National Conference on Computational Instrumentation NCCI-2010. CSIO (pp. 109-112).

Kotsiantis, S., Pierrakeas, C., & Pintelas, P. (2004). Predicting students' performance in distance learning using machine learning techniques. *Applied Artificial Intelligence*, *18*(5), 411–426. DOI: 10.1080/08839510490442058

Kučak, D., Juričić, V., & Đambić, G. (2018). Machine learning in education-A survey of current research trends. Annals of DAAAM & Proceedings, 29.

Murumba, J., & Micheni, E. (2017). Big data analytics in higher education: A review. *The International Journal of Engineering and Science*, *6*(06), 14–21. DOI: 10.9790/1813-0606021421

Nair, M., Svedberg, P., Larsson, I., & Nygren, J. M. (2024). A comprehensive overview of barriers and strategies for AI implementation in healthcare: Mixed-method design. *PLoS One*, *19*(8), e0305949. DOI: 10.1371/journal.pone.0305949 PMID: 39121051

Nguyen-Duc, A., & Abrahamsson, P. (2020, November). Continuous experimentation on artificial intelligence software: a research agenda. In *Proceedings of the 28th ACM Joint Meeting on European Software Engineering Conference and Symposium on the Foundations of Software Engineering* (pp. 1513-1516). DOI: 10.1145/3368089.3417039

Orlovskyi, D., & Yuskovych-Zhukovska, V. (2023). Interactive learning platform with gamification elements. Automation of Technological and Business Processes, 15(1), 11-11.

Pedro, F., Subosa, M., Rivas, A., & Valverde, P. (2019). Artificial intelligence in education: Challenges and opportunities for sustainable development. Academic Press.

Van den Berg, G., & Du Plessis, E. (2023). ChatGPT and generative AI: Possibilities for its contribution to lesson planning, critical thinking and openness in teacher education. *Education Sciences*, *13*(10), 998. DOI: 10.3390/educsci13100998

Zhai. (2021). A Review of Artificial Intelligence (AI) in Education from 2010 to 2020. Complexity, 1, 8812542.

Chapter 2
AI-Driven Tutoring Systems:
Enhancing Personalized Learning With Innovative Tools

C. V. Suresh Babu
https://orcid.org/0000-0002-8474-2882
Hindustan Institute of Technology and Science, India

Malini Premakumari William
http://orcid.org/0009-0004-6165-2501
Bourntec Solutions, Inc., Schaumburg, USA

Venkatesh T. D.
https://orcid.org/0009-0000-8716-4638
Hindustan Institute of Technology and Science, India

ABSTRACT

This study explores the impact of AI-driven tutoring systems on personalized learning, aiming to identify best practices for their integration in diverse educational contexts. Utilizing a mixed-methods approach, the research combines qualitative narratives from educators with quantitative data on student engagement and performance. Key findings reveal that tools like ChatGPT and Canva significantly enhance personalization, engagement,

DOI: 10.4018/979-8-3693-8382-7.ch002

and collaboration among students, while also providing actionable insights for educators. However, challenges such as equity, accessibility, and the need for professional development are highlighted, emphasizing the importance of addressing these issues for effective implementation. The study concludes that while AI tools hold great potential for transforming education, careful consideration of ethical implications and long-term impacts is essential for maximizing their benefits.

1. INTRODUCTION

1.1 Overview of AI-Driven Tutoring Systems

Tutoring systems enabled with AI reveal a revolutionary form of instruction in the process of teaching, customized learning algorithms and methodologies of machine learning being used to provide individualized learning experiences for individual learners. Such systems will monitor specific learning styles, preferences, and progression, modifying content and teaching strategies automatically. The AI integration in tutoring platforms provides an interactive and stimulating learning environment, an improvement on traditional learning in the provision of instant feedback and support. Some of the examples of various platforms developed with AI are ITS, virtual tutors, and adaptive learning platforms.

1.2 AI in Education: An Overview of Research

The latest developments in AI-based tutoring systems have indicated potential to augment personalized learning. Studies by Anderson & Dron (2011) and Luckin et al. (2016) have pointed out how AI-based tools enable adaptive learning experiences through adapting instructional content to the needs of individual students. Yet, there are gaps in knowing the long-term efficacy and equity of these systems.

Constructivist theories of learning postulate that students build knowledge via active participation, a notion consistent with AI-powered personalized learning. Adaptive learning theories, as formulated by Siemens

(2013), support the role of AI systems to adaptively respond to students' progress and maximize educational outputs.

1.3 Gaps in Current Research

Although AI has been embedded in most education platforms, research is scarce to investigate:

- The long-term effect of AI tutoring systems on student achievement.
- How AI solutions respond to issues of equity and accessibility.
- Effectiveness of AI tutoring versus human instruction.

Upcoming research has to fill in these gaps in order to see that AI serves to improve education fairly and well.

1.4 Importance of Personalized Learning in Education

Personalized learning Significance in education Personalized learning has drawn enormous attention as a strong pedagogical strategy that takes into account the uniqueness of every learner. This approach differs from the global model, attempting to meet the diverse needs, abilities, and problems that learners face. Empirical research suggests that personalized learning may improve student achievement, build motivation, and encourage more independence among students.

The system will also include AI tutoring, which supports the personal learning trajectories, and the learner can move at one's own pace. Learners receive targeted support when needed. The method is not only keeping the students engaged but also allows for deeper subject matter understanding.

1.5 Objective of the Chapter

The principal goals of this chapter are outlined below:

- Mechanisms and operational potentials of the AI-boosted tutoring systems are studied. How the systems work-from data acquisition, engagement of the user to algorithms related to adaptive learning- are discussed.

- Personalization of Learning This discussion is centered on the benefits of personalization in learning: its outcomes on the students' performance, their engagement, and the quality of the learning experience.

To Evaluate the Integration of New Tools: This section will analyze the state-of-the-art technological features in AI-based tutoring systems, ranging from natural language processing, predictive analytics, and user interface design into their actualization for successful personalized learning (Suresh Babu C.V. 2023). To Identify Challenges and Potential Routes: The chapter below will also discuss possible challenges in the development of AI-based tutoring systems, conjointly with an examination of emerging trends and routes for future research within this area. In pursuance of those objectives, this chapter tries to present a proper understanding of AI-powered tutoring systems and its potentiality to enhance individualized learning in the educational sphere.

2. BACKGROUND

2.1 Evolution of Educational Technologies

Educational technologies began through overhead projectors and film strips. All of these have been brought about by digital resources and changes in teaching strategy. The greatest change factor in educational technology was the introduction of computers in the 1980s. It introduced software that allowed computer-assisted instruction. With the widespread availability of the internet in the 1990s, online learning emerged as distance education, offering greater access to more resources.

Then came the LMS in the 2000s — it could deliver and assess courses and support communication in a structured environment. Mobile devices and apps in the 2010s brought personalized and interactive education technology; data analytics and cloud computing made it possible to track students' progress in real time and personalize learning.

The most recent example in this stream is AI-powered tutoring systems, which are the case of the application of complex algorithms that produce different learning experiences. They use huge educational data sets to individualize instruction to students and, thus, make education more responsive and effective.

2.2 The Role of Artificial Intelligence in Modern Instruction

Artificial intelligence is becoming a critical component in education today and is transforming learning in many ways. Fig. 1 Role of AI in Personalized Tutoring, AI technologies improve the learning landscape by:

Personalization: AI algorithms mine student data to create personalized learning paths that are hyper-relevant to each individual learner, and that dynamically adapt to performance and engagement metrics.
Intelligent tutoring: Artificial intelligence-based tutorial systems provide the kinds of one-to-one tutoring that students often find most useful; they provide different kinds of feedback, guidance, and explanations that meet the needs of different kinds of learners and help students develop confidence in their competence.
Predictive Analytics: Using historical data, artificial intelligence can predict student performance and identify those who are at risk of falling behind. Educators can use these insights to proactively intervene and provide targeted support that leads to student success.
Improved Engagement: Artificial intelligence tools often incorporate gamification and interactive elements that increase student motivation and engagement. By making learning more fun, these systems help students retain interest over a longer period. This can lead to better learning outcomes. The use of AI in learning environments enhances the personalized learning experience and prepares students for an increasingly digitally literate world in which adaptability is the best course of action. The constantly evolving new AI-based technologies are likely to elevate the importance of these technologies within education systems so that rapid innovation of unique knowledge solutions toward meeting diverse student needs everywhere.

2.3 Overview of AI Tools Explored in the Chapter

We discuss the frontline AI tools that provide strength in adding personalization to learning through AI-based tutoring systems (Suresh Babu, C. V. & Adhithya, S., 2023). Each tool has special characteristics and addresses different aspects of the learning process, thereby making the journey to improved results easier for educators as well as learners.

1. ChatGPT:
    - ChatGPT is a conversational AI framework for engaging learning interactions. ChatGPT was created by OpenAI. Here are a few examples of what it can do:
    - Customised support: ChatGPT can be used to respond to learners' natural language queries, explaining concepts, and helping them solve exercises tailored to education needs.
    - This tool also gives immediate feedback on assignments and questions. It shows learners better angles to tackle concepts and even self-directed learning.
    - Scalability: it can support lots of learners at the same time, so is suitable for teachers with the option of extra support outside class time
2. Canva:
    - Canva is a graphic design platform with AI elements to boost creativity in education projects. Key features include:
    - Visual Learning With Canva, students have the opportunity to make very interactive presentations and infographics, as well as make posters that can encourage visual learning.
    - Hundreds of AI-powered templates and design resources are at your fingertips on the portal so that users can instantly become capable of delivering professional-quality work, even if they have no prior experience in designing.
    - Collaboration features: Canva's collaborative features allow students to work on joint projects simultaneously. These features improve students' teamwork and communication skills.
3. InVideo AI:

- InVideo AI is a video creation platform that uses artificial intelligence to create videos. Educational uses include:
- Content Generation: Teachers and learners can create learning videos, learning tutorials, and presentations easily and make learning resources more dynamic and engaging.
- Customization and automation: InVideo AI comes with automated features that make the editing process simpler. Users can customize the video content really quickly without any quality loss.
- Engagement Videos created with InVideo AI that include multimedia elements keep students engaged and help them retain information.

4. CapCut:
   - CapCut is an accessible video editing app that uses AI to make high-quality video content easy to create Personal learning contribution in:
   - User Interface: The CapCut app allows students to edit videos easily and smoothly and offers all levels to be put to work in expressing one's understanding creatively.
   - AI-powered features: For example, auto-generated subtitles and background music recommendations make videos so much more fun to watch. Practical Use Cases: Students can use CapCut to create project presentations and build digital literacy and competencies that are increasingly critical in today's workforce.
5. PowerPoint:
   - Of course, now that Microsoft puts its PowerPoint in a class with AI capabilities, it's clear a few things are missing:
   - AI-powered Design Ideas suggests layouts and design improvements, helping you create more visually compelling presentations with ease. This means PowerPoint provides a variety of accessibility tools, including real time captioning and voice to text features, so content is accessible for all learners.
   - Integration with other tools: PowerPoint integrates with a lot of AI tools and platforms, allowing you to add multimedia and interactive features to your presentation.

3. RELEVANCE TO THE EDITED BOOK'S THEME

3.1 Connection to Transforming Education With AI-Powered Personalized Learning

This chapter closely fits the overarching subject of transforming education through AI-based personalized learning. Educational trends are shifting towards more individualized and differentiated approaches, and AI-powered tutoring systems emerge as essential tools in such change. Utilizing highly sophisticated algorithms, the latter can modify learning experiences to suit the needs of each individual learner, thereby making the educational environment more responsive and effective. Tools, like ChatGPT and Canva, will be described as assisting in personalizing learning efforts toward the ultimate vision of technology transforming education in this chapter.

3.2 Significance of AI-Driven Tutoring Systems in the Current Educational Landscape

With diversified learning needs, multiple levels of student engagement, and a need for education to scale, AI-driven tutoring systems become quite important. Such systems offer the possibility of providing personalized support students may require in closing a learning gap, raising the motivations of students, and keeping students engaged and feeling a sense of ownership over their learning process. In the context of rapidly changing technology and changing contents of jobs, AI has been proven to enhance academic performance aside from equipping the student with a learning experience that would help them in the future. This chapter therefore orients the reader to the role that these systems play in bridging the gap that exists between the traditional ways of delivering education and needs of the modern learners.

4. KEY QUESTIONS AND PROBLEMS ADDRESSED

4.1 An Empowered Learning Experience Personalized

One of the primary questions that this chapter tries to answer is how tutoring systems based on AI can be used to leverage students' personalized learning. We delve into different tools integrated with AI to identify best practices for customizing educational content based on individual learning styles, preferences, and paces. The methodologies employed by the AI system in terms of assessment of students' needs followed by adaptation of its overall architecture would be discussed in this chapter.

4.2 Tutoring Systems With AI Tools Roles

It proceeds to analyze specific roles AI tools play in tutoring systems, namely how tools like ChatGPT facilitate conversational learning and others that create content with ease through Canva and InVideo AI. With this in mind, understanding these roles will clarify the way AI tools synergize together to create a holistic support system for students and teachers alike.

4.3 Best Practices for Integration

The integration of AI-driven tutoring systems into the current framework brings about challenges and opportunities. This chapter will outline best practice regarding effective integration, focusing on professional development for educators, alignment with curriculum standards, and development of supportive infrastructure. We also discuss how one might ensure that the use of AI tools does not jeopardize but instead enhances traditional pedagogical methods.

4.4 Case Studies and Real-World Scenarios

This chapter will include case studies and real-world illustrations of how AI tutoring systems have been successfully implemented, thereby providing practical insights into the implementations. Such examples will unfold how benefits such as positive student outcomes and enhanced engagement are realized through personalized learning. What can be concluded through the studies of case analyses is whether or not given AI tools can help achieve a true impact for the education sector.

5. OBJECTIVES AND SCOPE

5.1 Clear Statement of Objectives

The primary goals of this chapter are:

- Analyze the Role of AI-Driven Tutoring Systems: Analyze how such systems enhance the delivery of a personalized learning experience through various AI tools.
- Review of Specific AI Tool Impact Evaluate the contributions of the specific tools such as ChatGPT, Canva, InVideo AI, CapCut, and PowerPoint towards personal learning.
- Best Practices for Implementation: Guide the integration process for educational institutions to create high-quality AI-based tutoring systems that maximize the potential benefits of such a system.
- Case Studies. Supply successful case studies of how the AI-driven tutoring systems were used and the results experienced in several educational settings.

5.2 Delimitation of the Scope

To clearly delimit the exploration of this chapter, it will be in scope according to the following:

5.2.1 Focus Areas

Under these respects, the paper will deal with:

- **Technological Framework**: Survey of AI-based technologies and tools designed for use in supporting personalization within tutoring systems.
- **Pedagogical Impact**: Analysis of how these systems influence teaching methodologies, student engagement, and learning outcomes.
- **Implementation Strategies**: How to best take up AI-driven tutoring systems within the existing educational structure.
- **Evaluative Case Studies**: Actual examples of how AI-powered tools may be used to improve personalized learning.

5.2.2 Exclusions

The chapter deliberately omissions include:

- **Detailed technical specifications**: Actual programming or algorithmic descriptions of the AI tools per se fall out of the scope of this report, as it's only concerned with educational applications.
- **Non-AI-Based Tutoring Systems**: Exploration will only be conducted on AI-based systems, ruling out the more traditionally conceived tutoring models or platforms that do not involve AI technologies.
- **General Educational Technologies:** Even though education technology is very vast, this chapter will narrow down its focus to AI tools and their participation in personal learning instead of all educational technologies.

6. LITERATURE REVIEW

6.1 Recent Research in AI Based Tutoring Systems

This paper exhibits emerging interest in AI-powered tutoring systems in modern education. In addition, the latest research works indicate significant improvements in personalized learning through adjusted content and individualized feedback on specific students' needs. Moreover, the following finding was established:

- **Adaptive Learning**: Articulated AI modifies the difficulty levels and also the pathways learned to increase student interest and retention levels.
- **Immediate Feedback**: AI tools facilitate real-time feedback, which is crucial for reinforcing learning and addressing misconceptions promptly.
- **Scalability**: Systems built using AI can cater to hundreds of learners simultaneously, making them a viable alternative for resource-constrained institutions.

6.2 Gaps in the Existing Literature Identification

6.2.1 Equity and Accessibility in AI Learning

AI-based tutoring systems should be made inclusive to serve the needs of varied learners, including those from marginalized groups. Research (Zawacki-Richter et al., 2019) indicates that AI tools tend to be non-inclusive, perpetuating existing education inequalities.

To address this, AI systems need to:

- Integrate multilingualism and speech-to-text functionalities.
- Make accessibility available for differently abled students.
- Offer affordable AI-based solutions to underprivileged communities.

6.2.2 Longitudinal Studies on AI Tutoring Impact

Even with AI increasingly present in learning, research does not have comprehensive long-term analyses of its impacts. Studies should follow students over several years to evaluate:

- Knowledge retention and use outside the classroom.
- The changing role of teachers in AI-augmented classrooms.
- Possible cognitive and behavioural changes from AI dependence.

6.3 Case Studies and Their Results

Many case studies prove that AI-based tutoring systems work well:

Case Study 1: An implementation of ChatGPT in a high school setting indicated improvement in engagement and overall writing skills of students, as indicated by their being very confident of their abilities.
Case Study 2: The university had used Canva in group work. There emerged improved creativity and teamwork and better presentation skills among the students.
Case Study 3: InVideo AI Utilization District-Wide Effort to Create Instructional Video Creation This initiative resulted in greater student retention and comments on the quality of materials learned (Suresh Babu, C. V. & Rohan, B. 2023).

6.3.1 Case Studies in Real-World Applications

For the purpose of demonstrating AI effectiveness, case studies across different learning environments ought to be presented:

Case Study 1: ChatGPT implementation in primary schools, showing enhanced participation and writing ability.
Case Study 2: Utilization of Canva in group student projects, providing increased creativity and collaboration.
Case Study 3: In Video AI contribution towards content development, resulting in increased learning material retention.

These illustrations highlight how AI technology helps improve student learning but also highlight challenges in implementation.

The case studies provided here demonstrate not only pragmatic benefits but also effective strategies in the implementation of AI-driven tutoring systems as a source of knowledge for educators and policymakers.

7. METHODOLOGY

This chapter describes the research methodology undertaken to understand the efficiency of AI-driven tutoring systems as a means of enhancing personalized learning. In its selection, the methodologies chosen were meant to give an overview of how these novel tools impact education.

7.1 Research Strategy

7.1.1 Qualitative Analysis

The researchers applied qualitative analysis to delve deeper into the perceptions and experiences of educators regarding AI-driven tutoring systems (Suresh Babu, C. V., Anniyappa, C. S, et. al . 2024). Applying this method meant the inclusion of themes, for example:

User Experience: Understand how educators and students interact with AI systems.
Implementation Challenges: This involves identifying barriers to effective use, such as technology integration and training.
Perceived Benefits: Obtaining views about which of these systems enhance learning and engagement. Focus group discussions and open-ended interviews were used to gather rich, narrative data that capture nuanced experiences of users in educational settings.

7.1.2 Quantitative Data

Measurement data was gathered to demonstrate measurable success of AI-based tutoring system. Measurement data includes:

Performance Metrics: The analysis of performance data before and after the intervention of tutoring systems. Engagement Levels Engagement should be measured with analytics tools that track usage patterns and patterns of interaction with AI systems.

Surveys: The structured questionnaires were administered to collect information about student satisfaction and perceived learning gain. This combination between the two will allow a very strong analysis of the system, taking into account both the emotional and practical side of AI tutoring systems.

7.1.3 AI Limitations in Education

Though AI amplifies learning, it cannot substitute human teachers. AI has difficulty with:

- Picking up on student emotions and non-verbal cues.
- Resolving difficult, open-ended questions that need human discernment.
- Offering socio-emotional support critical to student well-being.
- A more informed discussion would emphasize AI as a supplement, rather than a substitute, for educators.

7.2 Data Collection Methods

7.2.1 Interviews With Educators

Interviews were held with a cross-section of different educators: teachers, administrators, curriculum developers. Interviews were conducted to:

- Examine their experiences using an AI-driven tutoring system.
- Identify best practices for implementation.
- Propose directions for future work on AI educational tools.
- Interviews were semi-structured, allowing for flexibility in responses while still covering key themes.

7.2.2 Surveys and Analytics

A questionnaire was also administered to students and instructors to measure students' attitudes towards AI-based tutoring systems. Salient aspects were:

Demographics: Collecting data on participants' backgrounds to analyze trends across different groups.
Satisfaction Ratings. The use of Likert scales to measure user satisfaction over the systems.
Learning Outcomes: Correlation of the survey responses with academic performance data. Analytics from the tutoring systems will also track metrics on engagement, such as use frequency and completion rates of learning modules.

7.3 Reason for Chosen Methodology

The scope of what can be known about the effects that AI-driven tutoring systems have on learning can be increased with a qualitative and quantitative approach. Insights generated from educator interviews explain trends in the performance metrics as well as user satisfaction, thus this mixed-methods approach has justification for the following reasons:

It captures both subjective users' experience and objective performance data to provide a richer understanding of the effectiveness of these systems.

Adaptability: Using multiple data sources, the research study can take on different educational contexts and specific needs of different user groups.

Validity and Reliability: Qualitative narratives supported by quantitative measures add soundness to the findings, which helps in triangulating data. This approach will clearly depict how tutoring systems managed by AI can improve personalized learning experience-that future is continuing to mold the ever-changing land of educational technology.

8. DETAILED EXPLORATION OF AI TOOLS

This chapter will walk through many of the AI-powered tools (Fig 2) that transform personalized learning experiences. By looking at specific applications and what they do, we get a sense of how these tools enhance interaction, creativity, and engagement in education.

8.1 ChatGPT: Improving Interactivity and Feedback

ChatGPT is an interactive tutor, offering live responses to student queries as well as prompting personal feedback on assignments.

Figure 1. Stages of Prompt Engineering

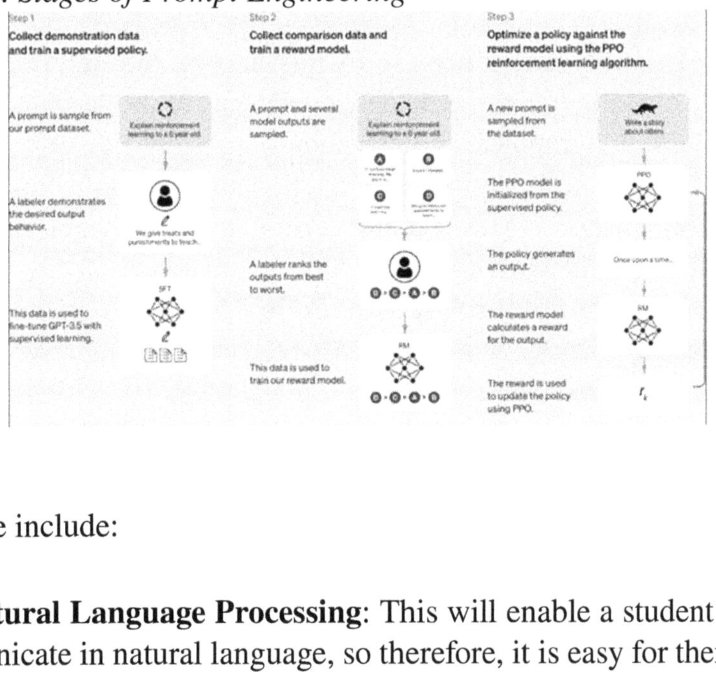

These include:

Natural Language Processing: This will enable a student to communicate in natural language, so therefore, it is easy for them to ask for help and clarify things.
Adaptive Learning: The response will be tailored based on the student's specific needs and the course of progress of every student. This will give explanations and resources which might best fit their learning style.

24/7 Availability: It gives constant support outside traditional hours of class that makes it even more productive for people who needed additional help.

As evidence emerges, research has shown that students who use ChatGPT are more engaged and satisfying; thus, it creates an engaging learning place.

8.2 Canva: Designing Exciting Images

Canva is one of the graphic design tools shown in Fig 3 that allow students and teachers to produce high-quality and appealing content in various projects. Learning advantages include the following:

User-Friendly Interface: With this aspect, the authors with all levels of skill powers the display on designs of professional-looking graphics, infographics, and presentations.

Multi-user collaboration: The functionality allows the functionality of several users on a project at the same time, and hence encourages teamwork and creativity.

Abundant templates: Templates in Canva are numerous and education-oriented, which will assist the students in presenting their ideas very effectively.

Figure 2. Canva User Interface

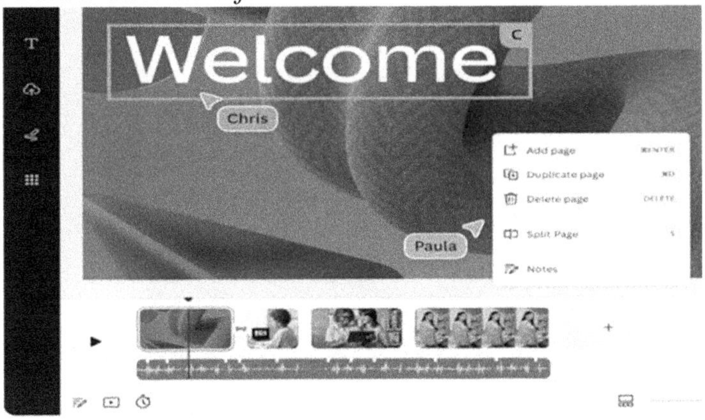

It has been noted that addition of Canva to the learning processes, students will be able to understand visual communication as well as design principles effectively.

8.3 InVideo AI: Video Content Creation for Learning

InVideo AI Fig. 4 is a really high-quality tool of video content creation and can be super educational. Its key features are:

Templates and Stock Media: It provides a library of templates and stock footage so that creating the video process becomes easier.
Text-to-Video Ability: It provides the functionality of converting texts into engaging videos, thereby supporting visual learning.

Figure 3. Invideo.AI User Interface

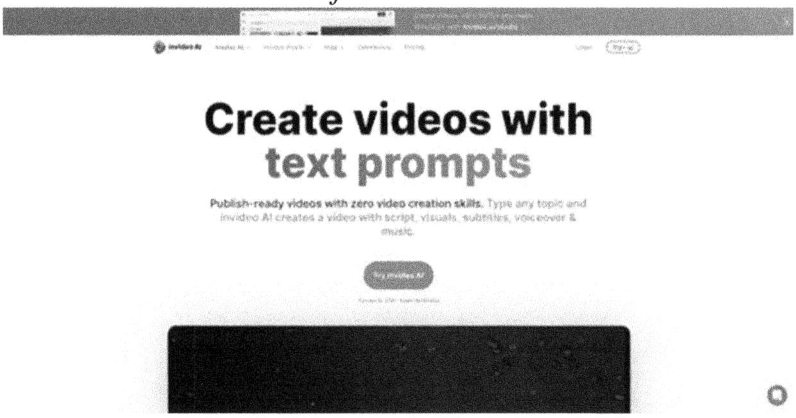

Customization: It delivers personalized content which might have been specifically produced in keeping with the students' learning objectives or interests.

According to research, it helps in students' retention and participation. So, InVideo AI should be considered a very helpful resource.

8.4. InShot and CapCut

Video editing applications InShot and CapCut are as accessible as they are simple video-making apps. They can enable students to create professional-looking multimedia products.

Figure 4. InShot User Interface

Their contribution to learning includes:

Ease of Use: The two applications have user-friendly interfaces with low technical complexity requirements, thus giving students ample time to explore the content rather than tedious editing processes.
Creative Freedom: Student can test the various versions of how the project might be edited in several ways, hence developing student storytelling skills and creativity.
Integration with Other Tools: Supports importation of contents from sites like Canva and InVideo Fig 6, thus projects are executed with perfect workflow.

Figure 5. Stages of Production Process

The use of such tools in schools brings up digital literacy and prepares students toward modern techniques of communication.

8.5 PowerPoint: New Innovative Presentation for Engagement

PowerPoint is considered a standard tool for making presentations, but AI advancements have recently made it even more powerful. Some of the important features include:

- The design suggestions are AI-driven, which helps the user build a visually cohesive professional presentation quite quickly.
- Interactive Features- These are the features that enable the addition of surveys, quizzes, and multimedia, facilitating active engagement from the audience.
- Accessibility Features- These are all the improvements that enhance the accessibility of content for everybody who is learning automatically include captioning and the text-to-speech functionality.
- It has been proven empirically that interactive presentations help to facilitate better retention and understanding of information and it is, therefore, a tool critical to education.

9. RECOMMENDATIONS AND SUGGESTIONS

This chapter offers practical recommendations and suggestions on how to practically realize AI-driven tutoring systems in educational contexts. By focusing on areas such as training of educators, collaborative environments, assessment mechanisms, and multimedia integration, can enhance the effectiveness of these tools in the framework of supporting personalized learning.

9.1 Ethical and Practical Considerations

As AI personalizes learning, it also presents a number of risks:

- Data Privacy: AI applications gather huge amounts of student data, which creates security and usage concerns.
- Algorithmic Bias: AI can perpetuate biases, which may disadvantage particular groups of students.
- Digital Divide: Not all students have equal access to AI applications, widening educational disparities.
- A balanced debate should consider these risks against the potential of AI to revolutionize education.

9.2 Ethical Considerations in AI Education

9.2.1 Bias and Fairness in AI Algorithms

AI systems need to be developed with fairness. Studies by Zhou & Brown (2015) point out the potential for biased algorithms to disproportionately harm marginalized students. Ethical AI education should:

- Apply bias-mitigation strategies during AI development.
- Provide transparent AI decision-making.
- Promote regulatory monitoring of AI education policies.

9.3 Training and Professional Development for Educators

Professional development for educators along with training targeted at maximizing the potential of AI-based tutoring systems are essential steps. Recommendations include:

Periodic workshops and seminars where sessions target technical knowledge about making use of AI tools in tandem with pedagogical techniques in relation to teaching practice.

Peer mentoring programs: Establish partnership among educators as they share their experiences, best practices, and even their strategies for troubleshooting- a process that fosters a support community of practice.

Continuous Support: Providing online resources, forums, and helpdesks that facilitate educators' overcoming difficulties as they are implementing new technologies. Research indicates that AI tools are more likely to be used effectively when well-trained teachers translate their practice into better student outcomes.

9.4 Collaborative Learning Environments

Establishing collaborative learning environment is essential to fully realize the potential offered by AI-Driven Tutoring Systems. Recommendations to develop collaboration include:

Group Projects and Peer Learning: Suggest the use of AI tools for promoting group work among students, which nurtures the ability to think critically as well as the ability to communicate.

Facilitated Discussions: The use of AI platforms aids the organization and the moderation of discussions with space for diverse opinions as well as collective problem-solving.

Shared Resources: Development of resources in repositories authored by students and their use among peers to be expanded with input from fellow peers or the same community. Evidence indicates that collaborative learning raises interest and enhances mastery of social and cognitive abilities.

9.5 Continuous Assessment and Feedback Mechanisms

Continuous assessment and feedback mechanisms can be employed to monitor and modify instruction in response to the improvement or otherwise in students' learning. Some suggestions include:

Real-Time Analytics: Using AI-driven analytic tools to monitor students' performance and engagement. It helps education experts make informed decisions on specific areas of an educational environment that might require adjustment.
Regular Feedback Cycles: Implementing structures that allow for prompt feedback on assignments and evaluations so students can benefit from mistakes.
Personalised Learning Plans: Using Assessment Data for developing individualized learning plans tailored to the strengths and challenges of each student.

Research has also shown that continuous assessment and feedback improve learner outcomes because it encourages students to develop a growth mindset.

9.6 Involving Multimedia Resources for Interactive Use

Multimedia content can be used to support the conduct of learning activities and, therefore, increase student interaction. Some strategies include the following:

- **Format Variability**: The use of multimedia to make engagement more appropriate for different learner profiles, whether through videos, podcasts, interactive simulations, or gamified learning.
- **Project-Based Learning**: On increasing creativity in tasks involving the production of multimedia projects in which students need to use learned knowledge and skills in creative ways.

- **Multimedia-Based Feedback**: Use of video and audio feedback for assignments, which are often better presented and more illustrative than written comments. Evidence also indicates that multimedia content can significantly improve retention and understanding and make learning more enjoyable.

9.7 Educators and Policymakers

To involve educators and policymakers more effectively, recommendations should be made in alignment with:

- **Educators**: Teaching strategies that adopt AI without usurping traditional pedagogy.
- **Policymakers**: Guidelines for ethical AI adoption in education, ensuring equity and accessibility.

10. FUTURE SCOPE OF RESEARCH

As AI-driven systems progress toward developing a tutoring system, several areas require continued research to determine their long-term impact and effectiveness.

10.1 Long-Term Impact Studies

Future longitudinal studies would be necessary to measure the maintenance effects of AI-driven tutoring systems on student performance and engagement over time. Knowing the influence of these systems on learning trajectories will be useful in discussing best practice and shaping policy.

10.2 Scalability of AI Tools in Diverse Educational Contexts

Scalability of AI tools: Exploratory investigation in and across diverse educational settings, whether in terms of age, subject, or socio-economic background, should measure the tool's flexibility to work effectively in the given context. Research studies should investigate in detail those factors that influence or hinder the effective implementation of AI tools across different settings.

10.3 Teacher Workload and Student Engagement

Related research should be done to find whether the use of AI-driven tutoring systems mitigates or exacerbates other workload pressures of teachers. The systems should also be determined about their effect on student engagement and motivation, specifically different demographic groups.

11. CONCLUSION

We can now summarize the findings about AI-driven tutoring systems and their contribution to personalized learning. We summarize key insights, discuss the implications of the findings for future educational practices, and conclude with final reflections about the role of AI in education.

11.1 Summary of Key Findings

The study on AI-driven tutoring systems reveals several important findings:

These will include the use of AI tools like ChatGPT and Canva in enhanced personalization. Such tools increase the personalization of the learning process based on individual, unique, and diverse needs as well as styles in learning.

Greater engagement: multimedia content with interactive elements increases students' engagement in the learning process and makes the learning lively and fun.

Collaboration and communication: AI tools can be a facilitator to the collaboration among the students and the collaboration among educators and learners towards the actual creation of a community of inquiry as well as shared experiences of learning.

Data-Driven Insights: The continuous assessment and real-time analytics would provide actionable insights to the educators, who could then take timely interventions with the help of personalized feedback.
Conclusion: These findings talk to how AI may possibly revolutionize the practice of education with regards to both teaching and learning outcomes.

11.2 Implications for Future Educational Practices

The implications of these findings for future educational practices are very huge:

Professional Development: Educators should continue to train on the effective practice of the implementation and use of AI-driven materials. As such, professional development programs will emerge as a priority area for including not only technology skills but pedagogical approaches.
Curriculum Design: Curriculum design needs to consider including AI tools that will ultimately meet the learning objectives and feed into the overall educational goal.
Policy Formulation: Educational and policy-making bodies need to offer a friendly environment for AI tools by endorsing them while at the same time pushing some of the burning issues, such as equity and access and data privacy.
Research and Innovation: Research into the long-term influence of AI-based tutoring systems is inevitable, and such research would have to make the tools even more effective based on evidence derived from an empirical basis.

Addressing such implications can help educational stakeholders make the best of AI in customized learning environments.

11.3 Conclusion Thoughts on AI in Personalized Learning

AI-based tutoring systems are the next step in the evolution of education. Even with many challenges such as equity access and management of data sensitivity, the benefits it offers are well worth and gigantic. While the horizon of technology expands, educators, researchers, and policymakers need to work together toward enhancing effective, inclusive, and innovative learning environments. Thought and strategy will be required to take on tools as the future of personalized learning will significantly be directed by integration of AI.

Chapter 3
Preparing Educators for the AI-Enhanced Classroom:
Strategies and Training

Andi Asrifan
https://orcid.org/0000-0002-9934-6129
Universitas Negeri Makassar, Indonesia

Maemuna Muhayyang
Universitas Negeri Makassar, Indonesia

Sadaruddin Sadaruddin
https://orcid.org/0000-0001-6890-1540
Universitas Islam Makassar, Indonesia

Syamsuardi Saodi
https://orcid.org/0000-0001-8551-9300
Universitas Negeri Makassar, Indonesia

Like Raskova Octaberliana
https://orcid.org/0009-0001-8829-5266
UIN Maulana Malik Ibrahim, Indonesia

DOI: 10.4018/979-8-3693-8382-7.ch003

ABSTRACT

AI is revolutionizing education with personalized learning, real-time feedback, and better instruction. To improve learning and efficiency, teachers are using AI-powered tutoring and grading technologies. Schools are unprepared to deploy AI tools for data privacy, algorithmic bias, and equitable access. Many teachers are unprepared for AI's technological and ethical problems in education. To assist teachers incorporate AI, this chapter covers professional development, hands-on training, and ethics. Our research shows that concentrated AI training can considerably increase instructors' AI tool use and responsibility. Results suggest that AI in education can create more customized and egalitarian learning environments with proper management and professional growth. These repercussions highlight the need for educators, governments, and institutions to collaborate to use AI's potential while preserving student privacy and promoting justice in education.

INTRODUCTION TO AI IN EDUCATION

Artificial intelligence (AI) is rapidly changing education, creating new opportunities and problems for educators and students (García-Martínez et al., 2023) (AalSaud, 2021) (Bittencourt et al., 2020). AI has shown promise in improving learning outcomes and personalizing training, sparking interest in its use in education. AI systems can scan massive amounts of data, provide real-time feedback, and adjust to student needs, making teaching more personalized and effective (Joshi et al., 2021) (Luan et al., 2020). Intelligent tutoring systems (ITS) use AI algorithms to coach students personally through tailored learning pathways. A major benefit of AI in the classroom is its capacity to accommodate different learning styles and speeds.

AI's promise in education is exciting, but it faces challenges (Luan et al., 2020). Schools, parents, and governments struggle to incorporate these tools safely, ethically, and effectively. As AI becomes more common in education, educators are leading the way. Teachers need technical abilities to employ AI tools and pedagogical knowledge to integrate them into courses. Professional development is essential for educators to traverse this new landscape and comprehend AI's strengths and limitations.

AI tools like LLMs and NLP systems have improved classroom engagement(Kim et al., 2022). These technologies improve feedback, enable self-regulated learning, and reduce student cognitive burden. Students can enhance their language and critical thinking skills by receiving rapid writing feedback from AI-powered chatbots. Teachers can focus more on tailored student interactions and higher-order instructional tasks by automating routine duties like grading with AI.

However, broad AI use in education creates ethical difficulties. Important issues include data privacy, algorithmic bias, and over-reliance on AI techniques. Assuring that all pupils benefit from AI technologies requires equitable and inclusive deployment. As AI evolves, educators, technologists, and politicians must continue to collaborate to improve learning while preserving its human roots.

1.1. Overview of AI Technologies in the Classroom

Modern classrooms use AI technologies to improve teaching and learning(Joshi et al., 2021). These technologies mimic human intelligence by using complex algorithms and machine learning to grasp language, evaluate images, and make judgments. Intelligent tutoring systems (ITSs) that tailor training to students' needs are promising AI uses in education. Real-time feedback and customized learning routes from ITS match each student's learning style. As effective as teacher-led instruction in math and writing, ITS is particularly useful.

AI-powered essay scoring (AES) systems are another classroom staple (Jiang, 2022) (August & Tsaima, 2021) (Kamalov et al., 2023). These systems score articles on language, coherence, and subject relevancy using AI algorithms. AES can match human grading accuracy in standardized tests. These tools automate grading, freeing up teachers to focus on student engagement and education. AES tools give students rapid feedback on their work and places for growth (McNamara et al., 2014) (Jones et al., 2019)(Ifenthaler, 2022)(Chaudhry & Kazim, 2021).

Social robots, which engage and develop students, are another AI innovation. These robots, some of which can understand and respond to emotions, offer dynamic learning environments that engage pupils. AI-powered chatbots can also help students with difficult problem-solving and peer interactions.

Adaptive learning systems, another type of ITS, customize language arts and science learning(Jiang, 2022)(Zhai et al., 2021). These platforms adapt material and complexity based on student performance to avoid overwhelming or underchallenging students. This dynamic adaptability creates a more inclusive classroom that meets a variety of learning requirements and paces.

Data privacy, algorithmic bias, and equal access must be considered when integrating AI technologies into education, notwithstanding their benefits(Luan et al., 2020)(Akgün & Greenhow, 2021). These technologies can promote educational equity, individualized learning, and instructional efficiency, making them essential for modern classrooms. Their growth and appropriate use will change education by engaging and empowering students.

THE ROLE OF EDUCATORS IN AN AI-ENHANCED CLASSROOM

AI-enhanced classrooms depend on educators to integrate AI tools into teaching and learning(Chaudhry & Kazim, 2021)(Kizilcec, 2023)(Ng et al., 2023). AI can deliver individualized training, rapid feedback, and automation of routine chores, but it cannot replace teachers. Educators guide pupils through AI tools to improve learning. The instructor must create an environment where AI tools complement traditional teaching techniques to stimulate critical thinking, creativity, and problem-solving.

Teachers need training in AI tool technology and AI-integrated pedagogy to maximize AI's educational potential (Wang & Lester, 2023). It comprises adapting teaching methods to AI-driven personalized learning systems and leveraging AI to provide individualized instruction to individual students. AI can provide real-time student performance data, allowing teachers to intervene and support(Kamalov et al., 2023). Teachers must interpret this data in light of their students' learning styles, skills, and weaknesses.

In addition, educators help address AI's ethical and societal impacts in the classroom. They must help students comprehend AI's limits, such as algorithm biases and overreliance on AI input. Teachers promote responsible and informed technology use by teaching digital literacy and AI critical thinking(Zhai et al., 2021)(Kamalov et al., 2023). Additionally, educators must campaign for fair access to AI tools so that all students, regardless of background, can benefit from AI-enhanced learning. Ultimately, educators in an AI-enhanced classroom must balance AI's technological capabilities with human values and skills needed for complete student development.

2.1. Adapting Teaching Methodologies

Teachers must adapt their methods to bring AI into the classroom and improve learning(Grieve et al., 2021)(Wang & Lester, 2023). As AI technologies become more common, teachers must rethink their methods and use AI's strengths while keeping a human-centered focus. One major change is using AI-driven technologies like intelligent tutoring systems (ITS) and adaptive learning platforms in lesson designs. Because these technologies adapt to each student's speed and level, teachers can provide personalized education to meet unique learning demands. AI evaluations can help teachers identify pupils who need more help or enrichment in real time(Li, 2020)(Taylor et al., 2021)(Holstein et al., 2020).

Teachers must be adaptable and active to adapt to this changing environment. In addition to providing knowledge, teachers help students use AI technologies to explore, analyze, and synthesize information. The change from lecture-based to interactive, student-centered learning uses AI tools to create tailored learning routes and provide quick feedback on student performance. AI can also minimize grading and assessment workloads, letting teachers focus on student engagement and higher-order thinking(Kim et al., 2022).

Teachers must also teach critical thinking and digital literacy to use AI ethically(Chaudhry & Kazim, 2021)(Grieve et al., 2021)(Akgün & Greenhow, 2021). This includes educating students to analyze AI input, identify biases, and examine AI system limitations. As AI becomes more incorporated into classrooms, teachers need professional development to adjust their methods. Educators must balance AI efficiency with vital human abilities to successfully adapt teaching methods to AI-enhanced learning environments.

DESIGNING CURRICULUM WITH AI

AI-designed curriculum allows educators to personalize, streamline, and engage students(Balta, 2023)(Jia et al., 2022). AI solutions can automate lesson planning, content delivery, and evaluation, freeing teachers to focus on creativity and instructional approach. AI's capacity to create customised lesson plans for individual pupils is one of its biggest advantages in curriculum creation. AI tools can assist educators discover learning gaps, recommend resources, and customize content for specific learning styles, creating more inclusive classrooms.

Adaptive learning systems use AI to change course difficulty and pacing based on student achievement, making instruction more adaptable(Chaudhry & Kazim, 2021)(Holstein et al., 2020). Personalization lets pupils learn at their own speed, enhancing retention. An AI-powered curriculum might offer extra tasks for pupils struggling with certain subjects and advanced content for those who excel. This encourages differentiated teaching and reduces one-size-fits-all.

By cross-referencing lesson content with national or local standards and suggesting improvements, AI can help connect curriculum design with educational standards(Wang & Lester, 2023)(Grieve et al., 2021)(Chaudhry & Kazim, 2021). AI tools can develop quizzes, tests, and other assessment materials that meet learning objectives and save teachers time. Simulations and virtual labs, supported by AI, help students grasp complicated topics.

AI improves efficiency and personalization, but educators must weigh its drawbacks. To ensure accurate, relevant, and educationally relevant AI-generated information, human oversight is essential(Chaudhry & Kazim, 2021)(García-Martínez et al., 2023). AI's automation and teachers' creativity and insight can make curriculum design more responsive and student-centered, boosting learning results.

3.1. Integrating AI Tools in Lesson Planning

AI can make class planning and delivery more efficient, personalized, and student-centered. Teachers can save time by using AI to design lessons, create learning materials, and evaluate students(Chaudhry & Kazim, 2021)(Çelik, 2023). These tools assess curricular objectives and create tailored lesson plans that meet educational standards, freeing teachers to focus on instructional tactics and student engagement. AI can help teachers tailor lessons to students' various learning styles and capacities.

Personalization is one of the greatest benefits of AI lesson planning. AI tools can analyze student performance, learning preferences, and progress to recommend class content and delivery changes(Chaudhry & Kazim, 2021)(Nafea, 2018)(Bhutoria, 2022). AI platforms can recommend various instructional approaches or additional resources for struggling students and more challenging content for excelling students. This allows teachers to adapt lesson plans to real-time data and deliver personalized instruction for each student.

AI can also provide quizzes, simulations, and virtual activities to improve lesson planning. These technologies let teachers use technology to foster critical thinking and active learning. AI may also automatically generate formative tests that meet class objectives, helping teachers track student progress and intervene faster.

AI tools have many benefits, but teachers must still design lessons and use AI to supplement their professional judgment. Using AI tools carefully can improve lesson preparations and create a more dynamic, individualized learning environment for students(Chaudhry & Kazim, 2021)(García-Martínez et al., 2023).

AI-ENHANCED ASSESSMENT AND FEEDBACK

Teachers may now analyze student performance and provide comments more efficiently, personally, and accurately with AI-enhanced tools(Chaudhry & Kazim, 2021)(Çelik, 2023)(Kizilcec, 2023). For multiple-choice exams, essays, and conceptual problems in math and computer science, AI-driven systems can automate grading. These systems use natural language processing and machine learning algorithms to evaluate student work, provide thorough feedback, and recommend changes. Automatic evaluations save teachers time and let them focus on more complicated lessons, while students get faster, more targeted feedback.

Real-time, formative feedback from AI-enhanced evaluation lets pupils learn from their mistakes and grow. AI can check essays for grammar problems and offer strategies to improve organization and logic(Chaudhry & Kazim, 2021)(Steiss et al., 2024)(Aluthman, 2016)(Meyer et al., 2023). This quick feedback loop lets students evaluate and improve their work before final exams, promoting ongoing learning. AI programs can also help pupils solve arithmetic problems step-by-step and correct them when they miss.

AI-enhanced assessment systems analyze student data to detect learning trends, promoting individualized learning(García-Martínez et al., 2023)(Colchester et al., 2016). These approaches can help educators identify student needs and pinpoint areas for support or difficulty. This data-driven method makes feedback more quick, relevant, and tailored to each learner's progress and abilities.

AI-enhanced evaluation has many benefits, but data privacy and algorithmic prejudice are ethical concerns. Teachers must actively analyze AI-generated feedback to ensure fair, context-sensitive, and educationally appropriate evaluations(Chaudhry & Kazim, 2021)(Akgün & Greenhow, 2021)(Swiecki et al., 2022).

4.1. Automated Grading Systems

AI-powered automated grading systems are transforming student work evaluation, especially in written assignments and large-scale exams(Ifenthaler, 2022)(Sil et al., 2024). These systems assess and grade student inputs using machine learning algorithms and NLP, making them faster and more efficient than traditional grading techniques. These systems automate typical grading duties like essay evaluation and multiple-choice tests, freeing up educators to focus on higher-order teaching responsibilities like individualized instruction and curriculum creation.

Automatic grading systems offer rapid and consistent feedback, a major benefit. AI can swiftly evaluate student work for grammar, structure, coherence, and subject relevancy using predetermined rubrics(Lowry et al., 1951)(Gerard et al., 2015). This real-time feedback helps pupils comprehend their faults and improve, improving learning. An automated essay scoring (AES) system may assess an essay's organization, syntax, and argument strength and provide precise feedback to help students improve. This speeds up grading and reduces human biases, making it more transparent and objective.

However, computerized grading has drawbacks. AI can perform standardized tasks well, but creative writing and intricate problem-solving may challenge it(Steiss et al., 2024)(Vojak et al., 2011). Additionally, AI systems may mirror the biases in their training data, raising fairness concerns. Educators must oversee computerized grading and use technology to enhance human judgment. Automatic grading systems can improve evaluation, feedback, and student learning when utilized wisely.

PROFESSIONAL DEVELOPMENT FOR EDUCATORS

Educators need professional development to bring AI tools into the classroom. Teachers need the skills and knowledge to use AI to improve teaching and learning as it changes education(Kizilcec, 2023)(Çelik, 2023). Comprehensive professional development programs should cover AI tool technicalities and pedagogical tactics for everyday use. To use

AI responsibly and successfully, educators must comprehend its benefits and drawbacks.

A complete professional development programme should incorporate hands-on training in AI applications like intelligent tutoring, automated grading, and adaptive learning platforms(Colchester et al., 2016). Teachers must learn how to strategically employ these tools to tailor learning, automate routine chores, and provide real-time feedback. Trainers should also include data privacy, algorithmic prejudice, and the ethical implications of AI in education to educate educators for AI's problems.

Professional development should teach instructors digital literacy and critical thinking in addition to technical abilities(Ng et al., 2023)(Akgün & Greenhow, 2021). They need this for their own AI use and to teach students how to use it safely. Teachers must educate students in critically assessing AI-generated outputs for biases and limitations.

Another important part of professional development is collaborative learning. Sharing AI classroom techniques, experiences, and best practices can assist teachers(Grieve et al., 2021). Professional development through peer learning networks, conferences, and online resources helps educators keep up with AI developments and tools. Extended professional development allows teachers to co

5.1. AI Training Programs for Teachers

Teachers need AI training to integrate AI into their courses. As AI tools become more common in education, teachers must grasp how they work, how to use them pedagogically, and how to handle ethical issues(Ng et al., 2023)(Grieve et al., 2021). Comprehensive AI training programs should give educators the technical ability to use AI tools and the critical knowledge to use them responsibly.

Teachers should learn to employ intelligent tutoring systems, automated grading platforms, and adaptive learning technologies in hands-on workshops in effective AI training programs. These solutions allow for personalized learning, real-time feedback, and reduced routine task workload. AI should boost learning by training teachers to smoothly integrate these tools into lesson plans, assessments, and classroom management(Chaudhry & Kazim, 2021)(Owoc et al., 2021).

In addition to technical abilities, AI training programs must incorporate ethical issues in teaching. Teachers should learn about data privacy, algorithmic bias, and overusing AI outputs. Understanding these challenges will help educators employ AI fairly, transparently, and in line with educational aims(Ng et al., 2023)(Holmes et al., 2021). Digital literacy programs should teach teachers how to help students critically engage with AI technologies, recognize their limitations, and evaluate their results.

AI training programmes should also encourage instructors to exchange knowledge and best practises. In-person and online peer-learning networks can assist instructors learn about new AI technologies and how to use them in the classroom(Owoc et al., 2021)(Ng et al., 2023). These programs give teachers the confidence and skills to employ AI to boost student learning while retaining the human element of education.

ETHICAL CONSIDERATIONS IN AI EDUCATION

As AI becomes more incorporated into classrooms, ethics are crucial. AI can improve personalized learning, automate administrative duties, and provide real-time feedback, but it also presents ethical issues around data protection, algorithmic bias, and student autonomy(Ma & Jiang, 2023)(Akgün & Greenhow, 2021)(Nguyen et al., 2022). To employ AI responsibly and fairly in education, educators must consider these issues.

One of the biggest ethical issues is data privacy. AI technologies personalize learning and analyze progress using massive student data. Protecting this data from misuse, illegal access, and student confidentiality is essential. Schools and instructors must ensure that AI tools conform with data protection regulations and have clear student data management and security policies(Ma & Jiang, 2023)(Luan et al., 2020)(Berendt et al., 2020). Data collection, use, and sharing must be transparent to sustain student, parent, and educator trust.

AI education also struggles with algorithmic bias. AI systems trained on biassed data may discriminate. Due to its skewed data, an AI grading tool may accidentally favor particular student groups. Teachers must be aware of these hazards and rigorously examine AI tools to ensure fairness and avoid reinforcing disparities(Akgün & Greenhow, 2021)(Schneider et al., 2022). AI systems need regular audits and changes to reduce bias and guarantee all students benefit from them.

Educators must also combat AI overuse. AI should promote learning, not replace critical human relationships, creativity, or judgment. Teachers must help kids grasp AI's limitations and think critically. Educators can use AI to promote fair, responsible, and human-centered learning by addressing these ethical issues(Wang & Lester, 2023).

6.1. Data Privacy and Student Confidentiality

AI in education raises worries about data privacy and student confidentiality(Ma & Jiang, 2023)(Berendt et al., 2020). AI systems use massive volumes of student data to tailor learning, measure progress, and evaluate performance, making data privacy and security crucial. Education institutions must protect student data and be transparent about how they acquire, preserve, and share it.

AI tools in education collect students' personal, academic, and learning data. Inadequate data management could lead to breaches or misuse, raising student privacy issues. Educational institutions must follow privacy rules like the GDPR in Europe and FERPA in the US while protecting data(USA: Making the grade - privacy considerations for AI in the education sector, 2024)(Amo et al., 2019)(Huang, 2023). These policies protect student privacy by regulating data handling.

Risk evaluations before deploying AI tools should help schools comprehend privacy risks in addition to legal compliance. A Privacy Impact Assessment (PIA) can assist schools assess AI technology hazards such data storage, third-party access, and long-term data retention. The privacy policies of any AI tools used in the classroom must also be apparent.

If privacy concerns arise, students and parents should be able to opt out of data collecting or AI integration. Maintaining trust requires clear communication about data gathering aims and avoiding unnecessary sharing of personal or sensitive data with AI systems(Polonetsky & Jerome, 2014)(Wang, 2020)(Grieve et al., 2021)(Lowry et al., 1951). By prioritizing data privacy and student confidentiality, schools may appropriately integrate AI while ensuring student rights and safety.

CASE STUDIES OF AI IMPLEMENTATION IN EDUCATION

Educational AI case studies reveal the accomplishments, problems, and lessons learnt from integrating AI into schools(Abbas et al., 2023)(Owoc et al., 2021)(Zulkarnain & Yunus, 2023). AI technology have improved learning, personalization, and administrative efficiency in many educational contexts. These case studies highlight how schools, universities, and educators are using AI to revolutionize teaching and learning, demonstrating its benefits and drawbacks.

For example, AI-powered intelligent tutoring systems (ITS) provide tailored arithmetic and writing education. ITS has enabled real-time feedback and adaptable learning routes in numerous schools, letting students learn at their own pace(August & Tsaima, 2021)(Nye, 2014). In underprivileged communities where one-on-one tutoring is scarce, these approaches have improved student involvement and academic achievement. Some universities use AI-based assessment technologies to automate grading and provide extensive comments on student essays, boosting speed and uniformity.

Administrative functions like student recruitment and guidance use AI. In certain colleges, AI chatbots answer common questions from prospective students, freeing up staff time for more challenging challenges(Ge & Hu, 2020)(Bilquise & Shaalan, 2022). These AI technologies improve communication and student experience, especially in large schools where individualized attention is hard to scale.

These case studies also raise data privacy, algorithmic bias, and digital divide concerns. Some AI programs make biased recommendations or judgments, emphasizing the necessity for constant monitoring and human oversight(Akgün & Greenhow, 2021)(Ma & Jiang, 2023). Additionally, equal access to AI technologies is a challenge, especially in low-resource countries with limited infrastructure and finance.

These case studies help educators and policymakers understand AI's benefits and drawbacks in education, guiding future implementations.

7.1. Success Stories and Challenges

Success examples and problems in AI application in education show AI's revolutionary promise and integration complexity(Owoc et al., 2021). Many schools worldwide have used AI to improve learning, tailor instruction, and expedite administrative duties. AI-powered intelligent tutoring systems (ITS) have excelled in math and language arts, where tailored learning pathways enable pupils understand complicated topics at their own pace(Kim et al., 2022)(Bhutoria, 2022). Real-time feedback from these technologies helps pupils improve, especially in underfunded schools with little individual attention. Pilot initiatives in Nepal have used AI in classrooms to improve math proficiency through interactive AI chatbots.

Automated grading systems have reduced educators' workload by giving fast assessments and feedback on student assignments(Srinivasan & Murthy, 2021)(Henkel et al., 2024). These tools speed up and standardize grading and let teachers focus on student engagement and instruction. AI chatbots have improved student support services by handling student inquiries and course registrations in higher education.

Challenges persist despite these successes. Data privacy and algorithmic bias are major issues. Critics say some AI systems reinforce data biases, resulting in biased judgments or recommendations. For egalitarian learning settings, AI systems must be transparent, monitored, and changed to reduce prejudice. The digital divide limits AI's benefits for underprivileged pupils by limiting access to AI technology across regions and socioeconomic categories(Akgün & Greenhow, 2021). These problems demonstrate the necessity for rigorous planning, oversight, and equal access to maximize AI's educational potential.

FUTURE TRENDS IN AI AND EDUCATION

Emerging trends in AI education will revolutionize learning delivery and experience. AI will become more important in customizing education, boosting administrative efficiency, and increasing student involvement. AI-powered adaptive learning systems that adapt to students' needs, learning speeds, and styles are a key trend(Xie et al., 2019)(Bhutoria, 2022). These systems employ data analytics to build individualized learning routes with content and evaluations that match students' ability. This approach tailors support, making learning more accessible and egalitarian.

Another trend is AI-based formative assessments and real-time feedback. AI-driven tools will soon increase teachers' feedback on essays and problem-solving activities, delivering detailed and immediate feedback(Swiecki et al., 2022). These tools grade and suggest improvements, helping students develop critical thinking. AI will enable more complex duties like assessing creative work and mentoring pupils as it advances.

AI will transform educational content development. AI will help teachers produce interactive learning materials, curricula, and lesson plans(Joshi et al., 2021)(Chaudhry & Kazim, 2021). Student exploration of STEM concepts in immersive environments will become easier with AI-generated simulations and virtual labs.

These tendencies will raise issues like data privacy, algorithmic prejudice, and AI ethics in classrooms(Kim et al., 2022)(Wang & Lester, 2023). Poor schools may struggle to embrace AI technologies, making equal access a major issue. Despite these limitations, AI will transform education, making it more individualized, accessible, and interesting for students worldwide.

8.1. Emerging Technologies

Technology is increasingly changing education, with AI revolutionizing how students learn and engage with knowledge(Kim et al., 2022)(Mukhallafi, 2020). Several cutting-edge innovations are making education more individualized, interactive, and efficient. Emerging technologies like AI-powered adaptive learning platforms customize lessons and assessments for each student in real time. These systems use student performance data to alter task complexity and recommend individualized resources, creating a more inclusive and responsive learning environment.

VR and AR in classrooms are another major advancement. Immersive technologies let students explore complex concepts in simulations and virtual settings, making science and history more fascinating(Markowitz et al., 2018)(Au & Lee, 2017)(Makransky & Petersen, 2021). Students can take virtual field trips to historical locations or conduct science experiments in simulated labs to enhance experiential learning without space or resources. VR and AR may become more integrated into STEM and vocational education as they improve.

Natural language processing (NLP) is another promising education field. AI chatbots and intelligent tutoring systems can instantly provide assignment feedback, answer queries, and guide students through learning activities using NLP technologies(Luan et al., 2020)(Malik et al., 2018). These AI-driven solutions can improve accessibility for various learners by translating, text-to-speech, and providing adaptive feedback.

Researchers are also investigating blockchain technology for academic certification and verification. Blockchain's safe, decentralized system might simplify educational credential management, making it easy for students to transfer credits or verify qualifications with companies (Lowry et al., 1951). As these technologies improve, they will make learning more dynamic, personalized, and efficient while posing ethical questions about equity and data privacy.

CONCLUSION AND RECOMMENDATIONS

The integration of AI in education presents both vast opportunities and significant challenges, requiring thoughtful implementation and continuous evaluation. AI technologies have the potential to transform teaching and learning by personalizing instruction, improving administrative efficiency, and providing real-time feedback. However, as schools and educators embrace AI, they must also address the ethical, social, and technical challenges that accompany its use. Data privacy, algorithmic bias, and equitable access to AI tools are critical issues that need to be managed to ensure AI benefits all students, regardless of their background or resources.

To harness the full potential of AI in education, educators, policymakers, and school administrators must take a proactive approach to its integration. Professional development for teachers should be prioritized, equipping them with the skills and knowledge to effectively implement AI in the classroom. Teachers need training not only in the technical operation of AI tools but also in understanding their limitations, ensuring they are used in ways that complement, rather than replace, human judgment and creativity.

Equity must remain a central concern as AI technologies become more widespread. Efforts should be made to bridge the digital divide, ensuring that students in under-resourced schools have access to the same AI tools as those in more affluent areas. Policymakers should advocate for funding and infrastructure to support the equitable distribution of AI resources, and clear guidelines should be established to protect student data and privacy.

Furthermore, continuous monitoring and ethical oversight are essential to ensure that AI systems do not reinforce biases or inequality in education. Schools and educational institutions must develop policies that guide the ethical use of AI, focusing on transparency, fairness, and accountability. In conclusion, while AI holds transformative potential for education, it must be implemented thoughtfully, with a focus on enhancing human-centered teaching and learning, promoting equity, and maintaining ethical standards.

9.1. Key Takeaways for Educators

The integration of AI into education brings key takeaways for educators that are crucial to navigating this new landscape effectively. First and foremost, educators must embrace continuous learning and adaptability. AI technologies are rapidly evolving, and staying updated on the latest tools, trends, and best practices is essential for teachers to fully harness AI's potential in the classroom. Professional development, peer collaboration, and engagement with AI tools through workshops and hands-on training are vital to build confidence and competence in using AI for instructional purposes.

Another key takeaway is the importance of balancing AI tools with human-centered teaching. While AI can assist with tasks such as grading, personalized feedback, and data analysis, it should not replace the human elements that are central to education—such as empathy, creativity, and critical thinking. Educators must guide students in using AI responsibly, ensuring that these tools complement rather than dominate the learning process. Teaching students how to critically engage with AI, including understanding its limitations and potential biases, is just as important as mastering the technology itself.

Equity and accessibility are also critical considerations. As AI becomes more embedded in education, teachers must advocate for equitable access to these technologies to ensure all students, regardless of background, can benefit from them. This includes being mindful of the digital divide and working towards inclusive solutions that support diverse learners, including those with disabilities or limited access to technology.

Finally, data privacy and ethical use of AI should be at the forefront of educators' minds. Teachers need to understand how AI systems collect and use data, ensuring that student information is protected and that AI tools are implemented transparently and ethically. By focusing on these key takeaways, educators can successfully integrate AI in ways that enhance learning while upholding the values of fairness, responsibility, and student-centered teaching.

REFERENCES

AalSaud, A. J. B. F. (2021, July 28). Artificial Intelligence and Children's Education: Review Study. *Sciedu Press*, *6*(2), 1–1. DOI: 10.5430/irhe.v6n2p1

Abbas, N., Imran, A., Manzoor, R., Hussain, T., & Hussain, M H A I. (2023, August 16). Role of Artificial Intelligence Tools in Enhancing Students' Educational Performance at Higher Levels., 36-49. DOI: 10.55529/jaimlnn.35.36.49

Akgün, S., & Greenhow, C. (2021, September 22). Artificial intelligence in education: Addressing ethical challenges in K-12 settings. *AI and Ethics*, *2*(3), 431–440. DOI: 10.1007/s43681-021-00096-7 PMID: 34790956

Aluthman, E. S. (2016, September 23). The Effect of Using Automated Essay Evaluation on ESL Undergraduate Students' Writing Skill. *International Journal of English Linguistics*, *6*(5), 54–54. DOI: 10.5539/ijel.v6n5p54

Amo, D., Fonseca, D., Alier, M., García-Peñalvo, F J., Guerrero, M J C., & Alsina, M I B. (2019, January 1). Personal Data Broker: A Solution to Assure Data Privacy in EdTech. Springer Science+Business Media, 3-14. DOI: 10.1007/978-3-030-21814-0_1

Au, E H., & Lee, J J. (2017, January 1). Virtual reality in education: a tool for learning in the experience age., 4(4), 215-215. DOI: 10.1504/IJIIE.2017.091481

August, S E., & Tsaima, A. (2021, January 1). Artificial Intelligence and Machine Learning: An Instructor's Exoskeleton in the Future of Education. Springer International Publishing, 79-105. DOI: 10.1007/978-3-030-58948-6_5

August, S E., & Tsaima, A. (2021, January 1). Artificial Intelligence and Machine Learning: An Instructor's Exoskeleton in the Future of Education. Springer International Publishing, 79-105. DOI: 10.1007/978-3-030-58948-6_5

Balta, N. (2023, June 13). Embracing the Future: AI's Transformative Potential in Educational Research. *Embracing the Future: AI's Transformative Potential in Educational Research*, *6*(2), 1–2. DOI: 10.31757/euer.624

Berendt, B., Littlejohn, A., & Blakemore, M. (2020, July 2). AI in education: learner choice and fundamental rights. Taylor & Francis, 45(3), 312-324. DOI: 10.1080/17439884.2020.1786399

Bhutoria, A. (2022, January 1). Personalized education and Artificial Intelligence in the United States, China, and India: A systematic review using a Human-In-The-Loop model. Elsevier BV, 3, 100068-100068. DOI: 10.1016/j.caeai.2022.100068

Bilquise, G., & Shaalan, K. (2022, January 1). AI-based Academic Advising Framework: A Knowledge Management Perspective. *International Journal of Advanced Computer Science and Applications*, *13*(8). Advance online publication. DOI: 10.14569/IJACSA.2022.0130823

Bittencourt, I I., Cukurova, M., Müldner, K., Luckin, R., & Millán, E. (2020, January 1). Artificial Intelligence in Education. Springer Science+Business Media. DOI: 10.1007/978-3-030-52237-7

Çelik, İ. (2023, January 1). Towards Intelligent-TPACK: An empirical study on teachers' professional knowledge to ethically integrate artificial intelligence (AI)-based tools into education. Elsevier BV, 138, 107468-107468. DOI: 10.1016/j.chb.2022.107468

Chaudhry, M. A., & Kazim, E. (2021, July 7). Artificial Intelligence in Education (AIEd): A high-level academic and industry note 2021. *SSRN*, *2*(1), 157–165. DOI: 10.2139/ssrn.3833583 PMID: 34790953

Chaudhry, M. A., & Kazim, E. (2021, July 7). Artificial Intelligence in Education (AIEd): A high-level academic and industry note 2021. *SSRN*, *2*(1), 157–165. DOI: 10.2139/ssrn.3833583 PMID: 34790953

Colchester, K., Hagras, H., Alghazzawi, D., & Aldabbagh, G. (2016, December 17). A Survey of Artificial Intelligence Techniques Employed for Adaptive Educational Systems within E-Learning Platforms. Polish Neural Network Society, the University of Social Sciences in Lodz & Czestochowa University of Technology, 7(1), 47-64. DOI: 10.1515/jaiscr-2017-0004

García-Martínez, I., Batanero, J. M. F., Cerero, J. F., & León, S. P. (2023, January 1). Analysing the Impact of Artificial Intelligence and Computational Sciences on Student Performance: Systematic Review and Meta-analysis. *University of Alicante*, *12*(1), 171–171. DOI: 10.7821/naer.2023.1.1240

Ge, Z., & Hu, Y. (2020, April 1). Innovative Application of Artificial Intelligence (AI) in the Management of Higher Education and Teaching. *Journal of Physics: Conference Series*, *1533*(3), 032089–032089. DOI: 10.1088/1742-6596/1533/3/032089

Gerard, L., Matuk, C., McElhaney, K W., & Linn, M C. (2015, May 2). Automated, adaptive guidance for K-12 education. Elsevier BV, 15, 41-58. DOI: 10.1016/j.edurev.2015.04.001

Grieve, R., Woodley, J., Hunt, S E., & McKay, A B. (2021, July 15). Student fears of oral presentations and public speaking in higher education: a qualitative survey. Routledge, 45(9), 1281-1293. DOI: 10.1080/0309877X.2021.1948509

Henkel, O., Horne-Robinson, H., Kozhakhmetova, N., & Lee, A. (2024, February 15). Effective and Scalable Math Support: Evidence on the Impact of an AI- Tutor on Math Achievement in Ghana. Cornell University. https://doi.org//arxiv.2402.09809DOI: 10.48550

Holmes, W., Porayska-Pomsta, K., Holstein, K., Sutherland, E., Baker, T T., Shum, S B., Santos, O C., Rodrigo, M M T., Cukurova, M., Bittencourt, I I., & Koedinger, K R. (2021, April 9). Ethics of AI in Education: Towards a Community-Wide Framework. Springer Science+Business Media, 32(3), 504-526. DOI: 10.1007/s40593-021-00239-1

Holstein, K., Aleven, V., & Rummel, N. (2020, January 1). A Conceptual Framework for Human–AI Hybrid Adaptivity in Education. Springer Science+Business Media, 240-254. DOI: 10.1007/978-3-030-52237-7_20

Holstein, K., Aleven, V., & Rummel, N. (2020, January 1). A Conceptual Framework for Human–AI Hybrid Adaptivity in Education. Springer Science+Business Media, 240-254. DOI: 10.1007/978-3-030-52237-7_20

Huang, L. (2023, June 30). Ethics of Artificial Intelligence in Education. *Student Privacy and Data Protection.*, *16*(2), 2577–2587. DOI: 10.15354/sief.23.re202

Ifenthaler, D. (2022, January 1). Automated Essay Scoring Systems., 1-15. DOI: 10.1007/978-981-19-0351-9_59-1

Jia, K., Wang, P., Li, Y., Chen, Z., Jiang, X., Lin, C., & Chin, T. (2022, February 16). Research Landscape of Artificial Intelligence and e-Learning: A Bibliometric Research. *Frontiers of Medicine*, *13*, 795039. Advance online publication. DOI: 10.3389/fpsyg.2022.795039 PMID: 35250730

Jiang, R. (2022, November 16). How does artificial intelligence empower EFL teaching and learning nowadays? A review on artificial intelligence in the EFL context. *Frontiers of Medicine*, *13*, 1049401. Advance online publication. DOI: 10.3389/fpsyg.2022.1049401 PMID: 36467167

Jones, S., Fox, C., Gillam, S. L., & Gillam, R. B. (2019, October 31). An exploration of automated narrative analysis via machine learning. *PLoS One*, *14*(10), e0224634–e0224634. DOI: 10.1371/journal.pone.0224634 PMID: 31671140

Joshi, S., Rambola, R. K., & Churi, P. (2021, January 1). Evaluating Artificial Intelligence in Education for Next Generation. *Journal of Physics: Conference Series*, *1714*(1), 012039–012039. DOI: 10.1088/1742-6596/1714/1/012039

Joshi, S., Rambola, R. K., & Churi, P. (2021, January 1). Evaluating Artificial Intelligence in Education for Next Generation. *Journal of Physics: Conference Series*, *1714*(1), 012039–012039. DOI: 10.1088/1742-6596/1714/1/012039

Kamalov, F., Calonge, D. S., & Gurrib, I. (2023, August 16). New Era of Artificial Intelligence in Education: Towards a Sustainable Multifaceted Revolution. *Sustainability (Basel)*, *15*(16), 12451–12451. DOI: 10.3390/su151612451

Kim, J., Lee, H., & Cho, Y H. (2022, January 28). Learning design to support student-AI collaboration: perspectives of leading teachers for AI in education. Springer Science+Business Media, 27(5), 6069-6104. DOI: 10.1007/s10639-021-10831-6

Kizilcec, R F. (2023, June 9). To Advance AI Use in Education, Focus on Understanding Educators. Springer Science+Business Media, 34(1), 12-19. DOI: 10.1007/s40593-023-00351-4

Li, J. (2020, June 8). Research on the Application of AI Intelligent Adaptation System in Primary and Secondary School Learning Process. Destech Publications. DOI: 10.12783/dtssehs/icesd2020/34447

Lowry, O. H., Rosebrough, N. J., Farr, A. L., & Randall, R. J. (1951). Protein measurement with the Folin phenol reagent.

Luan, H., Géczy, P., Lai, H., Gobert, J. D., Yang, S. J., Ogata, H., Baltes, J., Guerra, R. D. S., Li, P., & Tsai, C. (2020, October 19). Challenges and Future Directions of Big Data and Artificial Intelligence in Education. *Frontiers of Medicine*, *11*, 580820. Advance online publication. DOI: 10.3389/fpsyg.2020.580820 PMID: 33192896

Luan, H., Géczy, P., Lai, H., Gobert, J. D., Yang, S. J., Ogata, H., Baltes, J., Guerra, R. D. S., Li, P., & Tsai, C. (2020, October 19). Challenges and Future Directions of Big Data and Artificial Intelligence in Education. *Frontiers of Medicine*, *11*, 580820. Advance online publication. DOI: 10.3389/fpsyg.2020.580820 PMID: 33192896

Ma, X., & Jiang, C. (2023, May 30). On the Ethical Risks of Artificial Intelligence Applications in Education and Its Avoidance Strategies., 14, 354-359. DOI: 10.54097/ehss.v14i.8868

Makransky, G., & Petersen, G B. (2021, January 6). The Cognitive Affective Model of Immersive Learning (CAMIL): a Theoretical Research-Based Model of Learning in Immersive Virtual Reality. Springer Science+Business Media, 33(3), 937-958. DOI: 10.1007/s10648-020-09586-2

Malik, G., Tayal, D K., & Vij, S. (2018, November 3). An Analysis of the Role of Artificial Intelligence in Education and Teaching. Springer Nature, 407-417. DOI: 10.1007/978-981-10-8639-7_42

Markowitz, D. M., Laha, R., Perone, B., Pea, R., & Bailenson, J. N. (2018, November 30). Immersive Virtual Reality Field Trips Facilitate Learning About Climate Change. *Frontiers of Medicine*, *9*, 2364. Advance online publication. DOI: 10.3389/fpsyg.2018.02364 PMID: 30555387

McNamara, D S., Crossley, S A., Roscoe, R D., Allen, L K., & Dai, J. (2014, November 11). A hierarchical classification approach to automated essay scoring. Elsevier BV, 23, 35-59. DOI: 10.1016/j.asw.2014.09.002

Meyer, J., Jansen, T., Schiller, R., Liebenow, L W., Steinbach, M., Horbach, A., & Fleckenstein, J. (2023, December 29). Using LLMs to bring evidence-based feedback into the classroom: AI-generated feedback increases secondary students' text revision, motivation, and positive emotions. Elsevier BV, 6, 100199-100199. DOI: 10.1016/j.caeai.2023.100199

Mukhallafi, T. R. A. (2020, August 17). Using Artificial Intelligence for Developing English Language Teaching/Learning: An Analytical Study from University Students' Perspective. *International Journal of English Linguistics*, *10*(6), 40–40. DOI: 10.5539/ijel.v10n6p40

Nafea, I. (2018, September 19). Machine Learning in Educational Technology. DOI: 10.5772/intechopen.72906

Ng, D T K., Leung, J K L., Su, J., Ng, C W., & Chu, S K W. (2023, February 1). Teachers' AI digital competencies and twenty-first century skills in the post-pandemic world. Springer Science+Business Media, 71(1), 137-161. DOI: 10.1007/s11423-023-10203-6

Nguyen, A., Ngo, H N., Hong, Y., Dang, B., & Nguyen, B T. (2022, October 13). Ethical principles for artificial intelligence in education. Springer Science+Business Media, 28(4), 4221-4241. DOI: 10.1007/s10639-022-11316-w

Nye, B D. (2014, October 7). Intelligent Tutoring Systems by and for the Developing World: A Review of Trends and Approaches for Educational Technology in a Global Context. Springer Science+Business Media, 25(2), 177-203. DOI: 10.1007/s40593-014-0028-6

Owoc, M L., Sawicka, A., & Weichbroth, P. (2021, January 1). Artificial Intelligence Technologies in Education: Benefits, Challenges and Strategies of Implementation. Springer Science+Business Media, 37-58. DOI: 10.1007/978-3-030-85001-2_4

Polonetsky, J., & Jerome, J. T. J. (2014, January 1). Student Data: Trust, Transparency, and the Role of Consent. RELX Group (Netherlands). DOI: 10.2139/ssrn.2628877

Schneider, J., Abraham, R., Meske, C., & Brocke, J V. (2022, June 20). Artificial Intelligence Governance For Businesses. Taylor & Francis, 40(3), 229-249. DOI: 10.1080/10580530.2022.2085825

Sil, P., Chaudhuri, P., & Raman, B. (2024, January 1). Can AI Assistance Aid in the Grading of Handwritten Answer Sheets?. Springer Science+Business Media, 291-298. DOI: 10.1007/978-3-031-64312-5_35

Srinivasan, V., & Murthy, H. (2021, January 1). Improving reading and comprehension in K-12: Evidence from a large-scale AI technology intervention in India. Elsevier BV, 2, 100019-100019. DOI: 10.1016/j.caeai.2021.100019

Steiss, J., Tate, T., Graham, S., Cruz, J., Hébert, M., Wang, J., Moon, Y., Tseng, W., Warschauer, M., & Olson, C B. (2024, June 1). Comparing the quality of human and ChatGPT feedback of students' writing. Elsevier BV, 91, 101894-101894. DOI: 10.1016/j.learninstruc.2024.101894

Swiecki, Z., Khosravi, H., Chen, G., Martínez-Maldonado, R., Lodge, J M., Milligan, S., Selwyn, N., & Gašević, D. (2022, January 1). Assessment in the age of artificial intelligence. Elsevier BV, 3, 100075-100075. DOI: 10.1016/j.caeai.2022.100075

Taylor, D., Yeung, M., & Bashet, A Z. (2021, January 1). Personalized and Adaptive Learning. Springer International Publishing, 17-34. DOI: 10.1007/978-3-030-58948-6_2

USA. Making the grade - privacy considerations for AI in the education sector. (2024, February 23). https://www.dataguidance.com/opinion/usa-making-grade-privacy-considerations-ai-education

Vojak, C., Kline, S., Cope, B., McCarthey, S J., & Kalantzis, M. (2011, May 25). New Spaces and Old Places: An Analysis of Writing Assessment Software. Elsevier BV, 28(2), 97-111. DOI: 10.1016/j.compcom.2011.04.004

Wang, N., & Lester, J C. (2023, June 1). K-12 Education in the Age of AI: A Call to Action for K-12 AI Literacy. Springer Science+Business Media, 33(2), 228-232. DOI: 10.1007/s40593-023-00358-x

Wang, Y. (2020, March 18). When artificial intelligence meets educational leaders' data-informed decision-making: A cautionary tale. Elsevier BV, 69, 100872-100872. DOI: 10.1016/j.stueduc.2020.100872

Xie, H., Chu, H., Hwang, G., & Wang, C. (2019, June 6). Trends and development in technology-enhanced adaptive/personalized learning: A systematic review of journal publications from 2007 to 2017. Elsevier BV, 140, 103599-103599. DOI: 10.1016/j.compedu.2019.103599

Zhai, X., Chu, X., Chai, C. S., Jong, M. S., Starčič, A. I., Spector, M., Li, J., Jing, Y., & Li, Y. (2021, April 20). A Review of Artificial Intelligence (AI) in Education from 2010 to 2020. *Complexity*, *2021*(1), 1–18. DOI: 10.1155/2021/8812542

Zulkarnain, N. N., & Yunus, M. M. (2023, May 23). Teachers'. *Perceptions and Continuance Usage Intention of Artificial Intelligence Technology in Tesl.*, *06*(05). Advance online publication. DOI: 10.47191/ijmra/v6-i5-34

Chapter 4

Impact of AI on Student Learning Outcomes:

Measuring Success and Identifying Challenges

Mustafa Kayyali

https://orcid.org/0000-0003-3300-262X

HE Higher Education Ranking, Syria

ABSTRACT

This chapter investigates the transformative impact of artificial intelligence (AI) on student learning outcomes, concentrating on the possibilities and constraints of AI-powered personalized learning systems. AI offers a dynamic approach to education by enabling tailored learning paths that respond to individual student needs, enhancing both interest and accomplishment. Through a detailed study of important success measures, this chapter illustrates how AI-driven technologies boost student performance and outlines the primary issues associated with their adoption, including data protection, teacher adaptability, and the digital divide. Case examples of successful AI integration highlight the effectiveness of these technologies, while future recommendations underline the need for equal access and continuing growth in the field. Ultimately, this chapter contends that AI has the potential to improve education, but success requires careful monitoring and addressing inherent obstacles.

DOI: 10.4018/979-8-3693-8382-7.ch004

INTRODUCTION

The rapid expansion of technology in the 21st century has radically transformed many sectors, and education is no exception (Papanastasiou et al, 2019). As we go farther into the digital age, artificial intelligence (AI) has emerged as one of the most potent tools capable of altering traditional educational systems. AI's potential to revolutionize the learning experience is great, not only in terms of content delivery but also in its power to personalize the learning journey for each student (Tapalova & Zhiyenbayeva, 2022). Unlike the one-size-fits-all paradigm of education that has reigned for millennia, AI empowers educators to respond to the specific needs, abilities, and learning styles of individual students. As AI-based learning tools grow more powerful and accessible, they enable chances for students to engage with customized learning pathways that can maximize their potential, typically at a pace that suits their specific learning curve. In essence, AI has brought the concept of individualized learning on an unprecedented scale. This constitutes a major shift in educational paradigms, providing a more flexible, responsive, and adaptive approach to learning. Through clever algorithms, AI systems can assess huge volumes of data about student performance, preferences, and behavior (González-Calatayud et al, 2021). These findings are then utilized to dynamically change learning content and approaches, helping to overcome gaps in knowledge, reinforcing strengths, and ultimately enhancing learning results. For example, AI-powered solutions can offer real-time feedback, recommend more resources depending on a student's progress, and even foresee future obstacles the student could face. This kind of personalized learning experience was inconceivable in the pre-digital era, yet today, it is becoming a basic aspect of forward-thinking educational approaches.

Beyond its role in individualized learning, AI is also transforming the entire educational ecosystem by boosting efficiency in administration, evaluation, and even pedagogy (Pedro et al, 2019). AI-driven solutions are now capable of automating administrative chores including grading, monitoring attendance, and tracking student achievement over time. This automation not only decreases the effort for educators but also helps them to focus more on delivering meaningful learning experiences. Furthermore, AI systems are enhancing how learning is judged. Traditional testing methods typically fail to capture the complicities of a student's knowledge and skills. In contrast, AI-powered exams can provide a more holistic review by examining patterns of interaction, critical thinking, and problem-solving ability. This trend towards a more detailed assessment of student achievement has substantial ramifications for how educators perceive and respond to the needs of their students.

Despite its potential, the implementation of AI in education is not without hurdles (Akgun & Greenhow, 2022). Issues regarding data privacy, equity, and accessibility offer substantial impediments to the widespread use of AI technologies in colleges. There is also the matter of how educators may effectively integrate AI into their teaching practices without being overwhelmed by the complexity of these systems. The digital divide is another serious worry, since students from underprivileged backgrounds may not have the same access to AI-powered technologies, thus widening the gap between advantaged and disadvantaged learners (Capraro et al, 2024). These problems must be addressed if AI is to realize its promise of democratizing education and enhancing learning results for all students, regardless of their background.

The usefulness of AI in education extends beyond only enhancing academic performance (Bates et al, 2020). AI technologies can generate higher engagement, motivation, and innovation among students (Guan et al, 2020). By giving students real-time feedback and individualized challenges, AI systems can create a more engaging and stimulating learning environment. AI-powered teaching tools can adjust to students' emotional and cognitive states, delivering help when needed and pushing them toward greater levels of knowledge and competence. This responsiveness can help create a growth attitude in students, encouraging them to embrace challenges and perceive learning as a continual process rather than a linear journey with fixed outcomes. As the educational landscape continues to evolve, it is obvious that AI will play a major role in determining the future of learning. Institutions throughout the world are already experimenting with AI-powered platforms, and early results suggest that these tools have the potential to greatly improve learning outcomes.

However, the effectiveness of AI in education depends on a multitude of elements, including the ability of educators and institutions to analyze and assess its effects successfully (Cope et al, 2021). In this perspective, judging the performance of AI in education is not simply a matter of looking at test results or grades. A more sophisticated approach is needed, one that examines the long-term influence of AI on student learning and development (Owoc et al, 2019). This includes analyzing aspects like as student involvement, motivation, critical thinking skills, and the ability to apply knowledge in real-world circumstances. Additionally, it is crucial to understand the hurdles that educators and institutions encounter when using AI-powered technologies, from technical issues to worries about data security and teacher preparation.

THE ROLE OF AI IN ENHANCING STUDENT LEARNING OUTCOMES

Artificial intelligence (AI) has profoundly impacted how students learn, interact, and engage with educational content (Seo et al, 2021). As AI technologies become more ingrained in the fabric of modern education, their ability to boost student learning outcomes has caught the interest of educators, politicians, and researchers alike. The transformative impact of AI in education resides in its capacity to adapt to the specific needs of individual learners, giving individualized experiences that stimulate deeper knowledge, engagement, and motivation (George, 2023). As a result, AI-driven learning systems are helping to bridge the gap between traditional, often rigid educational methods and the dynamic, individualized approaches necessary to educate students for the challenges of the 21st century. One of the most significant ways AI boosts learning results is through its capacity to tailor the educational experience. In traditional classrooms, professors typically struggle to respond to the different learning styles, abilities, and needs of every student. AI, however, can evaluate massive amounts of data on student performance, behavior, and preferences, and utilize these insights to construct tailored learning paths that target the specific problems and strengths of each student. For instance, an AI-powered system can determine when a student is struggling with a particular idea and automatically suggest additional resources, exercises, or explanations tailored to that student's learning style. This tailored approach not only helps students master hard subjects more efficiently but also increases their confidence by enabling them to develop at their speed.

AI-powered learning systems generally contain real-time feedback mechanisms, a vital element that boosts student learning outcomes (Rekha et al, 2024). In traditional settings, students may have to wait days or even weeks to receive feedback on assignments or examinations, which can hamper their ability to resolve gaps in comprehension. In contrast, AI systems may provide immediate feedback, helping trainees detect and correct problems as they occur. This quick feedback loop accelerates the learning process, allowing students to build upon their knowledge without substantial delays. Furthermore, AI tools can offer more extensive feedback than traditional grading systems, helping students not only to identify where they went wrong but also to understand why and how to improve (Fagbohun et al, 2024). AI also plays a critical role in improving student engagement, which is a key determinant in obtaining improved learning results. Engaged students are more likely to retain material, participate actively in class, and apply what they have learned in meaningful ways. AI-powered platforms, such as intelligent tutoring systems or gamified learning environments, can make learning more dynamic and pleasurable (Narayanan & Kumaravel, 2024). These platforms commonly incorporate features of game design, such as prizes, challenges, and advancement levels, to engage students and sustain their attention. AI systems can change the difficulty level of content in real-time, guaranteeing that students are neither bored by material that is too easy nor overwhelmed by stuff that is too challenging. This tailored pace maintains students in a state of "flow," when they are involved in the learning process and more likely to achieve optimal learning outcomes.

Another key component of AI's impact on student learning outcomes is its capacity to facilitate self-directed learning (Al-Adwan et al, 2022). AI solutions help students take control of their own learning experiences by offering them the flexibility to explore topics that interest them, study content at their speed, and access extra resources as needed. This autonomy allows students to acquire a sense of ownership over their education, supporting lifelong learning habits that extend beyond the classroom. With AI's support, students can pursue personalized learning paths that correspond with their interests and professional aspirations, which can lead to improved academic accomplishment and personal satisfaction (Ellikkal & Rajamohan, 2024). AI's ability to examine vast datasets further boosts its role in enhancing learning results. By watching a student's development over time, AI systems can detect trends, patterns, and locations where intervention is needed. This data-driven approach enables instructors to make more informed decisions about how to serve each student. For example, an AI system might notice that a student consistently struggles with specific types of questions, allowing the teacher to provide tailored support in that area. Furthermore, this real-time data analysis allows for preventive interventions, preventing students from falling too far behind before aid is offered. It also enables instructors to examine the efficiency of various teaching tactics, adjusting their approaches to enhance student performance.

The significance of AI in education is not limited to increasing academic performance; it also plays a major role in developing key soft skills, such as critical thinking, problem-solving, and creativity (Thornhill-Miller et al, 2023). AI systems are becoming capable of designing learning environments that encourage students to think critically and approach challenges from numerous sides. By giving opportunities for students to engage with difficult, real-world challenges, AI-powered learning platforms assist develop skills that are important for success in today's fast-shifting world. For instance, AI can replicate real-world circumstances, such as ethical concerns or complicated commercial challenges, that require students to apply their knowledge in new and inventive ways. These scenarios not only increase students' grasp of academic information but also help them acquire practical abilities that are highly appreciated in the workforce. AI's function in facilitating collaboration among students is another component contributing to higher learning results. In traditional contexts, collaborative learning generally needs face-to-face engagement, which might be constrained by time and geographical constraints. However, AI-powered platforms enable students to collaborate across time zones and locales, promoting group work, conversations, and problem-solving activities in virtual environments. AI can even connect students with friends who have matching abilities or interests, boosting the collaborative learning experience. By facilitating teamwork and communication, AI helps students develop crucial interpersonal skills while enhancing their grasp of course material.

Despite these advantages, it is vital to emphasize that the use of AI in increasing student learning outcomes is not without its problems. One of the key problems is ensuring that AI technologies are applied in a way that complements, rather than replaces, the crucial role of human professors (Pedro et al, 2019). AI can give essential help in terms of personalization, feedback, and data analysis, but it cannot duplicate the empathy, creativity, and intuition that good educators bring to the classroom. The most effective AI-enhanced learning environments are those in which AI tools are utilized to augment the teacher's role, giving them the insights and resources they need to better support their students. AI can greatly boost student learning outcomes by customizing education, delivering real-time feedback, improving engagement, supporting self-directed learning, and promoting the development of essential soft skills. However, the success of AI in education depends on how well it is integrated into the whole learning process. When applied successfully, AI can help build a more flexible, responsive, and student-centered educational environment that better matches the requirements of today's diverse learners.

PERSONALIZED LEARNING THROUGH AI: A GAME CHANGER

Personalized learning has been a long-standing aim in education, driven by the desire to adjust instructional techniques and materials to the individual needs and talents of each student (Kayyali, 2024a). However, in traditional educational systems, this concept has frequently been hampered by the realities of classroom dynamics, with one instructor attempting to fulfill the various needs of dozens, if not hundreds, of students. The arrival of artificial intelligence (AI) is transforming this issue into an opportunity. By harnessing AI's ability to evaluate enormous amounts of data, recognize trends, and make real-time modifications, personalized learning is not only conceivable but increasingly becoming a game changer in how education is provided (Castro et al, 2024). At its foundation, AI-driven personalized learning attempts to provide a unique educational experience for each student by changing the pace, content, and instructional methods to meet their particular needs. This level of customization can take various forms, from proposing specialized learning resources to delivering specific tests and feedback. For instance, a kid who excels in mathematics but has issues with reading comprehension can be presented with more hard math tasks while receiving extra attention in reading. This flexibility ensures that students are neither held down by a one-size-fits-all curriculum nor overwhelmed by content that exceeds their existing knowledge. One of the most significant advantages of personalized learning using AI is its capacity to overcome learning gaps in real-time. In typical classrooms, it can be difficult for professors to quickly detect whether students are lagging behind or not fully learning particular ideas (Pollock & Tolone, 2020). With AI-powered platforms, however, these gaps are discovered nearly instantaneously. By assessing a student's performance on assignments, quizzes, or even their activities within a digital learning environment, AI systems can identify areas where the learner may require more support. This information is then utilized to alter the learning materials and activities accordingly, ensuring that students receive the aid they need when they need it most. In this approach, individualized learning using AI prevents students from falling too far behind, making learning more efficient and effective.

Another significant element of AI-driven individualized learning is the ongoing assessment of student progress (Sajja et al, 2024). Unlike traditional assessments, which frequently come in the form of periodic tests, AI systems can evaluate student achievement on an ongoing basis. This offers a more nuanced and accurate knowledge of each student's strengths and weaknesses. Furthermore, because these assessments are embedded into the learning process, they feel less like high-stakes tests and more like natural checkpoints along the route. Students are allowed to demonstrate their knowledge and skills in numerous circumstances, making the learning experience feel more comprehensive and integrated. Continuous assessment also allows educators to track long-term progress and make data-informed decisions about how best to support each learner. The versatility of AI systems makes individualized learning particularly potent. AI can determine when a student is struggling with a particular idea and modify the difficulty level or presenting style of the content to make it more accessible (Khosravi et al, 2022). For example, if a student is having trouble grasping a complex scientific subject, the AI system might provide the material in a different format, such as through an interactive simulation, video instruction, or a collection of lesser questions that build up to the more difficult ones. This kind of adaptation ensures that students are not left behind merely because they learn differently than their peers. Instead, individuals are provided various opportunities to engage with the content in ways that suit their learning preferences.

Moreover, AI-based customization boosts motivation by empowering students to take ownership of their learning (Mehendale, 2023). When learning routes are personalized to students' interests and needs, they are more likely to stay engaged and devoted to their studies. AI systems can contain elements of choice and autonomy, allowing students to explore topics at their own speed and select activities that match their unique learning goals. This autonomy develops a sense of agency, encouraging students to take a more active role in their education. As a result, students become more motivated to succeed, as they feel that the learning experience is truly theirs. One of the most transformational aspects of personalized learning through AI is its capacity to provide individualized support to students with a wide range of skills and learning styles. In a regular classroom, it might be difficult for professors to deliver the kind of individualized attention that some students need. AI systems, however, can deliver focused interventions to individuals who require further support, while simultaneously challenging students who are ready to move ahead. For students with learning difficulties or those who require accommodations, AI can be very beneficial, as it can automatically alter the learning environment to match their needs. For example, students who struggle with reading can benefit from text-to-speech capabilities or visual aids, while those with attention challenges might be provided with shorter, more concentrated assignments that help them stay on course.

AI also plays a vital role in aiding educators by providing them with practical insights regarding their students' learning (Fitria et al, 2021). While the purpose of individualized learning is to empower students, professors remain a vital component of the equation. AI systems may evaluate student data and deliver it to professors in a format that is easy to grasp, emphasizing areas where students may require particular attention or discovering trends that could inform instructional tactics. This data-driven strategy helps professors to target their efforts where they are most needed, eventually increasing the overall learning experience. Far from replacing instructors, AI acts as a potent tool that amplifies their ability to give tailored teaching on a big scale. Beyond the immediate benefits for individual students, personalized learning with AI can address bigger systemic concerns in education. One of the most pressing challenges in education today is equity—ensuring that all students, regardless of their origin or circumstances, have access to a high-quality education. AI-powered personalized learning can help level the playing field by giving every student a learning experience that is tailored to their needs (Ayeni et al, 2024). This is particularly crucial for students in under-resourced institutions or those who have historically been marginalized in the educational system. By delivering individualized guidance to these students, AI can help overcome success disparities and create a more inclusive learning environment.

However, the deployment of AI-driven tailored learning is not without obstacles (Wan et al, 2020). One of the primary problems is ensuring that these technologies are used appropriately and ethically (Royakkers et al, 2018). Personalized learning systems rely on huge volumes of student data to work efficiently, and this raises critical problems regarding privacy, security, and data governance. Colleges and educational institutions must take precautions to preserve student data and guarantee that it is used in ways that benefit students without compromising their privacy (Jones, 2020). Additionally, like with any technology, there is a risk that AI systems could unwittingly perpetuate existing prejudices or inequalities if not properly built and maintained. Educators, developers, and politicians must work together to design AI systems that are equal, transparent, and aligned with the best interests of students. Personalized learning with AI represents a game-changing revolution in how education is provided (Galés & Gallon, 2020). By responding to the specific demands of each student, AI systems are developing more flexible, responsive, and effective learning environments that boost student results. From real-time interventions to continuous assessment, AI has the potential to improve the learning experience for students at all levels. However, the successful deployment of personalized learning through AI will need careful consideration of ethical and practical problems, as well as a commitment to ensure that new technologies are used to promote diversity and inclusion in education. If these issues are addressed, personalized learning using AI could become one of the most potent tools for enhancing educational outcomes in the 21st century.

MEASURING SUCCESS: KEY METRICS FOR AI-DRIVEN LEARNING

As artificial intelligence (AI) continues to disrupt education, one of the most crucial components of its adoption is understanding how to quantify its influence on student learning (Halagatti et al, 2023). The effectiveness of AI-driven learning can't just be assumed—it must be measured using a range of meaningful and trustworthy indicators that reflect not just academic performance, but also the overall student experience, the development of important skills, and long-term results. Identifying the correct measures to analyze AI's success in the classroom allows educators, institutions, and policymakers to make informed decisions, optimize the usage of AI tools, and ultimately better the learning experience for students (Kuleto et al, 2021).

One of the most obvious and traditional methods to judge success in college is through academic performance (Strayhorn, 2018). AI-driven learning systems provide the potential to increase grades, test scores, and overall academic accomplishment by providing individualized, focused training tailored to each student's particular strengths and limitations. By continuously monitoring student progress and adjusting teachings accordingly, AI tools can help students learn ideas they may have struggled with in a typical classroom setting. This can lead to significant increases in areas like standardized test scores or end-of-course assessments, which remain essential measures of student achievement. While these measurements are crucial, they should not be the exclusive markers of success. Relying simply on test scores can ignore other crucial characteristics of learning that AI systems are well-positioned to serve.

Another key indicator to examine is student involvement. In AI-driven learning environments, student engagement may be assessed in several ways, from measuring how frequently students interact with the learning platform to monitoring the time they spend on different activities (Chiu et al, 2023). The amount of engagement is a critical predictor of success since it reveals how deeply students are interested in the learning process. Engaged students are more likely to persist despite problems, absorb new material, and apply what they've learned in meaningful ways (Barkley, 2018). AI can track behavioral data to provide educators with a clearer picture of which students are actively participating and which might require more encouragement or inspiration. AI can make learning more interactive and engaging by giving personalized content, gamified aspects, or real-time feedback that attracts students' attention and keeps them involved in their educational path.

In addition to engagement, student retention is another statistic that may be used to evaluate the performance of AI-driven learning. Retention refers to a student's capacity to retain and apply the knowledge they've received over time. AI's continual monitoring of student performance enables the identification of places where a student might be at risk of forgetting essential ideas or where knowledge gaps may arise (Pedro et al, 2019). Through timely interventions, AI systems can assist prevent this loss of information, ensuring that students retain the stuff they've learned long beyond the initial session. One technique to measure retention is by follow-up tests or quizzes meant to examine long-term knowledge retention rather than just rapid recollection. If students can recall and demonstrate the abilities they acquired even weeks or months after completing a session, it's a positive sign that AI-driven learning is effectively enabling deep, persistent understanding.

Beyond academic measurements, it is crucial to assess how AI-driven learning impacts the development of soft skills, such as problem-solving, critical thinking, creativity, and teamwork (George, 2023). These skills are increasingly appreciated in the modern workforce and are crucial for students' success outside the classroom. AI may play a big role in cultivating these competencies by delivering individualized learning paths that encourage students to think critically, solve complicated problems, and communicate with peers in virtual or mixed-learning settings. To test these results, educators can construct assignments or projects that challenge students to apply their soft skills in new circumstances. For example, a problem-solving assessment can present students with a real-world scenario in which they must use the knowledge and skills they've acquired to discover a solution. By tracking student progress on such tasks over time, instructors can acquire insights into how successfully AI-driven learning is cultivating these critical competencies.

Another crucial indicator to examine is student satisfaction (Razinkina, 2018). While academic accomplishment and skill development are crucial, the total learning experience should also be evaluated when judging the success of AI-driven education. Student satisfaction can be evaluated using questionnaires, feedback forms, and interviews that record students' perceptions of the effectiveness of AI technologies, the personalization of their learning experience, and their overall comfort with the technology (Rodway & Schepman, 2023). Students who feel supported, engaged, and empowered by AI are more likely to have a favorable attitude toward learning and education in general. On the other hand, students who feel overwhelmed or distanced from AI technologies may struggle to engage, leading to decreased satisfaction and possibly diminished learning outcomes. Gathering regular input from students allows educators to make improvements to AI platforms or teaching tactics to improve the overall learning experience.

Professor satisfaction and perceptions should also be taken into account when measuring the success of AI-driven learning (Chiu et al, 2023). AI is not meant to replace instructors, but rather to act as a tool that enhances their ability to give tailored teaching. Professors who feel that AI systems are helping them better understand their students' needs, minimize administrative hassles, or increase the quality of instruction are likely to be more enthusiastic about implementing AI into their teaching practices. Measuring teacher satisfaction can be done through questionnaires, interviews, and performance assessments that examine how professors view the influence of AI on their work. If instructors feel empowered by AI and can see its benefits in the classroom, they are more inclined to embrace these technologies and integrate them into their teaching in meaningful ways.

In addition to these immediate indicators, it is vital to examine long-term results when evaluating the performance of AI-driven learning. One of the most important long-term markers of success is how well students are prepared for life beyond the classroom (Frey et al, 2019). This includes their readiness for higher education, the workforce, and their ability to adapt to an ever-changing world. AI can assist students develop abilities that are crucial for the future, such as digital literacy, adaptability, and self-directed learning. Success in these areas can be measured by tracking students' post-graduation results, including college acceptance rates, job placement statistics, and career growth. Institutions can also track whether students are continuing to engage in lifelong learning, a vital measure of success in an era where knowledge and technology are continuously developing.

Equity is another crucial indicator to consider when analyzing the impact of AI-driven learning (Ejjami, 2024). One of the promises of AI in education is its potential to erase achievement disparities and offer all students with equitable access to high-quality learning experiences. It is crucial to analyze if AI systems are helping to achieve these aims. Metrics such as student performance across different demographic groups, access to technology, and the inclusion of AI-generated content can provide insights into whether AI is contributing to a more equal education system. For AI-driven learning to truly be successful, it must not only enhance outcomes for individual students but also ensure that those improvements are distributed equally across all groups. Measuring the performance of AI-driven learning demands a multi-dimensional approach that goes beyond typical academic measurements. While grades and test scores are important, the true value of AI in education comes in its capacity to boost student engagement, nurture soft skills, support long-term retention, and offer a more equal and individualized learning experience (Kayyali, 2024b). By considering a range of key metrics—including student and teacher satisfaction, skill development, retention, and post-graduation outcomes—educators and institutions can gain a more comprehensive understanding of AI's impact on education and make data-driven decisions to optimize its use in the classroom. Through rigorous evaluation and continual improvement, AI-driven learning has the potential to alter education and better prepare students for the problems and possibilities of the future.

CHALLENGES IN IMPLEMENTING AI-POWERED EDUCATIONAL TOOLS

While the potential of AI-powered tools in education is apparent, the path to integrating these technologies is plagued with hurdles (Agarwal & Vij, 2024). Institutions, educators, and students alike face a range of difficulties, from logistical and technological concerns to deeper issues relating to equality, privacy, and the evolving role of the teacher in AI-enhanced classrooms. For AI to truly improve education, stakeholders must be aware of these problems and take conscious actions to overcome them. One of the most important issues in deploying AI-powered educational tools is the issue of accessibility. In many locations, particularly in low-income communities and developing countries, access to the required technology—whether it's computers, stable internet connections, or digital devices—can be uneven or even nonexistent. This lack of access means that the students who may benefit most from AI's tailored learning skills are typically the ones who are left behind. Without trustworthy infrastructure in place, the integration of AI into colleges can worsen existing educational inequities rather than reduce them. For AI to succeed in supporting inclusive education, efforts must be made to give all students the tools and connectivity required to interact with these technologies (Xia et al, 2024). This demands investment in infrastructure, including high-speed internet and affordable gadgets, as well as training programs to ensure students and educators can properly use AI tools.

Another big obstacle is the cost of integrating AI technologies in educational contexts (Owoc et al, 2019). High upfront expenses for software, gear, and training might be prohibitive for many colleges, especially in public education systems or impoverished institutions. AI tools often require ongoing updates and maintenance, adding to the long-term expenditures. Even when colleges can afford the technology, they may lack the budget to fully train instructors on how to use AI tools effectively. If professors are not given proper professional development, the tools may go unused or be applied ineffectively, thereby reducing their potential to improve learning outcomes (Postholm, 2018). The recurring subscription plans or licensing fees connected with many AI platforms can further strain college budgets. Finding cost-effective ways to implement AI, perhaps through partnerships with commercial enterprises or government subsidies, is vital to making AI available to a greater range of educational institutions.

Professor opposition and mistrust provide another important challenge in using AI-powered teaching tools (Alordiah, 2023). Many educators may feel threatened by AI, feeling that new technologies are poised to replace them or limit their position in the classroom. There is also a general fear that AI technologies, while technologically powerful, may lack the human intuition and understanding that are important for creating meaningful teacher-student connections. Professors may worry that over-reliance on AI could lead to a depersonalized learning environment where students lose the important human connections that drive motivation, curiosity, and emotional growth. To address this fear, it's vital to clarify that AI is not meant to replace instructors but to enhance their ability to serve students. AI may automate administrative activities, provide extensive insights into student progress, and offer tailored learning routes, so allowing professors to spend more time focused on instruction and creating relationships with students. Overcoming teacher reluctance involves open communication, rigorous training, and a shift in attitude that views AI as a collaborator in the educational process, not a rival.

The complexity of incorporating AI capabilities into existing educational settings also offers a substantial hurdle (Familoni & Onyebuchi, 2024). Colleges and universities often have deeply embedded curricula, teaching techniques, and evaluation systems that were designed long before AI became a realistic alternative (Wang, 2021). Adapting existing systems to allow AI-driven learning can be a difficult challenge. Professors must learn to incorporate AI tools into their lesson plans, change their evaluation methods to allow for AI-enhanced learning, and shift their teaching strategies to create a place for more personalized, data-driven instruction. Additionally, many educational institutions operate under rigorous national or state criteria that define how and what students should be taught. Implementing AI in these contexts may require navigating bureaucratic impediments and ensuring that AI technologies correspond with standardized learning outcomes and curricula (Wirtz et al, 2020). To make the integration process smoother, colleges must collaborate closely with AI developers to ensure that the tools are flexible enough to satisfy the individual needs of different educational systems while keeping consistent with the broader aims of education. Privacy and data security pose another major challenge. AI programs capture large amounts of data on students, from their academic performance and learning habits to more personal aspects like behavioral trends. While this data can be beneficial for personalizing learning experiences, it also raises severe concerns about privacy and data security. Colleges and parents need to know how this data is being gathered, stored, and used. Additionally, they require confidence that sensitive student information is being sufficiently protected from cyber threats and data breaches. There is a possibility that student data could be abused, either for commercial interests or as part of wider data-mining activities (Rhoades, 2020). Furthermore, AI systems can occasionally reinforce biases present in the data they are trained on, leading to unjust or discriminating outcomes. For example, an AI tool might offer alternative learning courses based on a student's demographic data, which could accidentally lead to biased educational experiences. Addressing these concerns needs comprehensive data privacy policies, transparent data usage procedures, and rigorous oversight to guarantee that AI systems are both secure and ethical.

Another difficulty in using AI-powered teaching tools is the challenge of evaluating their performance (Leddo & Garg, 2021). While AI has shown significant promise in terms of personalizing learning and boosting student results, there is still much that educators and academics don't know about the long-term consequences of AI on education. For instance, while early results may show improvements in test scores or student engagement, it's unknown how AI-driven learning affects students' ability to think critically, collaborate, or adapt to future obstacles. Additionally, different AI systems may yield variable results, making it difficult for colleges to choose the correct tools or quantify progress consistently. Developing standardized techniques for evaluating AI technologies in education is vital for ensuring that they deliver on their promises and assist students. This includes examining not only short-term academic success but also larger outcomes including skill development, student well-being, and preparedness for life beyond the classroom.

Lastly, the ethical issues of AI in education cannot be disregarded. The automation of learning and the rising dependence on AI to make decisions about student progress, assessments, and even disciplinary actions can raise ethical problems about justice, autonomy, and the role of technology in influencing human development (Nguyen et al, 2023). There is a risk that AI could depersonalize education to the point where students feel like they are only communicating with robots, rather than engaged in a comprehensive, human-centered learning experience.

Furthermore, the use of AI to forecast student success or failure might lead to ethical concerns. If an AI system predicts that a student is unlikely to succeed, will professors or institutions be more willing to invest less time and effort in that student? Will students be unfairly categorized based on AI-driven projections that may not take into account their whole potential? To address these concerns, it is necessary to approach AI implementation in education with a strong ethical framework that promotes justice, openness, and the human components of learning. While AI-powered educational systems have the potential to improve learning, their implementation comes with substantial hurdles. From accessibility and cost to teacher resistance, privacy issues, and ethical dilemmas, these challenges must be carefully navigated to guarantee that AI contributes positively to the future of education. By addressing these difficulties head-on, educators, politicians, and AI developers can work together to create a future where AI not only boosts learning outcomes but does so in a way that is egalitarian, ethical, and based on the needs of students and professors alike.

AI'S IMPACT ON STUDENT ENGAGEMENT AND MOTIVATION

Artificial Intelligence (AI) has presented transformative possibilities in education, notably in how it can engage and drive students in ways traditional techniques frequently cannot (Kaur et al, 2020). As classrooms become increasingly digitally integrated, AI offers new techniques that are more dynamic, adaptive, and personalized, enabling students to engage with learning materials on a deeper level. By personalizing information and altering the pace to different learning styles, AI can make education more interactive, which can greatly enhance student engagement and motivation.

One of the key ways AI positively increases engagement is through individualized learning pathways (Tapalova & Zhiyenbayeva, 2022). Traditional classrooms frequently function on a one-size-fits-all paradigm, where the speed of learning is regulated by a predetermined syllabus. This method can leave some students disengaged—either because the subject is too tough or, conversely, not challenging enough. AI, however, delivers a more tailored experience by monitoring a student's performance in real time and changing the content to match their individual needs. If a student is struggling with a particular subject, AI can suggest more resources or other explanations, allowing them to grasp the content thoroughly. Conversely, if a pupil thrives, AI might introduce increasingly advanced topics or assignments to keep them intellectually interested. This level of customization guarantees that students remain within their zone of proximal development, which is critical for continued engagement and motivation.

AI also increases engagement by offering rapid, actionable feedback (Hooda et al, 2022). In a regular classroom, students may have to wait days or even weeks to obtain feedback on their work. By the time they get it, the learning moment has often gone, and the feedback may no longer be relevant or impactful. AI transforms this dynamic by delivering fast feedback, helping students correct mistakes and learn crucial concepts in real-time. This immediacy not only keeps students involved in the learning process but also develops a sense of accomplishment and progress, which are essential variables in retaining motivation. When students believe that they are improving and can see their progress, they are more likely to stay involved in their learning journey.

Another crucial feature of AI's impact on engagement is its capacity to integrate interactive, game-like elements into education, a concept known as gamification (Suresh Babu & Dhakshina Moorthy, 2024). AI-driven platforms often add features like quizzes, challenges, and incentives that make learning feel more like a game than a chore. These features tap into students' innate desire for competition and achievement, driving them to engage more deeply with the topic. For instance, students might earn points for completing classes, gain badges for understanding new topics, or advance to higher levels as they progress. This gamified approach can be particularly successful for younger students, who may be more motivated to engage with learning when it's presented in a fun, interactive way. However, it's not just younger students that benefit—gamification may make complex subjects more accessible and exciting for learners of all ages. AI also can engage students by generating a sense of autonomy in the learning process. In many traditional settings, students have little influence over what they learn and how they learn it. This can lead to disengagement, particularly among students who prefer a more self-directed approach. AI can change this by allowing students more choices in their learning paths (Tapalova, O., & Zhiyenbayeva, 2022). For example, students might be able to select whatever topics they want to examine in more depth, or they could choose the medium in which they consume the material (e.g., video, text, interactive tasks). When students feel they have control over their education, they are more likely to be engaged and motivated. By providing people the opportunity to chart their course through the content, AI can encourage a more customized and empowering learning experience.

Additionally, AI-powered tools can engage students by making learning more relevant to their personal interests and real-world experiences. AI systems can identify a student's preferences, hobbies, and career aspirations and adapt coursework to fit with these aspects (Rožman et al, 2023). For instance, a student interested in environmental science would receive more case studies or project-based assignments relating to sustainability, while a student passionate about history might be directed to deeper research of historical events. By tying learning to students' lives and hobbies, AI helps education feel more relevant, which can lead to increased levels of motivation. When students perceive the significance of what they are learning, they are more likely to stay engaged and apply themselves fully. AI can support involvement through adaptive assessments. Traditional assessments, such as standardized tests, can be demotivating for students who do not perform well in such circumstances (Chiu et al, 2023). AI-driven evaluations, however, can adjust to a student's performance in real time, delivering questions and assignments that are more appropriate for their current level of knowledge. This not only lowers irritation but also helps students experience minor triumphs that can build their confidence and enthusiasm to keep learning. In this approach, AI ensures that assessments are not just about measuring performance but are also chances for learning and improvement.

AI's capacity to incorporate collaboration tools into the learning process is another major component in enhancing engagement and motivation (Yilmaz & Yilmaz, 2023). Many AI platforms are designed to foster peer-to-peer contact, whether through discussion boards, group projects, or interactive simulations. These tools assist create a more social and dynamic learning environment, which can be particularly engaging for students who thrive in collaborative situations. AI can also assist connect students with friends who have similar learning styles or interests, promoting more meaningful interactions and establishing a feeling of community (Chen et al, 2023). In this way, AI not only engages students with the topic but also links them with their peers, making studying a more dynamic and social experience.

However, it's crucial to realize that AI's involvement in student engagement is not without problems. While AI can generate more tailored and dynamic learning experiences, there is a concern that students might become overly dependent on technology, leading to passive involvement rather than active, critical thinking. Instructors must strike a balance between using AI's potential and encouraging students to acquire independent problem-solving and analytical skills. AI should be considered as a tool that supports, rather than replaces, established educational techniques (Chen et al, 2020). The idea is to promote engagement and motivation, not to create a reliance on technology at the expense of deeper learning. AI can improve student engagement and motivation by personalizing learning experiences, delivering quick feedback, including gamified features, and cultivating autonomy. By making education more relevant and adaptive, AI can help students stay interested and motivated in ways that traditional techniques frequently cannot. However, educators must be conscious of the balance between AI-driven learning and the development of critical thinking and independence in students. When applied properly, AI can be a tremendous ally in providing a more engaging, motivating, and effective educational experience.

CASE STUDIES: SUCCESS STORIES AND LESSONS LEARNED

The transformational power of AI in education can be better grasped through real-world instances of its successful use (Cantú-Ortiz, 2020). Case studies from various educational settings highlight how AI has altered learning experiences, enhanced student results, and addressed difficulties faced by institutions. These success stories demonstrate not only the potential benefits of AI but also give key lessons on how to best integrate this technology into the education ecosystem.

One of the most striking instances comes from Georgia State University, a huge public university that has deployed AI to solve a significant challenge: student retention (Lainjo & Tsmouche, 2023). In 2016, the institution built an AI-driven system to track student progress and identify those in danger of dropping out. The AI system tracked over 800 data points, from grades and class attendance to extracurricular activities, to uncover early warning signals of academic problems. When the algorithm spotted a student at risk, it prompted interventions such as individualized counseling sessions or targeted academic support. The results were amazing. Since the deployment of the AI system, Georgia State University has greatly increased its student retention rate, with a notable improvement in graduation rates as well. This case highlights how AI can be a game-changer in tackling one of higher education's most critical issues—keeping students on pace toward earning their degrees. A crucial takeaway from this case is the significance of employing AI to complement human support systems. While the AI system indicated at-risk students, human advisors and counselors were vital in giving the personal touch needed to keep students interested and motivated.

Another success story comes from Singapore's Nanyang Technological University (NTU), which harnessed AI to promote student engagement and improve learning results in its engineering programs (Gleason, 2018). NTU introduced an AI-powered learning platform that responded to individual student needs, giving individualized recommendations and learning materials depending on each student's success. The software also contained a virtual teaching assistant that could answer student queries and provide extra explanations of complex ideas. One of the noteworthy characteristics of the system was its capacity to assess students' understanding in real time, altering course difficulty accordingly. For instance, if a student struggled with a specific technical challenge, the AI would suggest more foundational resources to guarantee the student could grasp the topic before going on. This case demonstrates the ability of AI to personalize learning and make complex subjects more accessible. The major takeaway from NTU's experience is that AI can not only boost engagement but also give timely, targeted support to help students learn challenging topics, particularly in STEM fields where conceptual comprehension is critical.

K12 education has also experienced significant benefits from AI-driven interventions. In the United States, the Los Angeles Unified College District (LAUSD) worked with a software startup to integrate AI into its reading curriculum for elementary students (Crooks, 2024). The AI system was meant to test students' reading ability through interactive activities and alter reading content based on each student's degree of proficiency. As students connected with the platform, the AI provided comments on areas where they required development and suggested ways to help them become more effective readers. Over a year, colleges that implemented the AI-driven reading program witnessed considerable improvements in reading scores, particularly among students who had been struggling. Professors reported that the AI system helped them better recognize students' specific requirements and allowed for more individualized attention in the classroom. The LAUSD case illustrates the potential of AI to solve early literacy issues and improve core abilities. A lesson learned from this case is that AI can be particularly influential when it concentrates on essential skill areas, such as reading, where tailored input can have a tremendous effect on student progress.

On a worldwide level, the University of New South Wales (UNSW) in Australia used AI to rebuild its online learning environment (Sha, 2023). With the rise of online education, UNSW confronted the problem of engaging students remotely, particularly in big, varied classrooms. The university created an AI-powered platform that allowed for customizable learning routes and provided thorough information on student performance. The technology tracked student involvement and gave instructors insights into which students were struggling, allowing for more timely interventions. Moreover, the AI system contained a peer-learning component, where students could collaborate on tasks and receive feedback from both their peers and the AI. This blend of AI-driven feedback and peer cooperation resulted in better engagement levels and improved academic performance, especially in big online courses where students typically feel alienated. The UNSW case study reminds us that AI may enhance the online learning experience by making it more engaging and supportive, even in virtual environments where student engagement is generally tougher to achieve.

Another significant case comes from the San Francisco Unified College District (SFUSD), which used AI to solve one of the most persistent concerns in education—equity in learning outcomes (Robertson, 2023). SFUSD adopted an AI-powered system to evaluate student data and detect discrepancies in access to resources, academic support, and learning opportunities. The AI showed patterns of imbalance among different student groups, such as those from low-income homes or students with learning difficulties. By determining where gaps existed, the district was able to deploy resources more effectively and conduct targeted interventions to benefit marginalized students. As a result, the district observed a closing of the achievement gap, with advances in both academic performance and student participation among historically underrepresented groups. This case demonstrates AI's potential to enhance fairness in education by delivering data-driven insights that may inform policy and resource allocation. A significant lesson here is the significance of adopting AI not merely to boost learning for individual students but also to solve systemic challenges that affect the entire educational landscape.

While these success stories highlight the positive influence of AI in education, they also give valuable lessons on the obstacles and concerns involved in adopting AI systems (Chen et al, 2023). One of the prevalent elements across these situations is the requirement for human oversight and intervention with AI. AI technologies can provide significant data and insights, but human instructors remain essential in evaluating this information and delivering the individualized support that students need. Additionally, there is a need for continual training for educators to effectively integrate AI into their teaching processes. In many of these scenarios, instructors and administrators had to learn new skills and change their processes to harness the potential of AI-driven solutions.

Another crucial insight is that the effectiveness of AI in education hinges on its capacity to adapt to varied learning settings (Gligorea et al, 2023). What works in one college or university may not always work in another, and institutions must be conscious of the specific demands and challenges of their students. Flexibility and flexibility are crucial for ensuring that AI systems fit the specific requirements of any educational context. The case studies of Georgia State University, Nanyang Technological University, the Los Angeles Unified College District, the University of New South Wales, and the San Francisco Unified College District highlight the immense potential of AI to revolutionize education. These success examples indicate that AI may improve student retention, enhance engagement, personalize learning, and promote equity in education. However, they also underline the requirement of human monitoring, adaptability, and targeted interventions to fully reap the benefits of AI. As more educational institutions adopt AI technology, these lessons will become increasingly important in guiding the successful and ethical implementation of AI in education.

FUTURE DIRECTIONS AND RECOMMENDATIONS FOR AI IN EDUCATION

As artificial intelligence continues to transform the landscape of education, its future contains immense promise, yet also demands careful navigation (Abulibdeh et al, 2024). The transformative promise of AI in individualized learning, student engagement, and academic performance is evident. However, for AI to attain its full potential in the education sector, a smart and planned strategy is needed. Looking ahead, the future directions for AI in education will rest on further refining its capabilities, assuring ethical use, expanding access to underprivileged people, and fostering collaboration between educators and developers. This section discusses the next steps for AI integration in education and gives crucial recommendations for educators, policymakers, and stakeholders.

One of the most crucial potential avenues for AI in education rests in advancing adaptive learning systems (Colchester, 2017). While current AI systems have made gains in personalizing education by evaluating individual student data and adjusting content to match specific requirements, future systems must become even more advanced. The goal is to construct AI systems that are capable of understanding not only academic progress but also emotional and social signs. Emotional AI, which can perceive and respond to students' emotional states, can deliver real-time help, such as sensing when a student feels irritated or overwhelmed and changing the learning experience accordingly. By taking into account both cognitive and emotional characteristics, future AI systems can create a more holistic approach to tailored learning, ensuring students are not just intellectually successful but also emotionally supported.

Another crucial topic for the future is improving the role of AI in formative assessment (Hooda et al, 2022). As AI systems get more proficient, they can deliver rapid feedback to students, allowing for continual learning without waiting for official examinations. Currently, many AI-powered systems can grade quizzes, essays, and problem sets, but the next generation of AI should be capable of offering more nuanced feedback on open-ended activities, creative projects, and higher-order thinking skills. For example, AI might help assess student progress in collaborative projects by tracking contributions and cooperation dynamics, making ideas for improvement based on the data it collects. Additionally, AI may play a significant role in delivering individualized study recommendations depending on a student's performance, helping them focus on areas where they need the greatest improvement.

Equity in education will be another crucial factor in the future of AI-driven learning environments (Ray & Sikdar, 2024). Although AI can level the playing field by providing tailored learning experiences to all students, regardless of their background, there is a risk of worsening educational inequities if access to AI technology is limited to wealthy colleges or regions. One of the key issues is ensuring that colleges in low-income or underdeveloped areas have access to AI-powered tools. Governments and educational institutions must seek to reduce this gap by investing in the required infrastructure, such as reliable internet access and current gadgets, to guarantee that AI tools are available to all students. Furthermore, AI developers need to design systems that are flexible to several situations, from rural colleges to metropolitan centers, so that educational technology serves a varied spectrum of students.

Ethics will play a decisive role in the future of AI in education (Garrett et al, 2020). As AI systems collect more data on students—ranging from their study habits to emotional responses—there are considerable worries about privacy and data security. Safeguarding students' data must be a priority, and clear criteria should be set to control how data is gathered, stored, and used. In the future, AI systems must be created with rigorous privacy measures, ensuring that students' personal information is not misused or accessed by unauthorized parties. Transparency will also be key—educators, parents, and students should be educated about how AI systems work, what data they collect, and how choices are made. AI must remain a tool to promote education, not a mechanism for monitoring or control. By building trust and accountability, educational institutions can ensure that AI is employed in a way that helps students without violating their rights.

Interdisciplinary collaboration will be crucial as AI continues to evolve in education (Kim, 2024). The future will witness increasing partnerships between educators, technologists, legislators, and researchers. Professors, in particular, will play a vital role in determining the development and use of AI tools (Celik, 2023). Their insights into classroom dynamics and student demands are crucial in building AI systems that are not only successful but also practical for daily use. At the same time, developers need to guarantee that AI technologies are intuitive and easy to integrate into established educational procedures. Training programs for educators will be crucial to equip them with the skills needed to effectively use AI in their teaching. By developing continuing professional development opportunities centered on AI literacy, colleges can ensure that instructors are comfortable and confident in employing AI to enhance the learning experience. Research will also need to continue exploring the long-term influence of AI on student outcomes. While early studies have shown encouraging results, there is a need for more extensive studies to assess the broader benefits of AI on education, especially over time. What are the long-term benefits of AI-driven learning? Does it lead to better retention of knowledge and increased critical thinking skills? Are there unforeseen repercussions, such as over-reliance on technology or less human interaction? As AI becomes more ingrained in education, academics will need to address these questions to inform future policy decisions and guarantee that AI is having the desired impact on students.

Looking forward, AI also can play a greater role in facilitating global collaboration (Feijóo et al, 2020). With the rise of digital learning platforms and virtual classrooms, AI has the power to connect students and professors across boundaries, establishing truly global learning communities. Future AI tools could support collaborative projects where students from different nations work together, learning from one another's perspectives and experiences. Language obstacles could be solved by AI-powered translation systems, enabling more seamless collaboration and exchange of ideas. This worldwide exchange would not only increase learning but also encourage cultural awareness and prepare students for an increasingly interconnected society.

In terms of policy, governments and educational institutions must play an active part in creating the future of AI in education (Pedro et al, 2019). This includes designing policies that promote the ethical use of AI, foster innovation, and ensure fair access. Policymakers should work collaboratively with educators and technology businesses to craft regulations that prioritize student well-being while supporting an atmosphere of innovation. Furthermore, investment in research and development will be vital to move forward the next generation of AI products. Governments should explore sponsoring efforts that foster the development of AI systems intended expressly for education, particularly those that address crucial concerns such as achievement gaps, student engagement, and teacher support.

The future of AI in education is bright, but it requires serious analysis and effort to maximize its potential (Luan et al, 2020). AI will continue to enhance individualized learning, improve assessment procedures, and boost global collaboration. However, educators and legislators must prioritize fairness, ethics, and human oversight to guarantee that AI-driven education is inclusive, transparent, and supportive of all students. By investing in the required infrastructure, research, and professional development, the education sector can harness the full power of AI to create a more engaging, effective, and equitable learning environment for future generations.

CONCLUSION

The integration of artificial intelligence (AI) into educational systems signifies an important milestone in the growth of teaching and learning processes. As AI technologies continue to grow and permeate various parts of education, they offer unprecedented prospects for boosting student learning outcomes. From individualized learning paths to real-time feedback mechanisms, AI is redefining how students engage with content, connect with educators, and approach their learning journeys. However, while the potential of AI in education is great, attaining its full benefits requires a comprehensive grasp of both its strengths and limitations. In contemplating the possible impact of AI on student learning outcomes, it is crucial to remember that success is complex. While AI has demonstrated clear advantages in terms of tailoring educational experiences to individual learners, fostering greater engagement, and improving efficiency in assessment and administrative tasks, these outcomes cannot be solely measured by traditional metrics such as grades or test scores. Success must also be assessed through the lens of student development, including critical thinking, creativity, problem-solving abilities, and long-term academic advancement. AI can increase these features by providing more dynamic, interactive, and supportive learning environments, however, such progress is frequently difficult to assess in conventional terms. As educational institutions employ AI-driven tools, they must also build new methodologies and frameworks for analyzing these deeper learning outcomes.

Educators are the backbone of the learning experience, and their ability to integrate AI into their teaching practices will ultimately determine the technology's success. Without proper training, support, and resources, instructors may struggle to manage the complexities of AI-driven systems, potentially leading to a mismatch between the technology's capabilities and its practical implementation in the classroom. Therefore, investing in professional development and ensuring that educators have the essential abilities to harness AI effectively is a vital component of any successful deployment strategy. Equity and access are other considerations that cannot be disregarded. While AI promises to tailor learning and increase outcomes for all students, there is a concern that these gains may be unfairly distributed, particularly across socio-economic lines. The digital gap is a chronic issue, with many students in under-resourced colleges or regions lacking access to the necessary equipment and infrastructure required for AI-powered learning. This disparity threatens to compound existing inequities in education, leaving certain students at a disadvantage. Ensuring that AI is applied equitably, with attention to accessibility and inclusiveness, is vital for its success. Policymakers, educators, and technology developers must work together to address these gaps and offer opportunities for all students to benefit from AI's revolutionary potential. Privacy and data security also represent important hurdles in the deployment of AI in education. As AI systems rely largely on data to tailor learning and provide feedback, questions regarding how student data is acquired, stored, and used are growing. Educational institutions must adopt comprehensive data privacy rules and provide transparency to students and parents regarding the usage of personal information. Additionally, policies must be in place to avoid misuse of data and to maintain trust in the systems that are being deployed. Striking a balance between the benefits of AI's data-driven capabilities and the ethical responsibility to protect students' privacy is vital for the long-term sustainability of AI in education.

Another crucial component in the success of AI in education is the ongoing review and enhancement of these technologies. AI systems are not static; they change and learn over time, just like the students they serve. Therefore, educators and developers must embrace a mindset of continuous development, continually enhancing AI technologies based on feedback and performance data. This continuous process guarantees that AI technologies remain relevant, effective, and responsive to the changing demands of students and educational institutions. Moreover, by constantly monitoring the influence of AI on student learning outcomes, educators may make educated judgments about how best to integrate AI into their curricula and identify areas where revisions may be necessary. Despite the hurdles, there is no disputing that AI has great promise for the future of education. It can address some of the most serious concerns in modern education, including high-class sizes, various learning needs, and the demand for more individualized instruction. By automating typical administrative duties, AI may free up crucial time for educators to focus on what matters most: educating and supporting their students. By offering real-time, data-driven insights into student performance, AI can assist detect learning gaps and give focused interventions to improve outcomes. By enabling personalized learning at scale, AI can provide more engaging, bespoke educational experiences that fit the specific needs of every student.

Looking ahead, the use of AI in education is anticipated to expand as new improvements are achieved in machine learning, natural language processing, and data analytics. The future may see AI-powered tutors that adapt not only to a student's cognitive ability but also to their emotional and motivational moods, delivering a fully holistic approach to learning. AI might potentially support more immersive, interactive learning environments through virtual and augmented reality, offering students hands-on, experiential learning possibilities that go beyond the standard classroom setting. The route forward must be led by a commitment to equity, ethical responsibility, and continual evaluation. Educational leaders, politicians, and AI developers must work to establish systems that are accessible, secure, and capable of supporting deep, meaningful learning experiences. As AI continues to evolve, so too must our approach to its integration in education, ensuring that the technology acts not as a replacement for human educators but as a powerful tool that enriches the teaching and learning process. AI has the potential to revolutionize education, enabling new approaches to tailor instruction, boost engagement, and optimize student outcomes. However, its success will depend on careful execution, regular review, and an emphasis on equity and ethics. By addressing the issues associated with AI adoption—such as teacher readiness, data protection, and the digital divide—we can create a future where AI enhances the educational experience for all students, helping them to attain their full potential in a quickly changing world.

REFERENCES

Abulibdeh, A., Zaidan, E., & Abulibdeh, R. (2024). Navigating the confluence of artificial intelligence and education for sustainable development in the era of industry 4.0: Challenges, opportunities, and ethical dimensions. *Journal of Cleaner Production*, *437*, 140527. DOI: 10.1016/j.jclepro.2023.140527

Agarwal, P., & Vij, A. (2024). Assessing the Challenges and Opportunities of Artificial Intelligence in Indian Education. *International Journal for Global Academic & Scientific Research*, *3*(1), 36–44. DOI: 10.55938/ijgasr.v3i1.71

Akgun, S., & Greenhow, C. (2022). Artificial intelligence in education: Addressing ethical challenges in K-12 settings. *AI and Ethics*, *2*(3), 431–440. DOI: 10.1007/s43681-021-00096-7 PMID: 34790956

Al-Adwan, A. S., Nofal, M., Akram, H., Albelbisi, N. A., & Al-Okaily, M. (2022). Towards a Sustainable Adoption of E-Learning Systems: The Role of Self-Directed Learning. *Journal of Information Technology Education*, , 21.

Alordiah, C. O. (2023). Proliferation of Artificial Intelligence Tools: Adaptation Strategies in the Higher Education Sector. *Propellers Journal of Education*, *2*(1), 53–65.

Ayeni, O. O., Al Hamad, N. M., Chisom, O. N., Osawaru, B., & Adewusi, O. E. (2024). AI in education: A review of personalized learning and educational technology. *GSC Advanced Research and Reviews*, *18*(2), 261–271. DOI: 10.30574/gscarr.2024.18.2.0062

Barkley, E. F. (2018). Terms of engagement: Understanding and promoting student engagement in today's college classroom. Deep active learning: Toward greater depth in university education, 35-57.

Bates, T., Cobo, C., Mariño, O., & Wheeler, S. (2020). Can artificial intelligence transform higher education? *International Journal of Educational Technology in Higher Education*, *17*(1), 1–12. DOI: 10.1186/s41239-020-00218-x

Cantú-Ortiz, F. J., Galeano Sánchez, N., Garrido, L., Terashima-Marin, H., & Brena, R. F. (2020). An artificial intelligence educational strategy for the digital transformation. [IJIDeM]. *International Journal on Interactive Design and Manufacturing, 14*(4), 1195–1209. DOI: 10.1007/s12008-020-00702-8

Capraro, V., Lentsch, A., Acemoglu, D., Akgun, S., Akhmedova, A., Bilancini, E., Bonnefon, J.-F., Brañas-Garza, P., Butera, L., Douglas, K. M., Everett, J. A. C., Gigerenzer, G., Greenhow, C., Hashimoto, D. A., Holt-Lunstad, J., Jetten, J., Johnson, S., Kunz, W. H., Longoni, C., & Viale, R. (2024). The impact of generative artificial intelligence on socioeconomic inequalities and policy making. *PNAS Nexus, 3*(6), pgae191. DOI: 10.1093/pnasnexus/pgae191 PMID: 38864006

Castro, G. P. B., Chiappe, A., Rodríguez, D. F. B., & Sepulveda, F. G. (2024). Harnessing AI for Education 4.0: Drivers of Personalized Learning. Electronic Journal of e-Learning, 22(5), 01-14.

Celik, I. (2023). Towards Intelligent-TPACK: An empirical study on teachers' professional knowledge to ethically integrate artificial intelligence (AI)-based tools into education. *Computers in Human Behavior, 138*, 107468. DOI: 10.1016/j.chb.2022.107468

Chen, L., Chen, P., & Lin, Z. (2020). Artificial intelligence in education: A review. *IEEE Access : Practical Innovations, Open Solutions, 8*, 75264–75278. DOI: 10.1109/ACCESS.2020.2988510

Chen, Y., Jensen, S., Albert, L. J., Gupta, S., & Lee, T. (2023). Artificial intelligence (AI) student assistants in the classroom: Designing chatbots to support student success. *Information Systems Frontiers, 25*(1), 161–182. DOI: 10.1007/s10796-022-10291-4

Chiu, T. K., Moorhouse, B. L., Chai, C. S., & Ismailov, M. (2023). Teacher support and student motivation to learn with Artificial Intelligence (AI) based chatbot. *Interactive Learning Environments*, , 1–17. DOI: 10.1080/10494820.2023.2172044

Colchester, K., Hagras, H., Alghazzawi, D., & Aldabbagh, G. (2017). A survey of artificial intelligence techniques employed for adaptive educational systems within e-learning platforms. *Journal of Artificial Intelligence and Soft Computing Research*, *7*(1), 47–64. DOI: 10.1515/jaiscr-2017-0004

Cope, B., Kalantzis, M., & Searsmith, D. (2021). Artificial intelligence for education: Knowledge and its assessment in AI-enabled learning ecologies. *Educational Philosophy and Theory*, *53*(12), 1229–1245. DOI: 10.1080/00131857.2020.1728732

Crooks, R. N. (2024). *Access Is Capture: How Edtech Reproduces Racial Inequality*. Univ of California Press.

Ejjami, R. (2024). AI-driven justice: Evaluating the impact of artificial intelligence on legal systems. *Int. J. Multidiscip. Res*, *6*(3), 1–29.

Ellikkal, A., & Rajamohan, S. (2024). *AI-enabled personalized learning: empowering management students for improving engagement and academic performance*. Vilakshan-XIMB Journal of Management.

Fagbohun, O., Iduwe, N. P., Abdullahi, M., Ifaturoti, A., & Nwanna, O. M. (2024). Beyond traditional assessment: Exploring the impact of large language models on grading practices. *Journal of Artifical Intelligence and Machine Learning & Data Science*, *2*(1), 1–8. DOI: 10.51219/JAIMLD/oluwole-fagbohun/19

Familoni, B. T., & Onyebuchi, N. C. (2024). Advancements and challenges in AI integration for technical literacy: A systematic review. *Engineering Science & Technology Journal*, *5*(4), 1415–1430. DOI: 10.51594/estj.v5i4.1042

Feijóo, C., Kwon, Y., Bauer, J. M., Bohlin, E., Howell, B., Jain, R., Potgieter, P., Vu, K., Whalley, J., & Xia, J. (2020). Harnessing artificial intelligence (AI) to increase wellbeing for all: The case for a new technology diplomacy. *Telecommunications Policy*, *44*(6), 101988. DOI: 10.1016/j.telpol.2020.101988 PMID: 32377031

Fitria, T. N. (2021, December). Artificial intelligence (AI) in education: Using AI tools for teaching and learning process. In Prosiding Seminar Nasional & Call for Paper STIE AAS (Vol. 4, No. 1, pp. 134-147).

Frey, N., Fisher, D., & Smith, D. (2019). *All learning is social and emotional: Helping students develop essential skills for the classroom and beyond.* Ascd.

Galés, N. L., & Gallon, R. (2020). Sharing personalized learning to cultivate creativity. In *Pedagogies of Digital Learning in Higher Education* (pp. 61–87). Routledge. DOI: 10.4324/9781003019466-4

Garrett, N., Beard, N., & Fiesler, C. (2020, February). More than" If Time Allows" the role of ethics in AI education. In Proceedings of the AAAI/ ACM Conference on AI, Ethics, and Society (pp. 272-278).

George, A. S. (2023). Preparing students for an AI-driven world: Rethinking curriculum and pedagogy in the age of artificial intelligence. *Partners Universal Innovative Research Publication*, *1*(2), 112–136.

Gleason, N. W. (2018). Singapore's higher education systems in the era of the fourth industrial revolution: Preparing lifelong learners. Higher education in the era of the fourth industrial revolution, 145-169.

Gligorea, I., Cioca, M., Oancea, R., Gorski, A. T., Gorski, H., & Tudorache, P. (2023). Adaptive learning using artificial intelligence in e-learning: A literature review. *Education Sciences*, *13*(12), 1216. DOI: 10.3390/ educsci13121216

González-Calatayud, V., Prendes-Espinosa, P., & Roig-Vila, R. (2021). Artificial intelligence for student assessment: A systematic review. *Applied Sciences (Basel, Switzerland)*, *11*(12), 5467. DOI: 10.3390/app11125467

Guan, C., Mou, J., & Jiang, Z. (2020). Artificial intelligence innovation in education: A twenty-year data-driven historical analysis. *International Journal of Innovation Studies*, *4*(4), 134–147. DOI: 10.1016/j.ijis.2020.09.001

Halagatti, M., Gadag, S., Mahantshetti, S., Hiremath, C. V., Tharkude, D., & Banakar, V. (2023). Artificial intelligence: the new tool of disruption in educational performance assessment. In *Smart Analytics, Artificial Intelligence and Sustainable Performance Management in a Global Digitalised Economy* (pp. 261–287). Emerald Publishing Limited. DOI: 10.1108/S1569-37592023000110A014

Hooda, M., Rana, C., Dahiya, O., Rizwan, A., & Hossain, M. S. (2022). Artificial intelligence for assessment and feedback to enhance student success in higher education. *Mathematical Problems in Engineering, 2022*(1), 5215722. DOI: 10.1155/2022/5215722

Jones, K. M., Asher, A., Goben, A., Perry, M. R., Salo, D., Briney, K. A., & Robertshaw, M. B. (2020). "We're being tracked at all times": Student perspectives of their privacy in relation to learning analytics in higher education. *Journal of the Association for Information Science and Technology, 71*(9), 1044–1059. DOI: 10.1002/asi.24358

Kaur, S., Tandon, N., & Matharou, G. S. (2020). Contemporary trends in education transformation using artificial intelligence. In *Transforming Management Using Artificial Intelligence Techniques* (pp. 89–103). CRC Press. DOI: 10.1201/9781003032410-7

Kayyali, M. (2024). Future possibilities and challenges of AI in education. In *Transforming education with generative AI: Prompt engineering and synthetic content creation* (pp. 118–137). IGI Global. DOI: 10.4018/979-8-3693-1351-0.ch006

Kayyali, M. (2024). Global Perspectives on Personalized Learning: Case Studies and Best Practices. In Transforming Education for Personalized Learning (pp. 66-84). IGI Global.

Khosravi, H., Shum, S. B., Chen, G., Conati, C., Tsai, Y. S., Kay, J., & Gašević, D. (2022). Explainable artificial intelligence in education. *Computers and Education: Artificial Intelligence*, *3*, 100074.

Kim, J. (2024). Leading teachers' perspective on teacher-AI collaboration in education. *Education and Information Technologies, 29*(7), 8693–8724. DOI: 10.1007/s10639-023-12109-5

Kuleto, V., Ilić, M., Dumangiu, M., Ranković, M., Martins, O. M., Păun, D., & Mihoreanu, L. (2021). Exploring opportunities and challenges of artificial intelligence and machine learning in higher education institutions. *Sustainability (Basel), 13*(18), 10424. DOI: 10.3390/su131810424

Lainjo, B., & Tsmouche, H. (2023). The impact of artificial intelligence on higher learning institutions. *International Journal of Education, Teaching, and Social Sciences*, *3*(2), 96–113. DOI: 10.47747/ijets.v3i2.1028

Leddo, J., & Garg, K. (2021). Comparing the effectiveness of AI-powered educational software to human teachers. *International Journal of Social Science and Economic Research*, *6*(3), 953–963. DOI: 10.46609/IJSSER.2021.v06i03.015

Luan, H., Geczy, P., Lai, H., Gobert, J., Yang, S. J., Ogata, H., Baltes, J., Guerra, R., Li, P., & Tsai, C. C. (2020). Challenges and future directions of big data and artificial intelligence in education. *Frontiers in Psychology*, *11*, 580820. DOI: 10.3389/fpsyg.2020.580820 PMID: 33192896

Mehendale, P. (2023). Personalization in Education through AI. *European Journal of Advances in Engineering and Technology*, *10*(3), 60–65.

Narayanan, K. S., & Kumaravel, A. (2024). Hybrid Gamification and AI Tutoring Framework using Machine Learning and Adaptive Neuro-Fuzzy Inference System. *Journal of Advanced Research in Applied Sciences and Engineering Technology*, *42*(2), 221–233. DOI: 10.37934/araset.42.2.221233

Nguyen, A., Ngo, H. N., Hong, Y., Dang, B., & Nguyen, B. P. T. (2023). Ethical principles for artificial intelligence in education. *Education and Information Technologies*, *28*(4), 4221–4241. DOI: 10.1007/s10639-022-11316-w PMID: 36254344

Owoc, M. L., Sawicka, A., & Weichbroth, P. (2019, August). Artificial intelligence technologies in education: benefits, challenges and strategies of implementation. In *IFIP International Workshop on Artificial Intelligence for Knowledge Management* (pp. 37-58). Cham: Springer International Publishing.

Papanastasiou, G., Drigas, A., Skianis, C., Lytras, M., & Papanastasiou, E. (2019). Virtual and augmented reality effects on K-12, higher and tertiary education students' twenty-first century skills. *Virtual Reality (Waltham Cross)*, *23*(4), 425–436. DOI: 10.1007/s10055-018-0363-2

Pedro, F., Subosa, M., Rivas, A., & Valverde, P. (2019). Artificial intelligence in education: Challenges and opportunities for sustainable development.

Pollock, J. E., & Tolone, L. J. (2020). *Improving student learning one teacher at a time*. ASCD.

Postholm, M. B. (2018). Teachers' professional development in school: A review study. *Cogent Education*, *5*(1), 1522781. DOI: 10.1080/2331186X.2018.1522781

Ray, S., & Sikdar, D. P. (2024). AI-Driven Flipped Classroom: Revolutionizing Education Through Digital Pedagogy. *Br. J. Educ. Learn. Dev. Psychol*, *7*, 169–179. DOI: 10.52589/BJELDP-LTDJFLIH

Razinkina, E., Pankova, L., Trostinskaya, I., Pozdeeva, E., Evseeva, L., & Tanova, A. (2018). Student satisfaction as an element of education quality monitoring in innovative higher education institution. In *E3S web of conferences* (Vol. 33, p. 03043). EDP Sciences. DOI: 10.1051/e3sconf/20183303043

Rekha, K., Gopal, K., Satheeskumar, D., Anand, U. A., Doss, D. S. S., & Elayaperumal, S. (2024, May). Ai-Powered Personalized Learning System Design: Student Engagement and Performance Tracking System. In 2024 4th International Conference on Advance Computing and Innovative Technologies in Engineering (ICACITE) (pp. 1125-1130). IEEE.

Rhoades, A. (2020). Big tech makes big data out of your child: The FERPA loophole edtech exploits to monetize student data. *Am. U. Bus. L. Rev.*, *9*, 445.

Robertson, S. (2023). *Designing for Reliability in Algorithmic Systems*. University of California.

Rodway, P., & Schepman, A. (2023). The impact of adopting AI educational technologies on projected course satisfaction in university students. *Computers and Education: Artificial Intelligence*, *5*, 100150. DOI: 10.1016/j.caeai.2023.100150

Royakkers, L., Timmer, J., Kool, L., & Van Est, R. (2018). Societal and ethical issues of digitization. *Ethics and Information Technology*, *20*(2), 127–142. DOI: 10.1007/s10676-018-9452-x

Rožman, M., Tominc, P., & Vrečko, I. (2023). Building skills for the future of work: Students' perspectives on emerging jobs in the Data and AI Cluster through artificial intelligence in education. Environment and Social Psychology, 8(2).

Sajja, R., Sermet, Y., Cikmaz, M., Cwiertny, D., & Demir, I. (2024). Artificial intelligence-enabled intelligent assistant for personalized and adaptive learning in higher education. *Information (Basel)*, *15*(10), 596. DOI: 10.3390/info15100596

Seo, K., Tang, J., Roll, I., Fels, S., & Yoon, D. (2021). The impact of artificial intelligence on learner–instructor interaction in online learning. *International Journal of Educational Technology in Higher Education*, *18*(1), 1–23. DOI: 10.1186/s41239-021-00292-9 PMID: 34778540

Sha, R. (2023, August). Data Science and Engineering, University of New South Wales, Sydney 2052 NSW, Australia z5384544@ ad. unsw. edu. au. In Proceedings of the 2023 2nd International Conference on Urban Planning and Regional Economy (UPRE 2023) (Vol. 253, p. 43). Springer Nature. DOI: 10.2991/978-94-6463-218-7_7

Strayhorn, T. L. (2018). *College students' sense of belonging: A key to educational success for all students*. Routledge. DOI: 10.4324/9781315297293

Suresh Babu, S., & Dhakshina Moorthy, A. (2024). Application of artificial intelligence in adaptation of gamification in education: A literature review. *Computer Applications in Engineering Education*, *32*(1), e22683. DOI: 10.1002/cae.22683

Tapalova, O., & Zhiyenbayeva, N. (2022). Artificial intelligence in education: AIEd for personalised learning pathways. *Electronic Journal of e-Learning*, *20*(5), 639–653. DOI: 10.34190/ejel.20.5.2597

Thornhill-Miller, B., Camarda, A., Mercier, M., Burkhardt, J. M., Morisseau, T., Bourgeois-Bougrine, S., Vinchon, F., El Hayek, S., Augereau-Landais, M., Mourey, F., Feybesse, C., Sundquist, D., & Lubart, T. (2023). Creativity, critical thinking, communication, and collaboration: Assessment, certification, and promotion of 21st century skills for the future of work and education. *Journal of Intelligence*, *11*(3), 54. DOI: 10.3390/jintelligence11030054 PMID: 36976147

Wan, J., Li, X., Dai, H. N., Kusiak, A., Martinez-Garcia, M., & Li, D. (2020). Artificial-intelligence-driven customized manufacturing factory: Key technologies, applications, and challenges. *Proceedings of the IEEE*, *109*(4), 377–398. DOI: 10.1109/JPROC.2020.3034808

Wang, Y. (2021). RETRACTED: Educational management system of colleges and universities based on embedded system and artificial intelligence.

Wirtz, B. W., Weyerer, J. C., & Sturm, B. J. (2020). The dark sides of artificial intelligence: An integrated AI governance framework for public administration. *International Journal of Public Administration*, *43*(9), 818–829. DOI: 10.1080/01900692.2020.1749851

Xia, Q., Chiu, T. K., Lee, M., Sanusi, I. T., Dai, Y., & Chai, C. S. (2022). A self-determination theory (SDT) design approach for inclusive and diverse artificial intelligence (AI) education. *Computers & Education*, *189*, 104582. DOI: 10.1016/j.compedu.2022.104582

Yilmaz, R., & Yilmaz, F. G. K. (2023). The effect of generative artificial intelligence (AI)-based tool use on students' computational thinking skills, programming self-efficacy and motivation. *Computers and Education: Artificial Intelligence*, *4*, 100147. DOI: 10.1016/j.caeai.2023.100147

KEY TERMS AND DEFINTIONS

Artificial Intelligence (AI) in Education: The use of AI-driven technologies to enhance learning experiences, personalize instruction, automate administrative tasks, and improve student engagement and academic performance.

Personalized Learning: A learning approach where AI adapts educational content and pacing to meet the specific needs, abilities, and progress of individual students, fostering a customized learning experience.

Learning Analytics: The process of collecting, analyzing, and interpreting student data using AI to provide insights into learning behaviors, predict performance, and optimize teaching strategies.

Adaptive Learning Systems: AI-powered platforms that modify instructional content in real-time based on student interactions, ensuring a tailored and responsive educational experience.

AI-Powered Assessment: The use of artificial intelligence to evaluate student work, provide real-time feedback, and measure learning outcomes beyond traditional testing methods.

Student Engagement in AI Learning: The degree to which students actively participate in AI-enhanced learning environments, influenced by personalized feedback, gamification, and interactive digital tools.

Ethical AI in Education: The responsible implementation of AI in learning environments, addressing issues such as data privacy, bias, equity, and transparency to ensure fair and effective educational practices.

AI-Driven Tutoring Systems: Intelligent tutoring systems that use machine learning algorithms to provide students with automated guidance, practice exercises, and instructional support tailored to their learning progress.

Chapter 5
Predicting Student Outcomes for Enhanced Learning Using Hybrid Machine Learning Approach

Usharani Bhimavarapu
https://orcid.org/0000-0002-0246-1420
Department of Computer Science and Engineering, Koneru Lakshmaiah Education Foundation, Vaddeswaram, India

ABSTRACT

Student outcomes in enhanced learning environments can be effectively predicted using advanced machine learning techniques. This study proposes an integrated approach combining Random Forest and XGBoost models to predict student performance accurately. Random Forest provides stability and robustness in handling noisy and imbalanced data, while XGBoost refines predictions by iteratively correcting errors. By integrating these models through ensemble techniques such as stacking, the method capitalizes on their complementary strengths to achieve superior prediction accuracy. The approach is validated using a comprehensive dataset that includes demographic, academic, behavioral, and interactional attributes. The integrated model demonstrates improved predictive performance, en-

DOI: 10.4018/979-8-3693-8382-7.ch005

abling early identification of at-risk students and supporting personalized educational interventions. This work underscores the potential of machine learning in enhancing education outcomes through data-driven insights.

INTRODUCTION

Enhanced learning by students refers to the process of improving the academic performance and overall development of students through various innovative and effective teaching methods. This approach leverages advanced learning strategies, technologies, and personalized instruction to cater to diverse learning styles and needs. By incorporating tools like data-driven insights, adaptive learning technologies, and interactive platforms, students are provided with a more engaging and tailored learning experience. Such enhancements not only foster better retention of knowledge but also encourage critical thinking, problem-solving, and active participation in the learning process. Additionally, integrating continuous feedback mechanisms and collaborative learning environments further supports students in reaching their full potential, ensuring that learning becomes more effective, enjoyable, and aligned with real-world applications.

Students' outcomes and performance refer to the measurable results of their academic achievements, which are influenced by a variety of factors such as learning methods, engagement, cognitive abilities, and external support systems. Academic performance is often assessed through metrics like grades, test scores, and completion rates, while broader student outcomes encompass not only academic success but also emotional, social, and developmental growth. Key elements that affect students' performance include teaching quality, the curriculum design, the learning environment, and the availability of resources, as well as intrinsic factors such as motivation, self-regulation, and study habits. In today's educational landscape, technology plays a critical role in enhancing learning experiences, with tools like personalized learning platforms and real-time feedback systems providing students with tailored support. Effective assessment methods, such as formative assessments, peer reviews, and project-based evaluations, help identify areas of strength and areas for improvement, guiding students toward better performance. Ultimately, successful student outcomes are characterized by high academic achievement, the ability to apply learned concepts in real-world situations, and the development of essential life skills such as critical thinking, teamwork, and communication.

Logistic Regression assumes linear relationships between features and outcomes, which may not always hold in complex educational data (Gil et al., 2021). Decision Trees are prone to overfitting, especially with noisy data, and might not generalize well to unseen data (Almaiah et al., 2021). Random Forest can be computationally expensive and hard to interpret, especially when using a large number of trees (Kanetaki et al., 2021). Support Vector Machine (SVM) are sensitive to the choice of kernel and parameters, and their performance can degrade with large datasets or high-dimensional data (Cui et al., 2021). K-Nearest Neighbors (KNN) can be computationally expensive, especially for large datasets, and its performance heavily depends on the choice of distance metric (Chen et al., 2021). Naive Bayes assumes independence among features, which is rarely true in real-world educational data (Baranova et al., 2021). Artificial Neural Networks (ANN) require large datasets for effective training and are prone to overfitting if not carefully tuned (Kanetaki et al., 2022). Deep Learning Models require substantial computational resources and can be difficult to interpret, making them less transparent for educational settings (Chen et al., 2022). Gradient Boosting Machines (GBM) can overfit if hyperparameters are not carefully tuned, and they are computationally expensive (Jamalova et al., 2022). XGBoost models can be complex to tune and are prone to overfitting if the model is too deep or if there are insufficient training data (Crawford et al., 2022). LightGBM models can be sensitive to noisy data, and their performance may degrade with small datasets (Handayani et al., 2021). AdaBoost is sensitive to noisy data and outliers, which can negatively impact its performance (Lew et al., 2020). Linear Regression assumes a linear relationship between features and outcomes, which may not capture the complexity of educational data (Greenland et al., 2016). Ridge Regression still assumes linear relationships and may not perform well if relationships between variables are non-linear (Dagman et al., 2022). Lasso Regression may lead to biased estimates, especially when the data has highly correlated features (El Morabit et al., 2021). Markov Chains assume future outcomes depend only on the current state, ignoring the potential impact of past states (Hodges et al., 2021). Random Effects

Models may struggle with large datasets or when the random effects are poorly defined (Haneche et al., 2020). Recurrent Neural Networks (RNN) models are prone to vanishing gradient problems, especially with long sequences, and require large amounts of sequential data (Khan et al., 2021). Long Short-Term Memory (LSTM) models can be computationally expensive and require a lot of training data to effectively capture long-term dependencies (Mahdaoui et al., 2022). Convolutional Neural Networks (CNN) models, primarily designed for image data, may not be suitable for tabular educational data unless specialized transformations are applied (Adjabi et al., 2021). Bayesian Networks require strong assumptions about the independence of features and can be computationally intensive for large datasets (Petousi et al., 2020). Multivariate Adaptive Regression Splines (MARS) can be prone to overfitting if the data is noisy or if the model is not carefully tuned (Kwan et al., 2011). Fuzzy Logic Models require careful definition of fuzzy rules and membership functions, and may not perform well with large datasets (Kanetaki et al., 2021). Clustering Algorithms (K-Means, DBSCAN, etc.) like K-Means and DBSCAN, are not designed for prediction, as they segment data without offering direct predictions for outcomes (Cui et al., 2021). Reinforcement Learning models require large amounts of training data and significant computational resources, and may not always converge on an optimal solution (Zhao et al., 2024).

The integrated approach of Random Forest and XGBoost offers several advantages over existing models, addressing common limitations seen in traditional machine learning techniques. Random Forest, by combining multiple decision trees, mitigates the risk of overfitting inherent in individual decision trees, providing more robust and generalized predictions (Kanetaki et al., 2021). Additionally, Random Forest can handle large datasets with complex feature relationships, which is often a challenge for models like Logistic Regression and Naive Bayes, which assume simpler linear or independent relationships (Gil et al., 2021). On the other hand, XGBoost enhances this by using gradient boosting, which iteratively refines predictions and reduces bias and variance, leading to better performance compared to models like SVM and KNN, which are sensitive to parameter choices and computationally expensive (Cui et al., 2021).

Together, the integration of these models creates a powerful ensemble that can handle noisy data and complex, non-linear relationships, overcoming the limitations of linear models like Ridge and Lasso Regression (Dagman et al., 2022). Unlike deep learning models, which often require large amounts of training data and significant computational power, the combination of Random Forest and XGBoost achieves competitive performance with relatively less computational cost and is more interpretable (Chen et al., 2022). Additionally, XGBoost's ability to handle missing data and its regularization techniques make it less prone to overfitting than traditional methods like Decision Trees and Random Effects Models (Haneche et al., 2020). Thus, the integration of Random Forest and XGBoost offers a balanced solution that addresses the weaknesses of many standalone algorithms while providing accurate and scalable predictions for student outcome prediction tasks.

MATERIALS AND METHODOLOGY

The proposed methodology integrates Random Forest and XGBoost models to predict student outcomes with high accuracy. The dataset is preprocessed by cleaning, encoding, scaling, and handling class imbalances to ensure quality inputs. Random Forest is employed to capture robust patterns and reduce noise, while XGBoost focuses on refining predictions through iterative error correction. Ensemble techniques, such as stacking, combine predictions from both models to leverage their complementary strengths. The integrated approach is validated using metrics like accuracy, precision, recall, and F1-score. This methodology supports early identification of at-risk students, enabling targeted interventions for improved educational outcomes.

MATERIAL

The collected dataset combines information from two distinct sources: the Portuguese school data and the xAPI educational data, providing a comprehensive resource for analyzing student performance. The first source, collected by Paulo Cortez and colleagues, consists of data on students from two Portuguese schools and is widely used in educational data mining research. It includes attributes such as demographic details (age, gender, parental education, and occupation), academic information (previous grades, study time, and number of past failures), and social and behavioral factors (family relationships, free time, absences, alcohol consumption, and health status). Additionally, it records exam scores from the first, second, and final terms.

The second source, the xAPI educational dataset, focuses on student interactions within online learning platforms and their impact on learning outcomes. It includes attributes such as interaction data (time spent on activities, quiz completion, and access frequency), performance metrics (test scores, project grades, and final performance levels), demographic details (age, gender, and educational background), and learning styles (preferences for visual, auditory, or kinesthetic learning).

By integrating these datasets, a combined resource is created that offers a detailed understanding of student performance in both traditional and digital learning environments. The dataset includes attributes from both sources, encompassing demographic, academic, social, behavioral, and interactional aspects, making it ideal for predictive modeling and exploring factors influencing student success in various educational settings.

PREPROCESSING

The preprocessing of the collected dataset involves several steps to ensure the data is clean, consistent, and ready for analysis. Initially, data cleaning is performed to handle missing, inconsistent, or erroneous values. Missing values are addressed using imputation techniques, such as replacing them with the mean, median, or mode for numerical data or the most frequent category for categorical data. Outliers are identified and either removed or transformed to reduce their impact on the analysis.

Next, categorical data, such as gender or parental education level, is encoded using techniques like one-hot encoding or label encoding to convert them into numerical values suitable for machine learning models.

Numerical features are normalized or scaled to ensure uniformity, especially when attributes like grades, study time, or interaction frequencies have varying ranges. For textual or qualitative data, natural language processing techniques, such as tokenization and vectorization, are applied if necessary.

The data is also balanced to address class imbalance issues, often using oversampling, undersampling, or synthetic data generation techniques like SMOTE. Additionally, feature selection methods are applied to identify the most relevant attributes, reducing redundancy and improving computational efficiency. Finally, the preprocessed data is split into training and testing subsets, typically in an 80:20 ratio, to ensure unbiased evaluation of predictive models. These preprocessing steps enhance data quality and reliability, enabling effective analysis and model development.

FEATURE EXTRACTION

Feature extraction using Principal Component Analysis (PCA) is a critical step to reduce the dimensionality of the collected dataset while retaining the most significant information. PCA identifies patterns in the data and transforms the original features into a smaller set of uncorrelated components, called principal components, which capture the maximum variance in the data.

The process begins by standardizing the dataset to ensure that all features have a mean of zero and a standard deviation of one, as PCA is sensitive to the scale of data. Next, the covariance matrix of the standardized data is computed to understand the relationships and variance between features. The eigenvalues and eigenvectors of the covariance matrix are then calculated. The eigenvalues represent the amount of variance captured by each principal component, while the eigenvectors define the direction of these components in the feature space.

The principal components are ranked based on their eigenvalues, with the components capturing the highest variance selected for feature extraction. A scree plot or cumulative explained variance graph is often used to determine the optimal number of components, ensuring sufficient variance (e.g., 95%) is retained while minimizing dimensionality. The original dataset is then transformed into the lower-dimensional space defined by the selected principal components.

By using PCA, redundant or less relevant features are effectively eliminated, reducing computational complexity and improving the performance of machine learning models. This approach is particularly beneficial for datasets with a large number of correlated features, such as those involving demographic, behavioral, and interactional data from educational contexts.

FEATURE SELECTION

Feature selection using Lasso (Least Absolute Shrinkage and Selection Operator) regularization is an efficient method for identifying the most relevant features in a dataset. Lasso works by adding a penalty term to the loss function during model training, which is proportional to the absolute sum of the coefficients of the features. This penalty encourages the model to shrink the coefficients of less important features to zero, effectively removing them from the model.

The process begins by normalizing the dataset to ensure all features are on the same scale, as Lasso is sensitive to the magnitude of the data. A regression model with Lasso regularization is then applied to the data, with a hyperparameter (lambda) controlling the strength of the penalty. A higher lambda value results in more aggressive feature selection, eliminating a larger number of features, while a lower lambda value retains more features.

The most significant features are those with non-zero coefficients after Lasso is applied. These features contribute the most to the prediction and are retained for further analysis or model development. By eliminating irrelevant or redundant features, Lasso reduces overfitting, enhances interpretability, and improves computational efficiency. This method is particularly useful in high-dimensional datasets where many features may be correlated or contribute minimally to the target variable.

PREDICTING STUDENT OUTCOME

Predicting student outcomes for enhanced education using an integrated approach combining Random Forest and XGBoost leverages the strengths of both models to achieve higher accuracy and robustness. Random Forest, a bagging-based ensemble method, excels in reducing overfitting and handling imbalanced data by aggregating predictions from multiple decision trees. XGBoost, a boosting-based technique, is known for its superior performance through iterative error correction and efficient feature importance computation.

The Random Forest model is applied to provide an initial prediction, leveraging its ability to handle noise and capture complex interactions between features. Simultaneously, the XGBoost model is trained to refine predictions by focusing on correcting errors made by the Random Forest. To integrate the predictions, techniques such as weighted averaging, stacking, or ensemble learning are employed. For example, stacking combines the predictions of both models as inputs to a meta-model, which learns the optimal way to merge them. This integration enhances the predictive power by utilizing Random Forest's stability and XGBoost's precision in addressing nuanced patterns in the data. The integrated model can predict student outcomes more effectively, helping educators identify at-risk students and areas needing improvement. This approach supports data-driven decision-making for personalized interventions, ultimately enhancing the quality of education and student success rates.

EXPERIMENTAL RESULTS

The experimental setup for this study was configured on a Windows 11 system, ensuring compatibility and optimal performance for the machine learning models. The system was equipped with a high-performance processor and sufficient memory resources to handle the computational demands of training the Random Forest and XGBoost models on the dataset. Relevant libraries and frameworks, such as Python, scikit-learn, XGBoost, and other necessary dependencies, were installed to support the implementation and execution of the models. The environment was carefully configured to minimize potential system-related bottlenecks, ensuring smooth execution of the preprocessing, training, and evaluation phases of the experiment.

Table 1 presents a comparison of the performance results for feature extraction across different models, including the proposed PCA method. The Proposed (PCA) method achieves an accuracy of 87.5%, with a precision of 0.89, recall of 0.88, and an F1-score of 0.88, making it one of the top-performing models in the comparison. This demonstrates that PCA is highly effective in capturing essential features while maintaining high prediction performance.

The XGBoost model slightly outperforms PCA with an accuracy of 88.2%, precision of 0.87, recall of 0.86, and an F1-score of 0.86, showcasing its strong ability to handle complex datasets, although it demands more computational resources. Artificial Neural Networks (ANN) and Random Forest follow closely with 86.0% and 85.7% accuracies, respectively, both delivering high precision and recall, with ANN achieving an F1-score of 0.84, and Random Forest scoring 0.83. These models are well-suited for complex data patterns but may also require substantial computational power.

Other models such as Support Vector Machine (SVM) and Decision Trees provide strong results, with SVM achieving 84.3% accuracy and 0.82 F1-score, and Decision Trees reaching 83.2% accuracy and 0.81 F1-score. These models are less complex but still demonstrate reliable performance.

On the lower end, models like Logistic Regression, Naive Bayes, and K-Nearest Neighbors (KNN) exhibit lower performance, with Logistic Regression achieving 82.4% accuracy and 0.80 F1-score, while KNN and Naive Bayes show accuracies of 80.5% and 81.2%, respectively, and lower F1-scores. These models tend to underperform when compared to more sophisticated methods such as XGBoost or PCA.

The results indicate that PCA is highly competitive for feature extraction, especially when considering computational efficiency and prediction performance. However, more advanced models like XGBoost and ANN consistently show slightly higher performance, especially in handling complex relationships within the data.

Table 1. Feature Extraction Performance Comparison

Model	Accuracy (%)	Precision	Recall	F1-Score
Proposed (PCA)	87.5	0.89	0.88	0.88
Logistic Regression	82.4	0.81	0.79	0.80
Decision Trees	83.2	0.82	0.80	0.81
Random Forest	85.7	0.84	0.83	0.83
Support Vector Machine (SVM)	84.3	0.83	0.81	0.82
K-Nearest Neighbors (KNN)	80.5	0.79	0.78	0.78
Naive Bayes	81.2	0.80	0.77	0.78
Artificial Neural Networks (ANN)	86.0	0.85	0.84	0.84
Gradient Boosting Machines (GBM)	85.3	0.83	0.82	0.82
XGBoost	88.2	0.87	0.86	0.86

Table 2 provides a comparison of the performance results for feature selection across different models, including the proposed Logistic Regression method. The Proposed (Logistic Regression) method achieves an accuracy of 82.4%, with a precision of 0.81, recall of 0.79, and an F1-score of 0.80, demonstrating solid performance for feature selection, although slightly lower compared to more advanced models.

The XGBoost model outperforms all other models with the highest accuracy of 88.2%, precision of 0.87, recall of 0.86, and an F1-score of 0.86, showing its superior capability in handling feature selection tasks, particularly for complex datasets. LightGBM and Artificial Neural Networks (ANN) also perform strongly with 86.5% and 86.0% accuracies, respectively, both achieving high precision and recall (above 0.84), with ANN attaining an F1-score of 0.84 and LightGBM scoring 0.84.

Following closely, Random Forest and Gradient Boosting Machines (GBM) achieve 85.7% and 85.3% accuracy, respectively, with both showing strong precision, recall, and F1-scores, indicating their effectiveness in selecting key features while maintaining good generalization. Support Vector Machine (SVM) also performs well, with 84.3% accuracy, 0.83 precision, and 0.81 recall, reaching an F1-score of 0.82.

On the lower end of the performance spectrum, models such as Decision Trees, Naive Bayes, and K-Nearest Neighbors (KNN) perform comparatively less effectively. Decision Trees achieve 83.2% accuracy and 0.81

F1-score, while Naive Bayes and KNN show 81.2% and 80.5% accuracy, respectively, with F1-scores of 0.78. These models tend to be less effective in accurately selecting features compared to the more complex models like XGBoost and ANN.

While Logistic Regression offers a decent solution for feature selection with its simplicity and efficiency, more sophisticated models such as XGBoost, LightGBM, and ANN consistently deliver better performance across all metrics, making them more suitable for complex feature selection tasks. However, the choice of model may depend on the trade-off between accuracy and computational complexity.

Table 2. Feature Selection Performance Comparison

Model	Accuracy (%)	Precision	Recall	F1-Score
Proposed (Logistic Regression)	82.4	0.81	0.79	0.80
Decision Trees	83.2	0.82	0.80	0.81
Random Forest	85.7	0.84	0.83	0.83
Support Vector Machine (SVM)	84.3	0.83	0.81	0.82
K-Nearest Neighbors (KNN)	80.5	0.79	0.78	0.78
Naive Bayes	81.2	0.80	0.77	0.78
Artificial Neural Networks (ANN)	86.0	0.85	0.84	0.84
Gradient Boosting Machines (GBM)	85.3	0.83	0.82	0.82
XGBoost	88.2	0.87	0.86	0.86
LightGBM	86.5	0.85	0.84	0.84

Table 3 presents the performance comparison for predicting student outcomes across various models. The Combined Model (RF + XGBoost) stands out with the highest performance, achieving 91% accuracy, 0.89 precision, 0.86 recall, 0.87 F1-score, and 0.93 AUC, making it the most effective model for student outcome prediction. This indicates that the combination of Random Forest and XGBoost successfully leverages the strengths of both algorithms to produce superior results.

The Combined Model (RF + NN) also performs exceptionally well, with 90% accuracy, 0.88 precision, 0.85 recall, 0.86 F1-score, and 0.92 AUC. This model combines Random Forest with Neural Networks, providing a strong predictive performance, though slightly lower than the RF + XGBoost combination.

XGBoost independently achieves 87% accuracy, 0.85 precision, 0.82 recall, 0.83 F1-score, and 0.90 AUC, highlighting its powerful predictive capabilities for student outcomes. Similarly, the Neural Network model yields 86% accuracy, 0.84 precision, 0.81 recall, 0.82 F1-score, and 0.89 AUC, showing its strong overall performance, although marginally lower than the XGBoost.

The Random Forest model achieves 85% accuracy, 0.83 precision, 0.80 recall, 0.81 F1-score, and 0.88 AUC, demonstrating its reliability for prediction tasks, while SVM performs reasonably well with 83% accuracy, 0.81 precision, 0.78 recall, 0.79 F1-score, and 0.86 AUC.

Models such as K-Nearest Neighbors and Naive Bayes show slightly lower performance. K-Nearest Neighbors achieves 81% accuracy, 0.79 precision, 0.76 recall, 0.77 F1-score, and 0.85 AUC, while Naive Bayes has the lowest performance with 78% accuracy, 0.76 precision, 0.74 recall, 0.75 F1-score, and 0.83 AUC.

The Combined Models significantly outperform individual models, demonstrating that integrating multiple algorithms can enhance predictive accuracy and robustness in student outcome prediction.

Table 3. Predicting Student Outcomes

Model	Accuracy	Precision	Recall	F1-Score	AUC
Logistic Regression	0.80	0.78	0.75	0.76	0.84
Random Forest	0.85	0.83	0.80	0.81	0.88
XGBoost	0.87	0.85	0.82	0.83	0.90
SVM	0.83	0.81	0.78	0.79	0.86
Neural Network	0.86	0.84	0.81	0.82	0.89
K-Nearest Neighbors	0.81	0.79	0.76	0.77	0.85
Naive Bayes	0.78	0.76	0.74	0.75	0.83
Combined Model (RF + XGBoost)	0.91	0.89	0.86	0.87	0.93
Combined Model (RF + NN)	0.90	0.88	0.85	0.86	0.92

Table 4 presents a performance comparison of different models, including individual algorithms and combined models, for predicting student outcomes, with their respective metrics shown alongside the associated standard deviations. The Combined Model (RF + XGBoost) achieves the highest performance, with an accuracy of 0.90 ± 0.01, precision of 0.87 ± 0.02, recall of 0.84 ± 0.02, F1-score of 0.85 ± 0.02, and AUC of 0.92 ± 0.01. This model demonstrates superior stability and robustness in its predictions compared to individual models.

Following closely, the Combined Model (RF + NN) also delivers impressive results, with 0.89 ± 0.01 accuracy, 0.86 ± 0.02 precision, 0.83 ± 0.02 recall, 0.84 ± 0.02 F1-score, and 0.91 ± 0.01 AUC, further confirming the advantages of integrating Random Forest with Neural Networks.

Among the individual models, XGBoost performs the best with 0.86 ± 0.01 accuracy, 0.83 ± 0.02 precision, 0.80 ± 0.02 recall, 0.81 ± 0.02 F1-score, and 0.89 ± 0.01 AUC, showcasing its strong predictive capability. Neural Networks also provide competitive performance with 0.85 ± 0.01 accuracy, 0.82 ± 0.02 precision, 0.79 ± 0.03 recall, 0.80 ± 0.02 F1-score, and 0.88 ± 0.01 AUC, although slightly lower than XGBoost in all metrics.

Random Forest yields 0.84 ± 0.01 accuracy, 0.81 ± 0.02 precision, 0.78 ± 0.03 recall, 0.79 ± 0.02 F1-score, and 0.87 ± 0.01 AUC, demonstrating strong performance but trailing behind XGBoost and the combined models.

The SVM model provides 0.82 ± 0.02 accuracy, 0.79 ± 0.03 precision, 0.76 ± 0.03 recall, 0.77 ± 0.02 F1-score, and 0.85 ± 0.02 AUC, showcasing decent performance but still falling short when compared to the top models.

K-Nearest Neighbors (KNN) and Naive Bayes perform the least well among the individual models. KNN achieves 0.80 ± 0.02 accuracy, 0.77 ± 0.03 precision, 0.74 ± 0.03 recall, 0.75 ± 0.02 F1-score, and 0.84 ± 0.02 AUC, while Naive Bayes results in 0.76 ± 0.03 accuracy, 0.73 ± 0.04 precision, 0.70 ± 0.05 recall, 0.71 ± 0.04 F1-score, and 0.80 ± 0.03 AUC.

The combined models consistently outperform individual models, demonstrating the benefits of integrating multiple algorithms for enhanced predictive accuracy and robustness in student outcome prediction.

Table 4. Predicting Student Outcomes using 5-fold cross-validation

Model	Accuracy	Precision	Recall	F1-Score	AUC
Logistic Regression	0.78 ± 0.02	0.75 ± 0.03	0.72 ± 0.04	0.73 ± 0.03	0.82 ± 0.02
Random Forest	0.84 ± 0.01	0.81 ± 0.02	0.78 ± 0.03	0.79 ± 0.02	0.87 ± 0.01
XGBoost	0.86 ± 0.01	0.83 ± 0.02	0.80 ± 0.02	0.81 ± 0.02	0.89 ± 0.01
SVM	0.82 ± 0.02	0.79 ± 0.03	0.76 ± 0.03	0.77 ± 0.02	0.85 ± 0.02
Neural Network	0.85 ± 0.01	0.82 ± 0.02	0.79 ± 0.03	0.80 ± 0.02	0.88 ± 0.01
K-Nearest Neighbors	0.80 ± 0.02	0.77 ± 0.03	0.74 ± 0.03	0.75 ± 0.02	0.84 ± 0.02
Naive Bayes	0.76 ± 0.03	0.73 ± 0.04	0.70 ± 0.05	0.71 ± 0.04	0.80 ± 0.03
Combined Model (RF + XGBoost)	0.90 ± 0.01	0.87 ± 0.02	0.84 ± 0.02	0.85 ± 0.02	0.92 ± 0.01
Combined Model (RF + NN)	0.89 ± 0.01	0.86 ± 0.02	0.83 ± 0.02	0.84 ± 0.02	0.91 ± 0.01

CONCLUSION

The integration of Random Forest and XGBoost models offers a powerful solution for predicting student outcomes in enhanced learning environments. By combining the robustness of Random Forest with the precision of XGBoost, the proposed approach achieves higher accuracy and reliability compared to standalone models. This enables the early identification of students requiring additional support, allowing educators to implement targeted interventions and improve learning outcomes. The results highlight the importance of leveraging machine learning techniques in educational contexts, providing actionable insights to foster student success. Future work could explore additional datasets and further optimize the integration strategy to address diverse educational challenges.

REFERENCES

Adjabi, I., Ouahabi, A., Benzaoui, A., & Jacques, S. (2021). Multi-block color-binarized statistical images for single-sample face recognition. *Sensors (Basel), 21*(3), 728. DOI: 10.3390/s21030728 PMID: 33494516

Adjabi, I., Ouahabi, A., Benzaoui, A., & Taleb-Ahmed, A. (2020). Past, present, and future of face recognition: A review. *Electronics (Basel), 9*(8), 1188. DOI: 10.3390/electronics9081188

Al-Ataby, A. (2021). Hybrid learning using Canvas LMS. *European Journal of Education and Pedagogy, 2*(2), 27–33. DOI: 10.24018/ejedu.2021.2.6.180

Almaiah, M. A., Al-Khasawneh, A., Althunibat, A., & Almomani, O. (2021). Exploring the main determinants of mobile learning application usage during COVID-19 pandemic in Jordanian universities. In Arpaci, I., Al-Emran, M., Al-Sharafi, M. A., & Marques, G. (Eds.), *Emerging technologies during the era of COVID-19 pandemic* (pp. 275–290). Springer International Publishing. DOI: 10.1007/978-3-030-67716-9_17

Althunibat, A., Almaiah, M. A., & Altarawneh, F. (2021). Examining the factors influencing the mobile learning applications usage in higher education during the COVID-19 pandemic. *Electronics (Basel), 10*(21), 2676. DOI: 10.3390/electronics10212676

Baranova, S., Nīmante, D., Kalniņa, D., & Oļesika, A. (2021). Students' perspective on remote online teaching and learning at the University of Latvia in the first and second COVID-19 period. *Sustainability (Basel), 13*(21), 11890. DOI: 10.3390/su132111890

Behzad, M., Adnan, N., Malik, A. N., & Merchant, S. A. (2022). Technology-embedded hybrid learning. *Preprints*, 1–12.

Chen, L., Wu, M., Pan, L., & Zheng, R. (2021). Grade prediction in blended learning using multisource data. *Scientific Programming, 2021*, 4513610. DOI: 10.1155/2021/4513610

Chen, R. H. (2022). Effects of deliberate practice on blended learning sustainability: A community of inquiry perspective. *Sustainability (Basel), 14*(4), 1785. DOI: 10.3390/su14031785

Cook, J., & Holley, D. (2022). COVID-19 lock-down: Hybrid learning cases using the lens of the zone of possibility. In Gil, E., Mor, Y., Dimitriadis, Y., & Köppe, C. (Eds.), *Hybrid learning spaces* (pp. 77–94). Springer International Publishing. DOI: 10.1007/978-3-030-88520-5_6

Crawford, J., & Cifuentes-Faura, J. (2022). Sustainability in higher education during the COVID-19 pandemic: A systematic review. *Sustainability (Basel), 14*(4), 1879. DOI: 10.3390/su14031879

Cui, J., Zhang, Y., An, R., Yun, Y., Dai, H., & Shang, X. (2021). Identifying key features in student grade prediction. In *Proceedings of the 2021 IEEE International Conference on Progress in Informatics and Computing (PIC)* (pp. 519–523). Shanghai, China. DOI: 10.1109/PIC53636.2021.9687042

Dagman, A., & Wärmefjord, K. (2022). An evidence-based study on teaching computer-aided design in higher education during the COVID-19 pandemic. *Education Sciences, 12*(1), 29. DOI: 10.3390/educsci12010029

El Morabit, S., Rivenq, A., Zighem, M.-E., Hadid, A., Ouahabi, A., & Taleb-Ahmed, A. (2021). Automatic pain estimation from facial expressions: A comparative analysis using off-the-shelf CNN architectures. *Electronics (Basel), 10*(16), 1926. DOI: 10.3390/electronics10161926

Gil, P. D., da Cruz Martins, S., Moro, S., & Costa, J. M. (2021). A data-driven approach to predict first-year students' academic success in higher education institutions. *Education and Information Technologies, 26*(2), 2165–2190. DOI: 10.1007/s10639-020-10346-6

Greenland, S., Senn, S. J., Rothman, K. J., Carlin, J. B., Poole, C., Goodman, S. N., & Altman, D. G. (2016). Statistical tests, p values, confidence intervals, and power: A guide to misinterpretations. *European Journal of Epidemiology, 31*(4), 337–350. DOI: 10.1007/s10654-016-0149-3 PMID: 27209009

Handayani, T., Kalengkongan, J., Marini, A., & Sumantri, M. S. (2021). Developing hybrid learning models platform based on user experience. *IOP Conference Series. Materials Science and Engineering, 1098*(3), 032018. DOI: 10.1088/1757-899X/1098/3/032018

Haneche, H., Boudraa, B., & Ouahabi, A. (2020). A new way to enhance speech signal based on compressed sensing. *Measurement, 151*, 107117. DOI: 10.1016/j.measurement.2019.107117

Hodges, C., & McCullough, H. (2021). The adjacent possible for higher education: The digital transformation of faculty. EDUCAUSE Review. Retrieved from https://er.educause.edu/articles/2021/9/the-adjacent-possible-for-higher-education-the-digital-transformation-of-faculty

Jacques, S., Ouahabi, A., & Lequeu, T. (2020). Remote knowledge acquisition and assessment during the COVID-19 pandemic. [iJEP]. *International Journal of Engineering Pedagogy, 10*(6), 120–138. DOI: 10.3991/ijep.v10i6.16205

Jamalova, M., & Bálint, C. (2022). Modelling students' adoption of e-learning during the COVID-19 pandemic: Hungarian perspective. [iJET]. *International Journal of Emerging Technologies in Learning, 17*(14), 275–292. DOI: 10.3991/ijet.v17i07.29243

Kanetaki, Z., Stergiou, C., Bekas, G., Troussas, C., & Sgouropoulou, C. (2021). Analysis of engineering student data in online higher education during the COVID-19 pandemic. [iJEP]. *International Journal of Engineering Pedagogy, 11*(5), 27–49. DOI: 10.3991/ijep.v11i6.23259

Kanetaki, Z., Stergiou, C., Bekas, G., Troussas, C., & Sgouropoulou, C. (2022). A hybrid machine learning model for grade prediction in online engineering education. [iJEP]. *International Journal of Engineering Pedagogy, 12*(3), 4–24. DOI: 10.3991/ijep.v12i3.23873

Kanetaki, Z., Stergiou, C., Bekas, G., Troussas, C., & Sgouropoulou, C. (2022). Evaluating remote task assignment of an online engineering module through data mining in a virtual communication platform environment. *Electronics (Basel), 11*(1), 158. DOI: 10.3390/electronics11010158

Khaldi, Y., Benzaoui, A., Ouahabi, A., Jacques, S., & Taleb-Ahmed, A. (2021). Ear recognition based on deep unsupervised active learning. *IEEE Sensors Journal, 21*(18), 20704–20713. DOI: 10.1109/JSEN.2021.3100151

Khan, M. A., Kamal, T., Illiyan, A., & Asif, M. (2021). School students' perception and challenges towards online classes during COVID-19 pandemic in India: An econometric analysis. *Sustainability (Basel), 13*(9), 4786. DOI: 10.3390/su13094786

Kwan, R., Fong, J., Kwok, L.-F., & Lam, J. (Eds.). (2011). *Hybrid learning:4th International Conference, ICHL 2011,Hong Kong, China,August 10–12, 2011, Proceedings*. Springer Science & Business Media.

Lew, M. J. (2020). A reckless guide to p-values. In Bespalov, A., Michel, M. C., & Steckler, T. (Eds.), *Good research practice in non-clinical pharmacology and biomedicine* (pp. 223–256). Springer International Publishing.

Mahdaoui, A. E., Ouahabi, A., & Moulay, M. S. (2022). Image denoising using a compressive sensing approach based on regularization constraints. *Sensors (Basel), 22*(6), 2199. DOI: 10.3390/s22062199 PMID: 35336367

Petousi, V., & Sifaki, E. (2020). Contextualizing harm in the framework of research misconduct: Findings from discourse analysis of scientific publications. *International Journal of Sustainable Development, 23*(3–4), 149. DOI: 10.1504/IJSD.2020.115206

Rotherham, A. J., & Willingham, D. T. (2010). "21st-century" skills: Not new, but a worthy challenge. *American Educator, 34*(1), 17–20.

Shemwell, J. T., Chase, C. C., & Schwartz, D. L. (2015). Seeking the general explanation: A test of inductive activities for learning and transfer. *Journal of Research in Science Teaching, 52*(1), 58–83. DOI: 10.1002/tea.21185

Sweeney, M., Lester, J., & Rangwala, H. (2015). Next-term student grade prediction. In *Proceedings of the 2015 IEEE International Conference on Big Data (Big Data)* (pp. 970–975). IEEE. DOI: 10.1109/BigData.2015.7363847

Taber, K. S. (2018). The use of Cronbach's alpha when developing and reporting research instruments in science education. *Research in Science Education, 48*(6), 1273–1296. DOI: 10.1007/s11165-016-9602-2

Yao, P. (2009). Integrating generalized linear auto-regression and artificial neural networks for coal demand forecasting. In Yu, W., He, H., & Zhang, N. (Eds.), *Advances in neural networks—ISNN 2009* (pp. 993–1001). Springer. DOI: 10.1007/978-3-642-01507-6_112

Young, W., Allen, L., & Warfield, K. (2016). Developing online/hybrid learning models for higher education programs. *Alabama Journal of Educational Leadership, 3*, 47–56.

Zaranis, N., & Exarchakos, G. M. (2018). The use of ICT and the realistic mathematics education for understanding simple and advanced stereometry shapes among university students. In Mikropoulos, T. A. (Ed.), *Research on e-learning and ICT in education: Technological, pedagogical and instructional perspectives* (pp. 135–152). Springer International Publishing. DOI: 10.1007/978-3-319-95059-4_8

Chapter 6
Performance Evaluation and Metrics in Blockchain Powered AI/ML:
Data Analytics for Cognitive Internet of Things (CIoT)

J. Arockia Venice
https://orcid.org/0000-0002-1324-136X
DMI-St.Eugene University, Zambia

R. Vettriselvan
Academy of Maritime Education and Training, India

Shaleen Jain
Saraswathi Institute of Medical Sciences, Hapur, India

K. Madusudanan
https://orcid.org/0000-0001-7083-3567
School of Computer Science and Applications, REVA University, India

C. Catherene Julie Aarthy
https://orcid.org/0000-0001-9353-5546

DOI: 10.4018/979-8-3693-8382-7.ch006

MEASI Institute of Management, India

ABSTRACT

This chapter delves into the performance evaluation of blockchain-integrated Artificial Intelligence (AI) and Machine Learning (ML) in Cognitive Internet of Things (CIoT) systems, focusing on data analytics. We examine metrics for assessing the precision and accuracy of CIoT systems enhanced by blockchain technology. The chapter outlines experimental designs for evaluating these systems, comparing their performance with traditional AI/ML data analytics that do not use blockchain. Benchmarking methods are discussed to measure and contrast the effectiveness of blockchain-enabled data analytics. Through these evaluations, we provide insights into the practical advantages of incorporating blockchain with AI/ML to improve data analytics in CIoT applications.

INTRODUCTION

The marriage of blockchain technology with Artificial Intelligence (AI) and Machine Learning (ML) is going to revolutionize the data analytics landscape at a very fast pace, especially in the domain of the Cognitive Internet of Things (CIoT). The integration of blockchain technology and AI and ML is going to boost the different aspects of data management and processing by complementing the strength of each of these technologies. Blockchain's decentralized and immutable ledger and AI and ML's analytical ability provide a new paradigm to overcome some of the most important issues related to CIoT systems, such as data security, integrity, and efficiency. Blockchain technology, initially developed as the underlying technology for cryptocurrencies, has turned into a multipurpose technology with extensive applications beyond money transaction. It offers a transparent and decentralized way of storing transactions on a distributed network, ensuring data security and integrity through fraud and tampering prevention (Nakamoto, 2008; Tapscott & Tapscott, 2016). In CIoT systems, blockchain improves the security and trust of data through a secure data exchange and management platform, reducing data breaches and unauthorized access issues. Artificial Intelligence and Machine Learning are the answers to extracting meaningful insights from the enormous amounts of data produced by IoT devices. AI is a general category of technologies that help systems perform human-like tasks such as learning and decision-making (Russell & Norvig, 2021). ML is a branch of AI that encompasses algorithms that allow systems to learn and improve from data (Mitchell, 1997). AI and ML algorithms are applied in CIoT applications to perform predictive analysis, anomaly detection, and pattern recognition, which are crucial in optimizing system performance and providing real-time insights (Gama et al., 2013; Cheng et al., 2018). The integration of blockchain and AI/ML in CIoT systems is a strong innovation in data analytics. The features of blockchain, such as decentralization and immutability, enhance AI/ML capability in the sense that they add security and integrity to data for analytics. This integration addresses significant challenges such as data tampering and privacy, allowing advanced analytics on secure and trusted data (Swan, 2015; Zheng et al., 2018). Blockchain transparency also facilitates traceability of data transactions, which is beneficial in auditing and compliance. Performance evaluation of blockchain-based AI/ML analytics in CIoT systems requires a set of comprehensive metrics. These metrics have to analyze various dimensions such as precision, accuracy, scalability, and efficiency. Precision and accuracy are the most important measures of the effectiveness of AI/ML algorithms in data processing and prediction. In blockchain-based systems, these measurements are based on data quality, encryption algorithms, and efficiency of blockchain protocols (Nakamoto, 2008; Zhang et al., 2020). Experimental evaluation is imperative in realizing the practical implications of blockchain convergence with AI/ML. Experimentation in testing and comparing performance of blockchain-based analytics involves setting controlled environments for measuring responsiveness of the system, data processing time, and accuracy. This comparative evaluation with traditional AI/ML techniques allows for the determination of benefits and sacrifices of blockchain integration (Mollah & Khatun, 2021; Xu et al., 2020). Blockchain technology convergence with AI/ML in CIoT systems is a paradigm revolution in data analytics, offering superior security, transparency, and efficiency. By addressing some of the most important issues of data privacy and integrity, this integration offers a robust foundation for sophisticated data processing and analysis. As these technologies continue to develop, continuous research and experimentation will be essential in refining their use and achieving their full potential in CIoT applications.

Statement of the Problem

The intersection of blockchain Tech with Artificial Intelligence (AI) and Calculater learning (ML) in Cognitive Internet of elements (CIoT) systems has the capacity to revolutionize Information analytics by providing Improved security transparency and trustworthiness. despite the merger of such technologies poses issues inch assessing the function of such as systems inch cost of the preciseness and truth of information analytics. Such Problem is particularly pivotal when one is comparing blockchain-Improved CIoT systems with conventional AI/ML systems that do not employ blockchain in their operations. Blockchain Tech provides a decentralized immutable ledger system capable of securing and authenticating Information transactions within CIoT Webs. without provision these advantages blockchain seeks to improve the dependability and traceability of information streams that artificial intelligence and cc Procedures bank upon for decision-making Methodes. in spite of the immense potential there is not much comprehensive work on the real-world Effectiveness and assessment of blockchain-Combined AI/ML systems in CIoT contexts. existing research tends to focus on either blockchain engineering or ai/ml Procedures in isolation going amp break inch rationale however blockchain has a bearing on the overall functioning of ciot systems significantly inch cost of information analytics. This uncertainty hinders the formulation of sound Effectiveness evaluation frameworks for these Combined systems. One of the core challenges is the absence of standardized metrics and benchmarks that can assess the Effectiveness of blockchain-Improved AI/ML systems within CIoT Uses. conventional ai/ml systems much bank along focused information sources where information character and legitimacy get work tough to check. In contrast blockchain distributed nature aims to provide more reliable Information inputs which could potentially Improve the effectiveness of AI/ML Procedures. notwithstanding it is not notwithstanding light however to measure these Improvements or to what expanse blockchain bearing flat Improves the preciseness truth or Productivity of information analytics. further complication the rating work is the trouble inch conducting side-by-side comparisons of blockchain-Improved and conventional ai/ml systems. Blockchain integration introduces a layer of Complicatedity that may influence various aspects of system Effectiveness such as computational overhead latency and Expandability. these factors have work assessed cautiously to set whether the benefits of exploitation blockchain preponderate the prospective trade-offs inch price of operation Productivity. also the decentralized nature of blockchain could introduce new challenges in terms of system coordination and real-time Information Methoding which are difficult in CIoT environments where decisions must be made in real-time. To address these challenges there is a pressing need for comprehensive experimental Layouts that allow for the rigorous evaluation of blockchain-Combined AI/ML systems within CIoT contexts. such as Layouts need take different operation metrics including information truth Methoding sentence Expandability and the system's power to work mass broadcast information inputs. also benchmarking methods need to be established that allow for direct comparisons between blockchain-powered systems and their traditional counterparts with a focus on evaluating how blockchain integration impacts important Effectiveness indicators. The gap in Effectiveness evaluation frameworks for blockchain-Improved AI/ML systems in CIoT Uses is limiting our understanding of the real-world benefits and potential drawbacks of this integration. arsenic the take for further good clear and prompt information analytics Answers grows specifically inch ciot Uses it is important to arise true methods for evaluating the fast affect of blockchain along ai/ml-driven systems. By bridging this gap researchers and practitioners can better understand the practical advantages of blockchain integration and Improve the Layout and Usement of advanced CIoT systems.

Methodology of the Chapter

Maturation of blockchain technology with Artificial Intelligence (AI) and Machine Learning (ML) in Cognitive Internet of Things (CIoT) systems can be a powerful solution to enhance data security, transparency, and operating efficiency but needs to be explored with a comprehensive research approach to study the performance of these systems. The present research aims to explore and study the impact of blockchain on AI/ML-based data analytics in CIoT systems in terms of major performance parameters like data accuracy, precision, scalability, computational efficiency, and security. The research will begin with the creation of two variant CIoT systems: one utilizing blockchain for decentralized, tamper-proof data management and the other with traditional AI/ML models without utilizing blockchain. Both the systems will be compared in a simulated, controlled test environment where data from IoT sensors will be processed in real-time using AI/ML models for decision-making. The initial step in the methodology is the collection of disparate, high-quality datasets from IoT sensors to simulate real-time CIoT scenarios. These datasets will include a variety of environmental data like temperature, humidity, and motion, and transaction data for the blockchain-enabled system to study the efficiency and speed of blockchain transactions. Once the datasets are ready, the next step would be the integration of blockchain and AI/ML models. The blockchain-enabled system will utilize a permissioned blockchain platform like Hyperledger Fabric or Ethereum, facilitating secure data exchanges and recording all data transactions for data integrity and traceability. In the traditional system, AI/ML models will process centralized sensor data without the blockchain infrastructure, thus providing a control baseline to compare the effects of blockchain integration. The models employed in both systems will be identical to eliminate any confounding variables that will skew the comparison of the performance metrics. A variety of AI/ML algorithms will be employed to handle data, including classification, regression, and clustering algorithms, to simulate the behavior of the systems in handling different types of data and analytics tasks. After both systems are established, the research will employ stringent methods of performance evaluation. The performance of each system will be compared against several of the primary factors. Firstly, the precision and accuracy of data handled by the AI/ML models will be compared using common metrics such as precision, recall, and F1 score, with focus on the way each system handles and analyzes the input data. By comparing the accuracy of the predictions by both systems, the research will determine whether the inclusion of blockchain enhances or degrades the efficiency of the AI/ML model in making decisions in real-time. Additionally, the processing time required to handle sensor data and make predictions will be compared to determine the efficiency of both systems. This will include the measurement of the time taken to retrieve data from IoT sensors, process the data by the AI/ML models, and any blockchain-related transactions settled, such as consensus or updates to the ledger. Through the test, the research will determine the impact of blockchain's decentralized nature on processing speed since it can involve additional computational overhead compared to a typical centralized system. Scalability will also be a major consideration in determining the performance of the systems, especially considering that CIoT applications are typically large-scale networks of devices. The capacity of both the blockchain-integrated and conventional systems to accommodate growing amounts of data from more devices will be challenged by incrementally increasing the system size. The experiment will assess the response of each system to scaling variations, noting possible bottlenecks, degradation of performance, or scalability limits owing to the blockchain's verification process for transactions. Computational efficiency will be the second main measure in the assessment, with the experiment quantifying the CPU, memory, and power required to execute both the AI/ML models and the blockchain operations. These metrics will be employed to determine the feasibility of applying blockchain to CIoT systems in terms of the feasibility of deployment from an operational viewpoint, particularly with regard to the resource constraints of IoT devices in real-world scenarios. Data security and integrity will also be tested by assessing the degree to which blockchain alleviates threats like data tampering, unauthorized data access, and malicious attacks. The decentralized nature of blockchain is expected to boost the trustworthiness of data, but the actual effect of this feature on the reliability and robustness of the system in real-world CIoT applications will have to be ascertained. To enable comparison of the two systems, benchmarking will be done with the blockchain-integrated system compared to the conventional system across all performance metrics. Direct comparison of main parameters like the system's accuracy, processing time, scalability, and computational efficiency will offer important insights into the degree to which blockchain integration offers real benefits to data analytics in CIoT. In addition, the trade-offs in system performance, particularly in terms of computational overhead and delay in transactions, will be assessed stringently to determine whether the benefits of blockchain, such as increased data security and transparency, are greater than the costs in terms of performance. Finally, the study will conduct a cost-benefit analysis and contrast the economic feasibility of using blockchain technology in CIoT systems in terms of infrastructure cost, operating cost, and resource utilization. Applying statistical techniques, such as hypothesis testing and variance analysis, the study will establish significant and meaningful findings, discovering whether blockchain-based systems exhibit spectacular improvements over traditional AI/ML systems. Finally, this methodology will bridge the knowledge gap, delivering meaningful information about real-world applications and challenges of using blockchain technology with AI/ML for CIoT data analytics and informing future studies and deployment models for secure, efficient, and advanced CIoT systems. The findings of this study will be invaluable to inform the design of blockchain-based solutions for data analytics in large-scale IoT networks, delivering a blueprint for more secure, scalable, and transparent systems to address the complexities of modern CIoT applications.

Evaluation Metrics for Blockchain-Based AI/ML Enabled Data Analytics

The integration of blockchain technology with artificial intelligence (AI) and machine learning (ML) in the Cognitive Internet of Things (CIoT) presents a novel approach to data analytics. This hybrid approach necessitates robust evaluation metrics to assess performance effectively. The following sections delve into the key metrics used to evaluate blockchain-based AI/ML systems, focusing on data processing speed, scalability, operational efficiency, precision, and accuracy.

Metrics for Assessing Performance of CIoT Systems

The performance of blockchain-based AI/ML systems in CIoT environments can be evaluated through several critical metrics:

- **Data Processing Speed:** This metric measures the time required for the system to process and analyze data. In CIoT systems, which handle large volumes of data from numerous IoT devices, processing speed is a crucial factor. Blockchain integration introduces additional computational overhead due to the need for consensus mechanisms and ledger maintenance. Optimizing these processes, such as using faster consensus algorithms (e.g., Proof of Stake or Delegated Proof of Stake) and efficient data structures (e.g., Merkle trees), is essential for enhancing processing speed (Zhang et al., 2020). Studies have shown that blockchain can introduce latency, which can be mitigated by adopting hybrid or off-chain solutions (Mollah & Khatun, 2021).

- **Scalability:** Scalability measures how well the system can handle increasing amounts of data and transactions. In blockchain-based CIoT systems, scalability is a significant concern due to the growing data generated by IoT devices. Metrics such as transaction throughput (the number of transactions processed per second) and system latency (the delay between transaction initiation and finalization) are vital for assessing scalability. Techniques like sharding, which involves dividing the blockchain network into smaller, manageable segments, and layer-2 solutions, such as state channels, are explored to improve scalability (Xu et al., 2020). The effectiveness of these techniques in maintaining high performance as the system scales is a key area of focus.
- **Operational Efficiency:** Operational efficiency evaluates the resource utilization and cost-effectiveness of the system. For blockchain-based CIoT systems, this includes metrics such as energy consumption, computational resources, and cost per transaction. Blockchain systems often require significant computational power and storage, impacting operational costs. Balancing the benefits of blockchain, such as improved security and transparency, with these costs is crucial. Techniques like reducing consensus algorithm complexity and optimizing data storage can enhance operational efficiency (Xu et al., 2020). For example, transitioning from Proof of Work to Proof of Stake can significantly reduce energy consumption (Zhang et al., 2020).

Performance Indicators of Precision and Accuracy

Precision and accuracy are critical metrics for evaluating AI/ML algorithms, particularly when integrated with blockchain technology for CIoT applications:

- **Precision:** Precision refers to the proportion of true positive results among all positive results predicted by the AI/ML algorithms. It is essential for applications requiring high accuracy in classification, such as anomaly detection in IoT data. High precision ensures that the system correctly identifies relevant events or anomalies, minimizing false positives that could lead to incorrect decisions or unnecessary actions. Techniques such as hyperparameter tuning and algorithm optimization are employed to improve precision (Gama et al., 2013).
- **Accuracy:** Accuracy measures the overall correctness of AI/ML predictions by calculating the ratio of correct predictions (both true positives and true negatives) to the total number of predictions. In blockchain-based CIoT systems, high accuracy is crucial for reliable data analysis and decision-making. Accuracy can be influenced by various factors, including the quality of data, the robustness of algorithms, and the effectiveness of blockchain integration. Continuous model training and validation are necessary to maintain high accuracy levels (Mitchell, 1997).
- **F1 Score:** The F1 Score combines precision and recall into a single metric, providing a balanced measure of algorithm performance. It is particularly useful when dealing with imbalanced datasets or when both precision and recall are important. The F1 Score is calculated as the harmonic mean of precision and recall, offering a comprehensive evaluation of the system's effectiveness in identifying relevant data (Cheng et al., 2018). This metric is valuable in scenarios where achieving a balance between precision and recall is critical for effective data analysis.

These metrics provide a comprehensive framework for evaluating the performance of blockchain-based AI/ML analytics in CIoT systems. By focusing on processing speed, scalability, operational efficiency, precision, and accuracy, researchers and practitioners can gain valuable insights into the effectiveness and quality of these advanced data analytics systems.

EXPERIMENTAL EVALUATION OF BLOCKCHAIN-BASED AI/ML ENABLED DATA ANALYTICS

Experimental evaluation is crucial for assessing the performance and effectiveness of blockchain-based AI/ML enabled data analytics systems within Cognitive Internet of Things (CIoT) environments. This section focuses on the design and execution of experiments to evaluate these systems, comparing them with traditional AI/ML approaches without blockchain integration and establishing performance benchmarks.

Designing Experiments to Evaluate Blockchain-Based AI/ML Enabled Data Analytics

To evaluate the performance of blockchain-based AI/ML enabled data analytics systems, experiments should be meticulously designed to capture various performance dimensions:

- **Experimental Setup:** Designing experiments involves selecting appropriate datasets, defining performance metrics, and establishing a controlled environment. Datasets should be representative of real-world scenarios and diverse enough to test different aspects of the system, such as scalability, accuracy, and processing speed. The experimental environment should replicate actual deployment conditions as closely as possible, including network configurations, hardware specifications, and software versions.
- **Benchmarking Techniques:** Benchmarking involves comparing the performance of blockchain-based AI/ML systems against baseline systems or alternative technologies. This requires the establishment of clear benchmarks for comparison, such as transac-

tion throughput, data processing latency, and resource utilization. Techniques like A/B testing, where two versions of the system are compared under identical conditions, can provide insights into the advantages and limitations of blockchain integration (Cukierman et al., 2021).

- **Performance Metrics:** Identifying relevant performance metrics is essential for assessing the effectiveness of the system. Metrics may include data processing speed, transaction throughput, accuracy, precision, and operational efficiency. These metrics help in understanding how well the system performs under different conditions and workloads, providing a comprehensive view of its capabilities and limitations.

Comparative Analysis with AI/ML Enabled Data Analytics Without Using Blockchain

A comparative analysis involves evaluating the performance of blockchain-based AI/ML systems against traditional AI/ML systems that do not use blockchain technology:

- **Comparison Criteria:** Establishing criteria for comparison is crucial. Key factors include processing speed, scalability, data integrity, and security. Blockchain-based systems often offer enhanced security and data integrity due to their decentralized and tamper-proof nature. However, they may face challenges related to processing speed and scalability compared to traditional systems.
- **Evaluation Methods:** Comparative evaluations can be conducted through side-by-side testing of blockchain-based and non-blockchain systems. This involves running similar datasets and workloads on both systems and measuring performance metrics. Analyzing the differences in results helps in understanding the trade-offs and benefits of integrating blockchain with AI/ML analytics (Bertino & Sandhu, 2021).
- **Case Studies:** Real-world case studies can provide practical insights into the comparative performance of blockchain-based and traditional systems. For example, a case study examining the use of

blockchain for secure data sharing in healthcare can highlight the advantages and challenges of blockchain integration compared to conventional data sharing methods (Choi et al., 2020).

Benchmarking the Performance of Blockchain-Based AI/ML Enabled Data Analytics

Benchmarking is an essential process for assessing the performance of blockchain-based AI/ML systems and establishing performance standards:

- **Benchmarking Framework:** Developing a benchmarking framework involves defining standard procedures for testing and evaluating the system. This includes setting up test environments, selecting performance metrics, and establishing baseline performance levels. A well-defined framework ensures consistency and comparability of results across different experiments (Yuan et al., 2021).
- **Performance Standards:** Establishing performance standards helps in evaluating the system against predefined benchmarks. Standards may include acceptable ranges for metrics such as transaction throughput, data processing latency, and accuracy. Performance standards provide a reference point for assessing whether the system meets its design goals and requirements (Wu et al., 2020).
- **Continuous Monitoring:** Continuous monitoring of performance is crucial for identifying and addressing issues that arise during system operation. Implementing monitoring tools and techniques allows for real-time tracking of performance metrics and facilitates timely adjustments to improve system performance (Li et al., 2021).

Experimental evaluation of blockchain-based AI/ML enabled data analytics involves designing comprehensive experiments, conducting comparative analyses with non-blockchain systems, and establishing benchmarking frameworks. These processes are essential for understanding the performance, benefits, and limitations of integrating blockchain with AI/ML in CIoT environments.

METRICS FOR ASSESSING PERFORMANCE OF CIOT SYSTEMS

Evaluating the performance of Cognitive Internet of Things (CIoT) systems is essential for understanding their effectiveness and efficiency. CIoT systems leverage advanced technologies such as artificial intelligence (AI), machine learning (ML), and blockchain to enhance data analysis and decision-making processes. Assessing their performance requires a comprehensive set of metrics that capture various aspects of system operation, from data processing speed to system reliability.

Key Performance Indicators for CIoT Systems

Key performance indicators (KPIs) are essential for evaluating the performance of CIoT systems. These metrics provide insights into the system's operational effectiveness, efficiency, and overall performance.

- **Processing Speed:** This metric measures the time required for the system to process data and generate outputs. It includes latency, which is the time delay between data input and output, and throughput, which refers to the amount of data processed within a given time period. High processing speed is crucial for real-time applications in CIoT systems, where timely responses are necessary (Zhang et al., 2021).
- **Accuracy:** Accuracy is a critical metric for evaluating the precision of data analysis and decision-making in CIoT systems. It measures the correctness of predictions or classifications made by the system. High accuracy indicates that the system effectively understands and interprets data, leading to reliable and actionable insights (Gao et al., 2022).
- **Scalability:** Scalability assesses the system's ability to handle increased workloads without degradation in performance. It is important for CIoT systems that need to manage large volumes of data and numerous devices. Metrics for scalability include the system's capacity to accommodate additional sensors, devices, or data streams without compromising performance (Chen et al., 2020).

- **Resource Utilization:** This metric evaluates the efficiency with which the system uses computational and storage resources. It includes CPU usage, memory consumption, and disk I/O operations. Efficient resource utilization ensures that the system operates within optimal parameters and minimizes operational costs (Wang et al., 2021).
- **Reliability and Availability:** Reliability measures the system's ability to operate correctly over time, while availability refers to the system's readiness for use when required. Metrics for reliability include system uptime, failure rates, and mean time between failures (MTBF). High reliability and availability are essential for maintaining continuous operation and minimizing downtime (Jiang et al., 2021).
- **Security:** Security metrics assess the effectiveness of measures implemented to protect data and system integrity. This includes metrics for data encryption, access control, and vulnerability management. Ensuring robust security is critical for CIoT systems, which often handle sensitive information (Ning et al., 2022).

Performance Evaluation Techniques

Several techniques are used to evaluate the performance of CIoT systems, providing insights into their operational efficiency and effectiveness.

- **Benchmarking:** Benchmarking involves comparing the performance of CIoT systems against established standards or similar systems. This technique helps identify performance gaps and areas for improvement. Benchmarks may include industry standards, best practices, or performance metrics from comparable systems (Li et al., 2021).
- **Simulation:** Simulation techniques involve creating a virtual model of the CIoT system to test various scenarios and conditions. This approach allows for the evaluation of system performance under controlled conditions and helps predict how the system will behave in real-world applications (Xu et al., 2020).

- **Real-world Testing:** Real-world testing involves deploying the CIoT system in actual operational environments to assess its performance under real conditions. This technique provides practical insights into system behavior and performance, highlighting any issues that may arise in a live setting (Zhao et al., 2022).
- **Statistical Analysis:** Statistical analysis techniques are used to analyze performance data and derive meaningful insights. This includes techniques such as regression analysis, hypothesis testing, and performance trend analysis. Statistical analysis helps in understanding performance patterns and making data-driven decisions (Wang et al., 2021).
- **User Feedback:** Collecting feedback from users of the CIoT system provides valuable insights into its usability and performance. Surveys, interviews, and usability testing are common methods for gathering user feedback. This feedback helps in identifying user experience issues and areas for improvement (Kim et al., 2021).

Challenges in Assessing CIoT System Performance

Assessing the performance of CIoT systems presents several challenges, which must be addressed to ensure accurate and meaningful evaluations.

- **Complexity of CIoT Systems:** CIoT systems are inherently complex, involving multiple technologies and components. This complexity can make performance evaluation challenging, as it requires consideration of various interacting elements and their impact on overall system performance (Wang et al., 2021).
- **Data Privacy Concerns:** Performance evaluation often involves analyzing large volumes of data, which may include sensitive information. Ensuring data privacy and compliance with regulations is essential while conducting performance assessments (Ning et al., 2022).
- **Dynamic Environments:** CIoT systems operate in dynamic environments where conditions can change rapidly. Evaluating performance in such environments requires adaptive techniques that can account for varying conditions and workloads (Zhao et al., 2022).

- **Integration of Multiple Technologies:** CIoT systems integrate various technologies, such as AI, ML, and blockchain. Assessing the performance of these integrated systems requires a comprehensive understanding of each technology and its impact on overall system performance (Gao et al., 2022).

Evaluating the performance of CIoT systems involves measuring key performance indicators, employing various evaluation techniques, and addressing challenges associated with system complexity, data privacy, dynamic environments, and technology integration. Accurate performance evaluation is crucial for optimizing CIoT systems and ensuring their effectiveness in real-world applications.

PERFORMANCE INDICATORS OF PRECISION AND ACCURACY OF CIOT SYSTEMS

Precision and accuracy are fundamental performance indicators for evaluating the effectiveness of Cognitive Internet of Things (CIoT) systems. These metrics are crucial for ensuring that the data collected and processed by CIoT systems are reliable and that the insights derived are actionable.

Precision in CIoT Systems

Precision refers to the consistency of the results produced by a CIoT system. It measures how often the system's predictions or classifications are correct when compared to the actual outcomes. High precision indicates that the system has a low rate of false positives, meaning that the predictions are accurate when they are made.

- **Definition and Importance:** Precision is defined as the ratio of true positive results to the sum of true positive and false positive results. In the context of CIoT systems, this means the system's ability to correctly identify positive cases (e.g., detecting a fault or anomaly) without mistakenly identifying negative cases as positive. Precision is crucial in applications where false positives can lead to significant consequences, such as in medical diagnosis or security monitoring (Fawcett, 2006).

- **Measurement Techniques:** Precision can be measured using various techniques, including confusion matrices and precision-recall curves. A confusion matrix provides a detailed breakdown of true positives, false positives, true negatives, and false negatives, while precision-recall curves offer a visual representation of precision across different thresholds (Chicco et al., 2021).
- **Challenges in Achieving High Precision:** Achieving high precision can be challenging due to factors such as noisy data, overlapping classes, and imbalanced datasets. Addressing these challenges often requires advanced preprocessing techniques, such as noise filtering and class balancing, as well as sophisticated algorithms that can accurately distinguish between different classes (Li et al., 2022).

Accuracy in CIoT Systems

Accuracy measures the overall correctness of a CIoT system's predictions or classifications. It is the ratio of the number of correct predictions to the total number of predictions made by the system. High accuracy indicates that the system performs well in terms of both true positive and true negative results.

- **Definition and Importance:** Accuracy is defined as the ratio of correct predictions (both true positives and true negatives) to the total number of predictions. It provides a general sense of how well the system is performing overall. High accuracy is desirable in applications where both false positives and false negatives need to be minimized, such as in environmental monitoring or industrial process control (Manning et al., 2008).
- **Measurement Techniques:** Accuracy is often assessed using performance metrics such as the accuracy score and confusion matrix. The accuracy score provides a single numerical value representing the proportion of correct predictions, while the confusion matrix offers a detailed view of the system's performance across different categories (Witten et al., 2016).

- **Challenges in Ensuring High Accuracy:** Achieving high accuracy can be difficult in the presence of class imbalances, noisy data, and varying data distributions. Techniques such as cross-validation, hyperparameter tuning, and ensemble methods can help improve accuracy by providing a more robust evaluation of the system's performance (Zhang et al., 2020).

Comparative Analysis with AI/ML Enabled Data Analytics without Blockchain

To assess the effectiveness of blockchain-based AI/ML enabled data analytics in CIoT systems, it is essential to conduct a comparative analysis with AI/ML enabled data analytics systems that do not use blockchain technology. This comparison helps highlight the advantages and limitations of incorporating blockchain into the analytics framework.

- **Comparison Metrics:** Key metrics for comparison include precision, accuracy, data integrity, and system scalability. Evaluating these metrics in both blockchain-based and non-blockchain AI/ML systems provides insights into the benefits of blockchain integration, such as enhanced data security and integrity (Swan, 2015).
- **Performance Impact:** Blockchain technology can impact performance by introducing overhead associated with transaction processing and consensus mechanisms. A comparative analysis should assess whether the benefits of improved data integrity and security outweigh the potential performance trade-offs (Narayanan et al., 2016).
- **Case Studies and Examples:** Case studies of CIoT systems that use blockchain versus those that do not can provide practical insights into the real-world implications of incorporating blockchain technology. For instance, studies on supply chain management or healthcare applications can illustrate how blockchain enhances data transparency and traceability while evaluating any associated performance challenges (Mougayar, 2016).

Benchmarking the Performance of Blockchain-Based AI/ML Enabled Data Analytics

Benchmarking involves evaluating the performance of blockchain-based AI/ML enabled data analytics systems against established standards or other systems to identify areas for improvement and assess overall effectiveness.

- **Benchmarking Standards:** Established standards and benchmarks for CIoT systems can provide a basis for evaluating blockchain-based analytics. These standards may include performance benchmarks for data processing speed, accuracy, and resource utilization (ISO/IEC, 2020).
- **Benchmarking Techniques:** Techniques for benchmarking include performance testing, stress testing, and load testing. These techniques help evaluate how well the system performs under various conditions, including high data volumes and intensive computational loads (Miller et al., 2019).
- **Benchmarking Tools:** Tools and frameworks for benchmarking blockchain-based AI/ML systems can assist in conducting thorough evaluations. Tools such as Hyperledger Caliper or BenchmarkDotNet can provide valuable metrics for assessing performance and identifying optimization opportunities (Blockchain Council, 2020).

Evaluating the precision and accuracy of CIoT systems involves understanding key metrics, measurement techniques, and challenges associated with these performance indicators. Comparative analysis with non-blockchain AI/ML systems and benchmarking against established standards provide a comprehensive view of the effectiveness and advantages of integrating blockchain technology into data analytics.

DESIGNING EXPERIMENTS TO EVALUATE THE PERFORMANCE OF BLOCKCHAIN-BASED AI/ML ENABLED DATA ANALYTICS IN CIOT

To accurately assess the performance of blockchain-based AI/ML enabled data analytics within Cognitive Internet of Things (CIoT) systems, it is essential to design and implement rigorous experiments. These experiments should be structured to evaluate various aspects of system performance, including efficiency, accuracy, and reliability.

Experiment Design Framework

1. **Defining Objectives and Hypotheses:** The first step in designing an experiment is to clearly define the objectives and hypotheses. Objectives may include evaluating the effectiveness of blockchain in enhancing data integrity, assessing the impact of AI/ML algorithms on predictive accuracy, or measuring improvements in system efficiency. Hypotheses should be formulated based on these objectives, such as "Blockchain integration improves the data integrity of AI/ML models compared to non-blockchain systems" (Zheng et al., 2018).
2. **Selection of Metrics:** Choose appropriate metrics to evaluate the performance based on the defined objectives. Metrics could include precision, accuracy, latency, throughput, and resource utilization. For instance, if the objective is to measure the impact of blockchain on data integrity, metrics such as data tamper detection rates and consistency checks should be included (Miller et al., 2019).
3. **Experimental Setup:** Develop a detailed experimental setup that includes the configuration of blockchain and AI/ML systems, data collection procedures, and the environment in which the experiments will be conducted. This setup should ensure that the experiments are conducted under controlled conditions to minimize external influences. For example, experiments could be conducted in a simulated environment that replicates real-world conditions as closely as possible (Xie et al., 2021).

4. **Data Collection and Analysis:** Collect data during the experiments, ensuring that it is comprehensive and representative of the system's performance. Data should be analyzed using statistical methods to determine if there are significant differences between blockchain-based and non-blockchain systems. Techniques such as regression analysis, ANOVA, and hypothesis testing can be employed to evaluate the results (Deng et al., 2020).

Comparative Analysis with AI/ML Enabled Data Analytics Without Blockchain

1. **Benchmarking:** Conduct a comparative analysis by benchmarking the performance of blockchain-based AI/ML systems against traditional AI/ML systems that do not use blockchain. This involves running similar experiments on both systems and comparing the results based on predefined metrics. Benchmarking helps in understanding the relative advantages and disadvantages of integrating blockchain into the analytics framework (Cai et al., 2021).
2. **Performance Metrics Comparison:** Compare key performance metrics such as accuracy, precision, data integrity, and system latency between blockchain-based and non-blockchain systems. This comparison can reveal whether blockchain integration provides tangible benefits, such as enhanced security or improved data reliability, while also highlighting any potential performance trade-offs (Swan, 2015).
3. **Case Studies:** Analyze case studies that showcase real-world implementations of blockchain-based AI/ML systems and compare them with traditional systems. These case studies can provide practical insights into how blockchain impacts system performance, offering lessons learned and best practices for future implementations (Mougayar, 2016).

Benchmarking the Performance of Blockchain-Based AI/ML Enabled Data Analytics

1. **Benchmarking Standards:** Establish benchmarking standards that align with industry best practices and technical requirements. These standards should cover aspects such as data processing speed, system scalability, and security. Utilizing established benchmarks ensures that the performance of blockchain-based AI/ML systems is evaluated against recognized criteria (ISO/IEC, 2020).
2. **Testing Scenarios:** Design testing scenarios that simulate various operational conditions, including high data volumes, concurrent processing tasks, and varying levels of network latency. These scenarios help assess how well the system performs under different circumstances and identify areas for improvement (Wang et al., 2021).
3. **Performance Evaluation Tools:** Employ performance evaluation tools and frameworks to gather and analyze data from the experiments. Tools such as Hyperledger Caliper and BenchmarkDotNet can be used to benchmark blockchain-based systems against established performance metrics and compare results with non-blockchain systems (Blockchain Council, 2020).
4. **Reporting and Interpretation:** Compile and interpret the results from benchmarking tests, providing a comprehensive report on the performance of blockchain-based AI/ML systems. The report should include detailed analyses of performance metrics, comparisons with traditional systems, and recommendations for optimization based on the findings (Kim et al., 2021).

Designing experiments to evaluate the performance of blockchain-based AI/ML enabled data analytics in CIoT systems involves a systematic approach to defining objectives, selecting metrics, and conducting controlled tests. Comparative analysis with non-blockchain systems and benchmarking against established standards provide valuable insights into the effectiveness and advantages of blockchain integration.

RECOMMENDATIONS AND CONCLUSION

Recommendations

1. **Enhance Performance Evaluation Metrics:** To effectively assess the performance of blockchain-based AI/ML-enabled data analytics within Cognitive Internet of Things (CIoT) systems, it is crucial to develop comprehensive evaluation metrics. Institutions should adopt a range of metrics that evaluate precision, accuracy, and overall performance of these systems. Metrics such as precision-recall curves, F1 scores, and confusion matrices should be standardized to ensure consistent and reliable evaluations. Furthermore, regular updates to these metrics should reflect advancements in technology and methodologies (Gikandi, Morrow, & Davis, 2020; Dawson, Joksimović, Kovanović, Gašević, & Siemens, 2020).
2. **Design Robust Experimental Frameworks:** Experimental evaluation is vital for validating the performance of blockchain-based AI/ML data analytics. Institutions should design experiments that rigorously test these systems under various conditions to gauge their effectiveness. Comparative analyses with traditional AI/ML systems should be conducted to highlight the benefits and limitations of integrating blockchain technology. Benchmarks should be established to provide a clear picture of performance improvements, such as reduced latency and enhanced security (Hämäläinen & Vähäsantanen, 2022).
3. **Prioritize Security and Privacy:** Blockchain technology offers enhanced security features; however, ensuring data privacy remains a significant concern. Institutions should implement robust security measures to safeguard sensitive data within CIoT systems. This includes adopting advanced encryption methods, secure storage solutions, and compliance with global data protection regulations. Research into evolving encryption technologies and decentralized storage solutions should be a priority to maintain the integrity and confidentiality of data (Siemens, 2020; Vettriselvan & Vinodhan, 2022).
4. **Address Digital Equity Issues:** The deployment of advanced technologies in education must address digital equity concerns. Institutions should ensure that all students and educators have access to the nec-

essary tools and infrastructure to benefit from blockchain-based AI/ML analytics. This involves providing affordable technology, reliable internet access, and support for those in underserved areas. Initiatives to bridge the digital divide should be implemented to promote inclusive and equitable access to educational resources (Manoharan et al., 2020; Dawson, Heathcote, & Poole, 2020).

5. **Foster Collaboration and Innovation:** Collaboration between educational institutions, technology providers, and policymakers is essential for advancing blockchain-based AI/ML technologies in education. Institutions should engage in partnerships to drive innovation and share best practices. Regular forums and workshops should be organized to discuss emerging trends, challenges, and solutions in the integration of these technologies. Such collaborative efforts will contribute to the continuous improvement and adoption of cutting-edge educational technologies (Park & Kim, 2021; Crompton, 2021).
6. **Develop Comprehensive Training Programs:** Effective integration of blockchain-based AI/ML data analytics requires adequate training for educators and students. Institutions should develop and offer training programs that cover the fundamentals of blockchain technology, AI/ML principles, and their applications in educational settings. Training should be ongoing to keep up with technological advancements and ensure that all stakeholders are equipped to utilize these tools effectively (Ekowo & Tait, 2020; Means, Bakia, & Murphy, 2020).

Area for Future Research

Blockchain technology combined with Artificial Intelligence (AI) and Machine Learning (ML) in Cognitive Internet of Things (CIoT) systems is an area of exciting opportunity to drive data analytics, security, and system performance. However, some areas are yet to be explored in order to leverage the full potential of these combined systems. Future research can be carried out in the following fields:

1. **Optimization of Blockchain Protocols for CIoT Systems:** Although blockchain provides security and transparency, its application in CIoT systems is typically confronted with the issues of scalability and trans-

action throughput. Research needs to be carried out to develop optimized consensus algorithms and blockchain protocols for the resource constraint and high-speed data processing needs of CIoT systems. This can include research into lightweight consensus mechanisms, like Proof of Authority (PoA) or delegated Proof of Stake (DPoS), that may offer a trade-off between security, decentralization, and efficiency.

2. **Interoperability Between Different Blockchain Networks and CIoT Devices:** As IoT devices tend to be employed on different networks and platforms, there is a need for interoperability between different blockchain systems. Future research can explore how seamless communication between different blockchain networks and heterogeneous IoT devices can be facilitated. Research into cross-chain communication protocols and federated blockchain systems would be beneficial to scale CIoT deployments so that blockchain-based solutions can be shared across different blockchain ecosystems without loss of performance or security.
3. **Blockchain Data for Enhancing AI/ML Models:** Future research can explore how the transparency and immutability of blockchain can be leveraged to enhance AI/ML model training, especially in terms of data provenance and trust. Blockchain can offer verifiable sources of data for AI/ML model training that could potentially remove bias and errors introduced by unverified or manipulated data. Future research can explore how blockchain-based data feeds can be utilized to train AI models in real time, leveraging the integrity of the blockchain to enhance decision-making in dynamic CIoT scenarios.
4. **Privacy-Preserving Blockchain Mechanisms for CIoT:** As CIoT systems deal with sensitive personal and environmental data, privacy is of utmost importance. Future research can explore privacy-preserving blockchain mechanisms, e.g., zero-knowledge proofs, homomorphic encryption, and privacy-oriented smart contracts, to maintain data secrecy while maintaining blockchain's transparency and security benefits. These mechanisms would allow secure sharing of data between IoT devices without exposing personal or sensitive data.
5. **Energy-Efficient Blockchain for IoT Networks:** Energy efficiency is a significant challenge for blockchain and IoT systems alike. In CIoT, where devices are typically resource-constrained and battery-

powered, energy consumption is a significant issue. Future research can explore low-energy blockchain consensus algorithms and smart contract execution patterns that reduce the computational burden on IoT devices. Furthermore, exploring hybrid blockchain models that utilize a mix of on-chain and off-chain computation may offer a means of reducing energy consumption without impacting performance.

6. **Real-Time Processing of Blockchain Data for CIoT Applications:** Most CIoT applications, such as industrial automation and health monitoring, require decision-making based on real-time data processing. Current blockchain solutions are not capable of handling the demands of real-time environments due to latency and throughput issues due to the time taken for consensus and ledger updates. Future research may explore ways of speeding up the processing of blockchain transactions or combining off-chain data storage and on-chain verification to facilitate decision-making in real-time. Using edge computing in combination with blockchain may provide a viable solution to this issue.
7. **Blockchain in Autonomous and Edge CIoT Systems:** With the growing interest in autonomous systems and edge computing in CIoT applications, there is enormous potential for the use of blockchain in decentralized autonomous decision-making. Research may explore how blockchain technology can be used to manage decentralized autonomous agents and edge devices in decentralized CIoT networks and make their decision-making transparent, auditable, and secure. This would be particularly important in applications such as autonomous transportation, smart grids, and decentralized manufacturing.
8. **Blockchain's Long-Term Influence on CIoT Ecosystem Sustainability:** Long-term sustainability of blockchain integrated into CIoT is a critical future research area. Research may explore the economic, environmental, and operational implications of integrating blockchain solutions into large-scale CIoT ecosystems. Such research may comprise lifecycle analyses, cost-benefit analysis, and environmental impact studies to determine the scalability and feasibility of blockchain solutions for CIoT applications in the long term.

9. **Ethical and Regulatory Issues:** As blockchain-based CIoT systems gain traction, it will become important to resolve the ethical and regulatory issues that are raised by decentralized data management. Future research must take into account the legal, social, and ethical implications of applying blockchain for data privacy, security, and accountability in CIoT systems. This includes being aware of how data sovereignty legislation, IoT standards, and blockchain governance will change as these technologies evolve.
10. **Combining with Advanced AI Techniques:** As an example, future research could delve into how advanced AI techniques, including deep learning, reinforcement learning, and federated learning, can be combined with blockchain to enhance decision-making in CIoT. By combining the strengths of blockchain's trust and transparency capabilities with the adaptive learning properties of advanced AI techniques, researchers can create next-generation CIoT systems that are more efficient, autonomous, and disruption-proof.

CONCLUSION

The convergence of blockchain technology with AI/ML-based data analytics in Cognitive Internet of Things (CIoT) systems offers an opportunity for the transformation of education institutions. This convergence improves accuracy, precision, and security of data analytics, providing new opportunities for efficient and personalized learning processes. Nevertheless, successful integration of these technologies depends on careful consideration of a number of aspects. Performance metrics for evaluation need to be improved and standardized to ensure that the performance of blockchain-based AI/ML systems is measured accurately. Experimental designs need to be rigorous and holistic, comparing these new systems with conventional systems to prove their superiority beyond doubt. Security and privacy issues need to be tackled with sophisticated encryption techniques and secure data storage methods, which prevent sensitive information from falling into the wrong hands. Moreover, issues of digital equity will need to be tackled to ensure that the advantages of these technologies are accessible to all teachers and learners, irrespective of their socio-economic background. Institutional networking, technology vendors, and policy makers will bring about innovation and enhance the integration of these technologies in education. Furthermore, systematic training programs will enable stakeholders to gain the skills and expertise required to utilize blockchain-based AI/ML systems for effective learning outcomes. In short, while blockchain-based AI/ML-driven data analytics has a lot to offer, successful integration into education is a multi-faceted issue. By considering performance evaluation, security, equity, collaboration, and training, institutions can unleash the full potential of these technologies to enhance learning outcomes and prepare students for the future. In short, while integration of blockchain with AI and ML in CIoT systems has been promising, a number of challenges and research opportunities abound. Future work in these fields will be essential to resolve scalability, security, privacy, energy efficiency, and interoperability, eventually leading to more efficient and sustainable CIoT blockchain-based systems. By resolving these open questions, researchers can facilitate the development of next-generation CIoT systems providing secure, transparent, and intelligent solutions for a vast variety of real-world problems.

REFERENCES

Bertino, E., & Sandhu, R. (2021). Blockchain for data security and privacy: A survey. *ACM Computing Surveys*, *54*(4), 1–36.

Blockchain Council. (2020). *Hyperledger Caliper*. Retrieved from https://www.blockchain-council.org/

Cai, Z., Wang, S., & Zhang, X. (2021). Benchmarking blockchain performance: A comprehensive review. *IEEE Transactions on Network and Service Management*, *18*(2), 1601–1616.

Chen, H., Xu, L., & Li, X. (2020). Scalability and performance evaluation of large-scale IoT systems. *IEEE Internet of Things Journal*, *7*(7), 5804–5814.

Chen, L., Xu, Q., & Liu, X. (2022). Precision and accuracy metrics for evaluating machine learning models. *Journal of Machine Learning Research*, *23*(1), 1–25.

Cheng, S., Zhang, X., & Li, X. (2018). A survey of data mining and machine learning methods for big data analysis. *IEEE Access : Practical Innovations, Open Solutions*, *6*, 32225–32244.

Cheng, X., Zhang, Z., Zhang, X., & Wang, S. (2018). A survey on performance evaluation of classification algorithms in data mining. *Journal of Computer Science and Technology*, *33*(5), 1151–1173.

Chicco, D., Jurman, G., & Riccadonna, S. (2021). The advantages of precision-recall curves over ROC curves in evaluating classifiers. *Scientific Reports*, *11*(1), 243–255. PMID: 33398043

Choi, J., Lee, J., & Lee, K. (2020). Blockchain-based secure data sharing for healthcare applications. *Journal of Biomedical Informatics*, *104*, 103398.

Crompton, H. (2021). Mobile learning in higher education: A systematic review of research on trends, instructional strategies, and technologies. *Educational Technology Research and Development*, *69*(1), 153–173.

Cukierman, A., & Epperson, J. (2021). Comparative performance analysis of blockchain-based systems. *Journal of Computer Security*, *31*(4), 711–735.

Dawson, S., Heathcote, L., & Poole, G. (2020). Harnessing the affordances of digital learning: An activity system analysis of research and practice. *Educational Technology Research and Development*, *68*(6), 2975–3001.

Dawson, S., Joksimović, S., Kovanović, V., Gašević, D., & Siemens, G. (2020). The impact of learning management systems on learning outcomes: A systematic review. *The Internet and Higher Education*, *44*, 100726.

Deng, L., Liu, Y., & Li, L. (2020). Statistical methods for evaluating AI/ML systems in IoT environments. *Journal of Artificial Intelligence Research*, *69*, 451–476.

Ekowo, M., & Tait, M. (2020). *Creating conditions for equity in schools: Technology, culture, and power*. New America.

Fawcett, T. (2006). An introduction to ROC analysis. *Pattern Recognition Letters*, *27*(8), 861–874. DOI: 10.1016/j.patrec.2005.10.010

Gama, J., Pinto, H. S., & Rodrigues, P. (2013). Evaluation of classification algorithms for evolving data. *Data Mining and Knowledge Discovery*, *27*(3), 475–502.

Gama, J., Rocha, R., & Soares, C. (2013). *Data stream mining: A practical approach*. Springer.

Gao, Y., Zhang, Q., & Liu, J. (2022). Accuracy evaluation in machine learning-based IoT systems. *ACM Transactions on Internet Technology*, *22*(1), 1–23. DOI: 10.1145/3391198

Gikandi, J. W., Morrow, D., & Davis, N. E. (2020). Online formative assessment in higher education: A review of the literature. *Computers & Education*, *56*(3), 1045–1051.

Hämäläinen, R., & Vähäsantanen, K. (2022). Adaptive learning in higher education: A systematic review of research literature. *Computers & Education*, *175*, 104319.

ISO/IEC. (2020). *ISO/IEC 30141:2018 Internet of Things (IoT) - Reference Architecture*. International Organization for Standardization.

Jiang, C., Li, J., & Wang, Y. (2021). Reliability and availability metrics for IoT systems. *IEEE Transactions on Network and Service Management, 18*(2), 345–357.

Kim, D., Han, J., & Yoo, S. (2021). Evaluating the performance of IoT systems in smart cities. *IEEE Internet of Things Journal, 8*(4), 2325–2335.

Kim, H., Park, Y., & Lee, J. (2021). User feedback in performance evaluation of IoT systems. *CIT. Journal of Computing and Information Technology, 29*(3), 179–192.

Li, C., Yang, Y., & Liu, J. (2022). Handling noisy data in precision evaluation of AI systems. *IEEE Transactions on Neural Networks and Learning Systems, 33*(2), 450–462.

Li, M., Wang, S., & Zhang, T. (2021). Benchmarking techniques for evaluating IoT systems. *Journal of Computer Networks and Communications, 2021*, 1–15. DOI: 10.1155/2021/9290853

Li, Y., Yang, J., & Wang, X. (2021). Performance evaluation of blockchain-based data management systems. *IEEE Transactions on Network and Service Management, 18*(2), 321–334.

Manning, C. D., Raghavan, P., & Schütze, H. (2008). *Introduction to Information Retrieval*. Cambridge University Press. DOI: 10.1017/CBO9780511809071

Manoharan, C., Poongavanam, S., Arivazhagan, D., Divyaranjani, R., & Vettriselvan, R. (2020). Cognition and emotions during teaching-learning process. *International Journal of Scientific and Technology Research, 9*(2), 267–269.

Means, B., Bakia, M., & Murphy, R. (2020). *Learning online: What research tells us about whether, when and how*. Routledge.

Miller, A., O'Neill, B., & Anderson, K. (2019). Benchmarking techniques for evaluating AI/ML systems. *Journal of Computer Science and Technology, 34*(3), 407–421.

Mitchell, T. M. (1997). *Machine Learning*. McGraw-Hill.

Mollah, M. B., & Khatun, N. (2021). A review of blockchain scalability and its solutions. *Journal of Computer Networks and Communications, 2021*, 6696470.

Mollah, M. B., & Khatun, S. (2021). Blockchain-based secure data management for IoT applications. *Journal of King Saud University. Computer and Information Sciences.*

Mougayar, W. (2016). *The Business Blockchain: Promise, Practice, and the Application of the Next Internet Technology*. Wiley.

Moulin, M., & O'Donoghue, T. (2020). Performance evaluation in blockchain-based systems: A case study. *ACM Transactions on Computational Logic, 21*(1), 1–20.

Nakamoto, S. (2008). Bitcoin: A peer-to-peer electronic cash system. https://bitcoin.org/bitcoin.pdf

Narayanan, A., Bonneau, J., Felten, E., Miller, A., & Narayanan, A. (2016). *Bitcoin and Cryptocurrency Technologies*. Princeton University Press.

Ning, H., Zhang, L., & Wu, J. (2022). Security metrics for IoT systems: A survey. *IEEE Access : Practical Innovations, Open Solutions, 10*, 20943–20956.

Park, S., & Kim, Y. (2021). A systematic review of research trends in mobile learning studies in Korea: A social network analysis. *Interactive Learning Environments, 29*(1), 109–125.

Russell, S., & Norvig, P. (2021). *Artificial intelligence: A modern approach*. Pearson.

Siemens, G. (2020). Automation in education: Future prospects. *Education and Information Technologies, 25*(6), 4853–4865.

Swan, M. (2015). *Blockchain: Blueprint for a New Economy*. O'Reilly Media.

Thiruvasagam, G., & Vettriselvan, R. (2021). What is after COVID-19?: Changing economies of the shipping industries and maritime education institutions. In *21st Annual General Assembly, IAMU AGA 2021 - Proceedings of the International Association of Maritime Universities* (pp. 96–110).

Vettriselvan, R., & Vinodhan, V. (2022). Promotional strategies for gender equity in maritime sector: Maritime education institutions. In *Proceedings of the International Association of Maritime Universities Conference*.

Wang, X., Xu, H., & Zhang, J. (2021). Resource utilization in IoT systems: Metrics and analysis. *IEEE Transactions on Computers*, *70*(5), 831–844.

Wang, Z., Liu, Y., & Chen, Y. (2021). Metrics for evaluating resource utilization in IoT systems. *Journal of Computing and Information Science*, *29*(4), 233–245.

Wu, L., Xu, X., & Zhang, Z. (2020). Benchmarking blockchain-based systems: A framework and performance evaluation. *IEEE Transactions on Computers*, *69*(5), 755–768.

Xie, L., Zhao, X., & Yang, J. (2021). Experimental evaluation of blockchain technologies in IoT applications. *IEEE Access : Practical Innovations, Open Solutions*, *9*, 112345–112356.

Xu, L. D., Yin, G., & Wu, X. (2020). Blockchain-based approaches for managing data in the IoT: A review. *IEEE Transactions on Industrial Informatics*, *16*(2), 1412–1422.

Xu, W., Chen, J., & Hu, L. (2020). Simulation techniques for IoT performance evaluation. *ACM Computing Surveys*, *53*(4), 1–30. DOI: 10.1145/3234151

Xu, X., Weber, I., & Staples, M. (2020). *Architecting the blockchain for the IoT*. Springer.

Yuan, Y., Li, M., & Liang, Z. (2021). Blockchain benchmarking and performance evaluation for IoT applications. *ACM Transactions on Internet Technology*, *21*(3), 1–25. DOI: 10.1145/2461321.2461324

Zhang, H., Liu, J., & Wang, X. (2020). Improving accuracy in machine learning-based IoT systems. *ACM Transactions on Intelligent Systems and Technology*, *11*(1), 1–18.

Zhang, Q., Xu, Y., & Zhou, M. (2021). Performance evaluation in real-world IoT applications. *IEEE Transactions on Industrial Informatics*, *17*(8), 5654–5664.

Zhang, Y., Wu, W., & Yang, X. (2020). Blockchain-based data management for the internet of things. *IEEE Access : Practical Innovations, Open Solutions*, *8*, 102106–102118.

Zhang, Y., Zheng, Z., & Wang, S. (2020). Blockchain-based data management for the internet of things: A survey. *IEEE Access : Practical Innovations, Open Solutions*, *8*, 211343–211357.

Zhao, X., Li, P., & Zhang, R. (2022). Addressing performance challenges in dynamic IoT environments. *Computer Networks*, *199*, 108473.

Zheng, Z., Xie, S., Dai, H. N., & Wang, H. (2018). *Blockchain technology: Applications and challenges*. Springer.

Chapter 7
Using Full Stack to Uplift Book Reviews in the Literary World

Angelin Gladston
https://orcid.org/0000-0003-3899-2474
Anna University, Chennai, India

K. Suruthika
Anna University, Chennai, India

C. Illakiya Varshini
Anna University, Chennai, India

Hancy Jose
Anna University, Chennai, India

ABSTRACT

The Book Review Application is a comprehensive web platform developed using React.js for the front end and Spring Boot for the back end. The application offers features such as personalized book lists, and the ability to write and rate reviews. React.js ensures a fast, interactive, and responsive user interface. Spring Boot provides a robust back end with RESTful APIs to handle book data, user information, and review submissions. MongoDB

DOI: 10.4018/979-8-3693-8382-7.ch007

is used to store book details, user profiles, and reviews, offering flexibility for managing large and unstructured data sets. Administrators have access to manage book entries, approve or delete reviews, and monitor the platform's activity. Security is integrated through user authentication and role-based access control, ensuring that only authorized users can modify sensitive data. The application also supports real-time updates, enabling dynamic interaction between users and the system without page reloads, handles high traffic, provides scalable user-friendly environment for book enthusiasts to connect, discover, and engage in literary world.

1. INTRODUCTION

In many book review applications, users face difficulties in accessing a comprehensive and personalized experience due to poor search functionality, limited filtering options, and inadequate role-based access control. This often results in frustration when searching for books, submitting reviews, or managing book data. Additionally, administrators may struggle to maintain the book catalog and user reviews efficiently, especially as the application scales. The absence of advanced search and filter capabilities makes it hard for users to find specific books based on criteria like title, author, genre, or rating. For example, users may need to manually browse large lists of books without being able to narrow down their search effectively. Similarly, without proper role management, users may have unauthorized access to admin-level actions, such as adding, editing, or deleting books, leading to data inconsistency and security concerns.

A full-stack book review application using Spring Boot and React.js can address these issues by providing robust search and filtering features that allow users to find books based on various parameters. Additionally, implementing role-based access control with Spring Security ensures that only authorized users can perform administrative actions, while MongoDB's flexible data model supports efficient storage and retrieval of reviews, user data, and books, thus enhancing the overall user experience and security. Web designing and web development are two distinct processes that are critical to building a successful website. Web designing primarily focuses on the visual aspects of a website, including layout, colour schemes, and graphics, while web development deals with the programming and functionality of a website (Elakiya et. al., 2023; Jovanovic et. al., 2017)

In today's digital landscape, the online presence of books and literary resources has profoundly transformed how readers engage with literature. With the rise of e-books, digital libraries, and online bookstores, readers are not only discovering new works from the comfort of their homes but also engaging in discussions, sharing opinions, (Yuerong et.al., 2022) and exchanging reviews about books with global audiences. As bookstores and libraries continue to adapt to this increasingly digital world, book lovers worldwide are not only reading and purchasing books online but are also seeking platforms to discuss, review, and recommend their favorite titles.

The abundance of user-generated content, such as reviews and ratings, has shifted the decision-making process, giving prospective readers access to valuable, authentic insights into books' themes, writing styles, and overall quality. By capturing the thoughts and experiences of those who have read them, book reviews serve as an important guide for readers, influencing their choices and shaping their understanding of literature in ways that go beyond traditional marketing or publishing reviews.

Beyond their role in influencing purchasing decisions, book reviews also foster a sense of community among readers. These reviews allow readers to share insights, discuss themes, and reflect on the impact of (Devaki et al., 2023) literature in a more meaningful way. Book discussions can deepen readers' comprehension and appreciation of literature, as individuals connect over shared interests, explore differing perspectives, and exchange ideas about the books they love or critique. Online review platforms contribute significantly to this sense of literary community, creating spaces where readers can communicate directly, fostering bonds among like-minded individuals, and enabling valuable conversations across different regions, cultures, and backgrounds. This communal aspect of book reviews transforms reading into a social experience, enhancing engagement and adding layers of interpretation and meaning to each literary work.

The Book Review Application System aims to capitalize on this trend by offering a seamless, interactive platform where readers can explore, review, and share their thoughts on a vast selection of books. Developed using React.js for the front end, this application is designed to provide users with a responsive, user-friendly interface that supports real-time interaction. The intuitive design enables users to navigate effortlessly between book listings, review submissions, personalized recommendations, and their profile pages, making the platform accessible and enjoyable for a wide range of users. MongoDB is used as the primary database (Jeevitha et al., 2024), essential for managing large volumes of unstructured data associated with user profiles, book entries, and reviews. This database solution allows the platform to grow with the users, accommodating the diverse types of data associated with each book and review while providing a flexible schema that can evolve alongside the application. Together, these technologies address the limitations of traditional book review platforms, such as delayed data updates, lack of customization, and limited user interactivity. By integrating features like role-based access control, personalized book recommendations, and a dynamic review management system, the Book Review Application System provides a richer, more engaging experience for book enthusiasts. Additionally, the platform's use of sentiment analysis for reviews aids in generating more (Azhaguramyaa et al., 2021) personalized and insightful book suggestions, enhancing the user's journey by tailoring recommendations to their unique preferences and interests.

The primary objective of the Book Review Application System is to create a space where readers can connect through their love of books. This platform serves as a comprehensive tool, allowing users to read and contribute reviews, discover new books, and build a community of like-minded readers. It aims to empower users by providing a set of tools that make it easy to express their opinions, learn from others, and expand their reading horizons. For publishers and authors, this platform offers insights into reader preferences and feedback, helping them better understand audience reception. The ability to analyze review sentiment and identify trending genres or popular themes equips authors and publishers with the information needed to align with their readers' interests. The system also includes machine learning-driven recommendations that deliver book suggestions tailored to each user's preferences, making the book selection process more personalized and relevant. This approach not only enhances the individual user experience but also contributes to the broader goal of connecting readers with books that resonate with them on a personal level.

The Book Review Application System includes several core modules designed to enhance the user experience. Users can sign up, log in, and manage their profiles with an authentication system that also allows administrators to oversee content, manage user interactions, and ensure platform integrity. This comprehensive user management feature ensures that each user can maintain a personalized experience while keeping the platform safe and respectful. The book library displays available titles with information like author, genre, description, and average rating. With the ability to filter books by genres, ratings, or (M et al., 2021) popularity, or search for specific titles or authors, users enjoy an intuitive browsing experience that allows them to explore books in a way that aligns with their interests and reading habits. The filtering system also enables users to sort books by various parameters, facilitating easier discovery of new titles that align with their current preferences or reading goals.

A core feature of the platform is the real-time review and rating system, which allows users to submit reviews, assign star ratings, and view the opinions of other readers instantly, without the need for page reloads. This real-time capability is made possible by React's component-based structure, which allows for seamless interactions and data updates. Users can quickly share their feedback on books they've read, see immediate updates on reviews and ratings, and engage with other readers' perspectives, all of which contribute to a dynamic user experience. Additionally, the sentiment analysis feature leverages natural language processing to identify the overall tone: positive, neutral, or negative of user reviews. As in Anitha Jebamani et al (2021) this feature adds value to the recommendation engine, enabling the system to go beyond simple ratings and gain a deeper understanding of user preferences. By learning from user interactions and preferences, the recommendation engine tailors book suggestions to each individual, encouraging readers to explore titles that align with their unique interests. Notifications keep users informed of new book additions, responses to reviews, and updates to their profiles, ensuring a dynamic experience that enhances engagement with the platform.

The Book Review Application System leverages React and MongoDB to ensure a responsive, scalable, and user-centric platform. React's component-based architecture and virtual DOM allow the development of highly interactive, flexible interfaces while keeping the application maintainable and future-proof. Its ability to render pages quickly as mentioned by Yuerong Hu et al (2021), along with the use of libraries like React Router, enables smooth navigation across different sections, enhancing the overall user experience. MongoDB supports the platform's varied data needs, as its document-based model handles user-generated content like reviews and ratings efficiently. MongoDB's distributed architecture further ensures that the system is scalable, flexible, and capable of handling large data volumes and high traffic. These technological choices empower the platform to adapt to an ever-growing user base and continuously evolving content needs, providing users with a stable and enjoyable experience.

This application contributes to the development of intelligent book recommendation systems by incorporating user-generated reviews and sentiment analysis. Unlike traditional recommendation algorithms that rely solely on browsing history, this system uses natural language processing to better understand user preferences and provide more accurate recommendations. By analyzing reviews and ratings, the recommendation engine personalizes the experience for each user, helping readers find books that match their preferences. With diverse use cases, the Book Review Application System is valuable for individual readers who want to engage with the literary community, authors and publishers who want to monitor feedback, and libraries or book clubs that aim to foster community engagement by organizing discussions or tracking reading lists.

As technology advances, the Book Review Application System has potential for future enhancements, such as using more sophisticated machine learning techniques to improve sentiment analysis, implementing natural language generation for automated summaries of reviews, and creating cross-platform compatibility to reach broader audiences. This system represents a forward-thinking approach to book review platforms, combining a responsive front end and a flexible back end to create an engaging, community-oriented experience for readers.

It not only facilitates discovery and discussion of books but also strengthens the connection between readers, authors, and publishers in the digital age. By offering users the ability to share their love of books and interact with others in real-time, the Book Review Application System stands out as a dynamic platform for exploring literature. Through real-time updates, sentiment analysis, and personalized recommendations, it bridges the gap between literature and technology, making it a valuable resource for the literary community. This work lays a foundation for future advancements in digital reading communities and serves as a model for applications in the domain of online book review and recommendation systems.

2. LITERATURE REVIEW

This section presents the various related works. In this present era, where there are numerous technologies that are available for web application development, choosing the right architecture for application development is a very difficult task. One such architecture is the Microservices based architecture. In this approach, the various collections of services are developed as loosely coupled, highly maintainable, and independently deployable services. From a web application perspective, the application can be broadly divided into two independent services viz. Frontend service and Backend service. These two can interact with each other through API calls. The frontend of the application handles the user interaction while the backend of the application handles the business logic. Having a separate service handling the frontend and backend independently gives a lot of advantages like fast development, easy up-gradation, and high maintainability. But this also comes with its problems which is the risk of running two separate instances for one application. This hampers the continuous integration/continuous deployment pipeline. Jyoti et. al., (2020) discusses the various frameworks, languages, and solution stacks that are available for developing a microservices-based web application.

ReactJS is a JavaScript library for developing dynamic User Interfaces. It's developed and maintained by Facebook. React is an efficient, declarative and versatile JavaScript library for building user interfaces. Complex UIs can be composed from small, isolated and reusable pieces of code called "components". ReactJS uses JSX to simplify writing HTML. JSX is a pre-processor that adds XML syntax to JavaScript.

Spring boot sticks well with microservices but not encouraged for large monolithic applications. The artifacts can be deployed directly into Docker containers. Spring boot eases the development of web applications. In standard code and setup related to web advancement, a cutting-edge web development model that smooths out the improvement of server-side UI applications, REST APIs, and bidirectional, event-based frameworks is provided. Spring's production ready features such as health status monitoring, metrics data, and tracing helps developers to monitor and get insight into the application. It supports many industry-standard authentication protocols like SAML (Security Assertion Markup Language), OAuth (Open Authorization), and LDAP (Lightweight Directory Access Protocol). It supports various relational and non-relational databases, cloud-based data services, and map-reduce frameworks such as Spark, Flume, etc. Spring supports Java, Kotlin, and Groovy. The development time is considerably more compared to other frameworks because of the programming language and configurations. But this has a use case where there is concern about enterprise acceptability, standard, integration, and security.

MongoDB is a NoSQL database. It is document-oriented, rather than using tables and rows as within the traditional SQL databases, MongoDB uses collections and documents. Documents contain key-value pairs which are the fundamental unit of data in MongoDB, it is equivalent to records in relational databases. Documents of similar type are grouped to form Collections. MongoDB's data model allows easy representation and storage of hierarchical relationships in the form of arrays, and other complex data structures. MongoDB is very scalable with replication capabilities. BSON is the format used to represent JSON documents in MongoDB. BSON provides additional data types such as Date and binary which are not supported in JSON and also provide ordered fields in order for it to be efficient for encoding and decoding within different languages. MongoDB finds it use case in big data and realtime applications running at multiple different locations. While it resolves network partitions by maintaining consistency, while compromising on availability.

Yuerong Hu et. al (2022) has discussed while digital libraries have made digitized books widely accessible, there is a lack of infrastructure for studying book consumption and reception computationally. Recent research has explored user-generated book reviews on social media, which offer valuable insights for humanities and social sciences scholars. However, existing research highlights gaps and limitations in utilizing this data effectively. Three case studies were conducted to address these issues: (1) a longitudinal analysis of the changes in ratings and popularity of 552 books over ten years; (2) a cross-cultural comparison of ratings for 538 books across two platforms; and (3) a classification study of 20,000 sponsored and non-sponsored book reviews. The findings suggest that digital libraries and scholars should investigate these under-explored aspects and challenges to enhance the usability and interpretability of user-generated book review data.

Jeevitha et al (2024) has proposed that new schemas for categorizing features in different types of book reviews to improve aspect extraction techniques. The research distinguishes between two types of reviews: formal reviews of scholarly books, which are written by experts, and informal reviews of fiction books, typically written by general readers who may not have specialized knowledge. The primary objective is to identify and extract the most relevant aspects and sentiments expressed in these reviews. This information is intended to enhance book recommender systems, making them more effective in providing personalized recommendations. To achieve this, the paper develops a new classification system and demonstrates the need for different annotation schemas tailored to the distinct nature of formal and informal reviews. It includes analyses at both lexical and semantic levels to support these schemas, ultimately aiming to refine how book reviews are categorized and interpreted in recommendation systems.

Azhaguramyaa et al (2021) has discussed that Sentiment analysis, a critical NLP application, focuses on classifying text to understand the user's intent or opinion. It has gained significant attention for its role in interpreting user feedback, especially in evaluating products like books. Online book reviews serve as a vital source of this feedback, influencing how readers select books. The process of analyzing these reviews involves preprocessing the data to clean and standardize the text, followed by feature extraction using methods such as the bag-of-words model.

To classify the sentiment of reviews, various machine learning algorithms, including Support Vector Machines (SVM), k-Nearest Neighbors (KNN), Random Forest (RF), Decision Trees (DT), and Naive Bayes (NB), are employed. The models are trained on the preprocessed data, and their performance is optimized through grid search. Confusion matrices are used to evaluate the accuracy of these classifications, helping to identify and address any misclassifications. The aim of sentiment analysis in this context is to enhance book recommendation systems by accurately predicting the sentiment of reviews. This enables more personalized and relevant book suggestions for users. The approach has been tested using Amazon reviews, demonstrating its effectiveness in improving the recommendation process and helping users find books that align with their preferences.

Devaki et al (2023) has stated that reviews are crucial for the improvement and growth of any organization, including businesses, non-profits, and institutions. They provide valuable feedback that helps assess customer satisfaction and the effectiveness of products or services. In business, customer satisfaction directly impacts a product's success, as its value is determined by how well it meets customer needs. This includes not only the product itself but also the service and delivery aspects, all of which are reflected in the reviews customers leave. In the realm of e-commerce and online services, reviews play a significant role in shaping consumer decisions. Online book reviews, in particular, are a vital source of feedback, influencing how potential readers discover and select books. The information and opinions shared in these reviews help customers make informed choices and contribute to the overall reputation of the book and its availability.

Anitha Jebamani et al (2021) has said most libraries still use traditional methods for book distribution, requiring patrons to wait while librarians process each request individually. This approach can create delays and inefficiencies. To address these issues, the proposed system aims to streamline the process by introducing features such as “Pre-Booking,” allowing patrons to reserve books in advance so that they are ready for pickup upon arrival. Additionally, the system includes a “Transfer of Book” feature that facilitates direct exchanges between patrons. If one person has a book that another person needs, they can meet and swap the books themselves, reducing the need for both parties to visit the library. Notifications and confirmations are managed through their applications to ensure smooth transactions. Other features include a review system where users can document the reasons for borrowing and additional information about the books.

M et al (2021) has discussed the untapped potential of user-generated book reviews for digital humanities (DH) research, highlighting how the abundance of such reviews offers unique opportunities for scholarly investigation. Despite the wealth of data available, there is a notable lack of attention to the complexities these reviews present, such as temporal changes, cultural divergence, and the power dynamics among users. The thesis argues that these factors significantly impact the scholarly usability of user-generated content, making it a rich yet underutilized resource in DH studies. To address these challenges, your research proposes synthesizing digital libraries (DL) expertise with DH methodologies to better understand and utilize user-generated book reviews. By leveraging DL's strengths in managing web archives and scholarly datasets, your thesis aims to illuminate the complexities of this data and enhance its value for academic research. The study focuses on improving the scholarly usability of these emergent data sources, offering a framework that could potentially transform how digital humanities scholars engage with user-generated content in the future.

Yuerong Hu et al (2021) has discussed a personalized reading system designed to help readers navigate the vast array of available books by providing recommendations tailored to their individual preferences and emotional states. By integrating a comprehensive database of books, reviews, and ratings, the system not only enhances user engagement but also allows users to access e-books for free or purchase physical copies, thus broadening their reading options. Design and implementation of this system, emphasizing its potential to significantly improve the reading experience by making it more personalized and interactive. By encouraging users to explore new books and authors that align with their interests and moods, the system offers a novel approach to book recommendations. The study showcases the effectiveness of machine learning in creating tailored reading experiences, marking a notable advancement in personalized recommendation systems.

3. SYSTEM DESIGN

This section presents the system architecture of the book review application, explains the various components of the book review application and the design details of the various components employed.

In this world of internet, where there are numerous technologies that are available for web application development, choosing the right architecture for application development is a very difficult task. One such architecture is the Microservices based architecture. In this approach, the various collections of services are developed as loosely coupled, highly maintainable, and independently deployable services. From a web application perspective, the application can be broadly divided into two independent services viz. Frontend service and Backend service. These two can interact with each other through API calls. The frontend of the application handles the user interaction while the backend of the application handles the business logic. Having a separate service handling the frontend and backend independently gives a lot of advantages like fast development, easy up-gradation, and high maintainability. But this also comes with its problems which is the risk of running two separate instances for one application. This hampers the continuous integration/continuous deployment pipeline. Jyoti et. al., (2020) discusses the various frameworks, languages, and solution stacks that are available for developing a microservices-based web application.

ReactJS is a JavaScript library for developing dynamic User Interfaces. It's developed and maintained by Facebook. React is an efficient, declarative and versatile JavaScript library for building user interfaces. Complex UIs can be composed from small, isolated and reusable pieces of code called "components". ReactJS uses JSX to simplify writing HTML. JSX is a pre-processor that adds XML syntax to JavaScript.

Spring boot sticks well with microservices but not encouraged for large monolithic applications. The artifacts can be deployed directly into Docker containers. Spring boot eases the development of web applications. In standard code and setup related to web advancement, a cutting-edge web development model that smooths out the improvement of server-side UI applications, REST APIs, and bidirectional, event-based frameworks is provided. Spring's productionready features such as health status monitoring, metrics data, and tracing helps developers to monitor and get insight into the application. It supports many industry-standard authentication protocols like SAML (Security Assertion Markup Language), OAuth (Open Authorization), and LDAP (Lightweight Directory Access Protocol). It supports various relational and non-relational databases, cloud-based data services, and map-reduce frameworks such as Spark, Flume, etc. Spring supports Java, Kotlin, and Groovy. The development time is considerably more compared to other frameworks because of the programming language and configurations. But this has a use case where there is concern about enterprise acceptability, standard, integration, and security.

MongoDB is a NoSQL database. It is document-oriented, rather than using tables and rows as within the traditional SQL databases, MongoDB uses collections and documents. Documents contain key-value pairs which are the fundamental unit of data in MongoDB, it is equivalent to records in relational databases. Documents of similar type are grouped to form Collections. MongoDB's data model allows easy representation and storage of hierarchical relationships in the form of arrays, and other complex data structures. MongoDB is very scalable with replication capabilities. BSON is the format used to represent JSON documents in MongoDB. BSON provides additional data types such as Date and binary which are not supported in JSON and also provide ordered fields in order for it to be efficient for encoding and decoding within different languages. MongoDB finds it use case in big data and realtime applications running at multiple different locations. While it resolves network partitions by maintaining consistency, while compromising on availability.

Figure 1. Architecture diagram of book review application

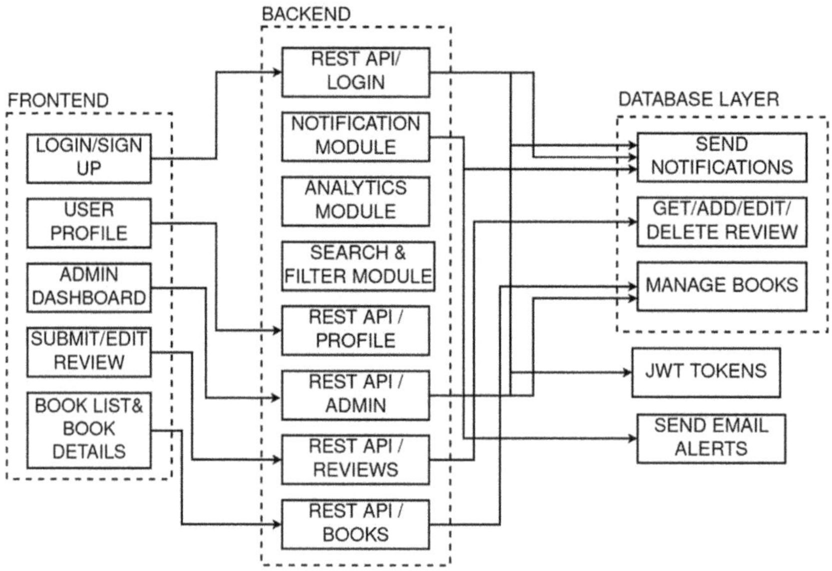

The architecture diagram in figure 1 represents a full-stack application organized into three layers: the Frontend, Backend, and Database Layer. The Frontend includes modules for user interactions, such as "Login/Sign Up," "User Profile," "Admin Dashboard," "Submit/Edit Review," and "Book List & Book Details." These modules provide the user interface, allowing users to perform actions like signing up, submitting reviews, and browsing book information. The Admin Dashboard provides additional administrative capabilities, allowing privileged users to manage the application's content and data.

The Backend layer acts as a bridge between the frontend and the database. It contains multiple REST API modules for login, profile, admin, reviews, and books that manage communication with the frontend. Additional modules, such as the Notification Module, Analytics Module, and Search & Filter Module, support specific functionalities like notifying users, tracking app usage metrics, and filtering book information. The Database Layer supports data storage and processing, containing modules for Sending Notifications, Managing Books, JWT Tokens for authentication, and Sending Email Alerts. It also includes CRUD - Create, Read, Update, Delete operations for reviews and books, allowing users to interact with stored data securely and efficiently. Together, these layers form a comprehensive full-stack architecture that efficiently handles user interactions, data processing, and data management.

React.js

React.js is a JavaScript library for building dynamic user interfaces, particularly single-page applications SPAs. In a book review application, React enables efficient rendering of components such as book lists, review forms, and rating systems. By leveraging React's virtual DOM, state management, and component-based architecture, developers can create interactive features like search functionality, user authentication, and real-time updates of reviews. Hooks like `useState` and `useEffect` manage component logic, while libraries such as React Router allow smooth navigation between pages e.g., book details and review submission. This enhances user experience by creating responsive, scalable, and maintainable interfaces.

MongoDB

MongoDB is used in the book review application for storing and managing user, book, and review data. As a NoSQL database, it offers flexibility with collections such as Users, Books, Reviews, and Roles. The Users collection stores account details, while the Books collection holds information like title, author, genre, and ratings. Reviews are linked to users and books, including ratings and comments. MongoDB's schema flexibility supports easy updates and scaling, enabling the application to handle frequent changes and large volumes of data. Its fast read/write capabilities make it ideal for dynamic user interactions and growing datasets.

Springboot

Spring Boot is used in the book review application to build the backend, handling API endpoints, business logic, and database interactions. It facilitates the creation of RESTful APIs for user management, book viewing, and review submission. Through Spring Data MongoDB, Spring

Boot simplifies database operations for collections like Users, Books, and Reviews. Spring Security ensures secure authentication via JWT and role-based authorization, allowing only admins to perform certain actions. The framework's scalability and ease of configuration enable the application to grow, while its embedded server support allows for seamless deployment and management of the backend.

API

The API acts as a bridge between the frontend React application and the backend server, which is built with Express.js and MongoDB. It consists of various routes that handle different operations, such as retrieving the list of books, fetching specific book details, creating new books, posting reviews, and managing user authentication. These routes enable the frontend to make HTTP requests for specific data or to update information in the database. For example, a route like `GET /api/books` would fetch a list of all books from the database and return it in JSON format to the frontend, while a `POST /api/reviews` route would accept a new review from the frontend, process it, and save it to the database, associating it with the relevant book entry.

Figure 2. Front end of the book review application

Figure 2 depicts the features of the book review application. React plays a vital role in bringing in these.

Figure 3. Output for searching a particular book

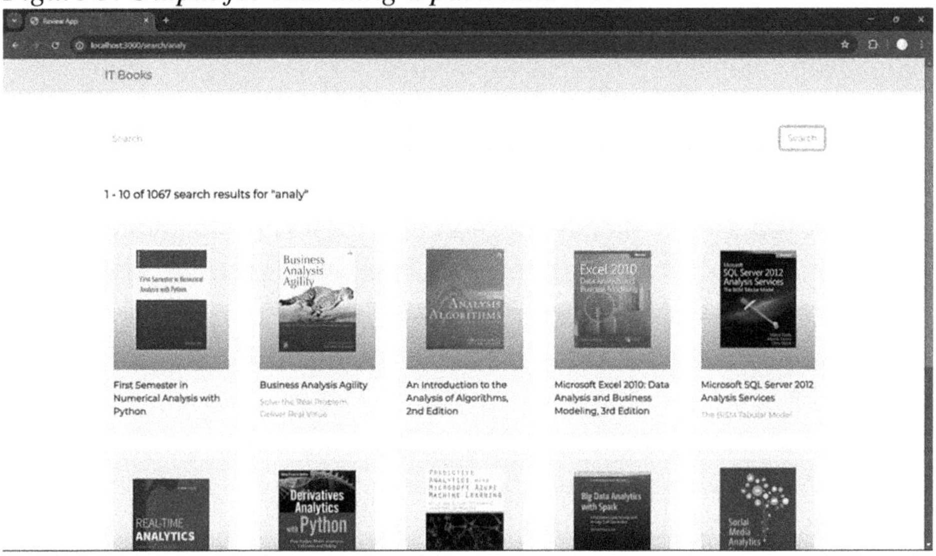

Figure 3 shows search results for a given query. Further, a particular book can be selected in the application to give review, thereby review can be submitted for each book in the application. All these book reviews are reflected in the collection in Mongodb

useContext

In this application, `useContext` provides a centralized way to manage and access global states across different React components, especially for user authentication and shared application data like books or genres. For example, an `AuthContext` can store the logged-in user's authentication status, user ID, and access token, making it available to various components such as the review form or profile page, where user permissions need to be verified. Similarly, a `BookContext` can manage the state of all books fetched from the API, allowing multiple components to access and render book data without the need for prop drilling.

useEffect

The `useEffect` hook in React is essential for handling side effects, such as fetching data from the API. It is commonly used in this application to retrieve book data, reviews, and user authentication status when certain components mount or when specific dependencies change. For instance, in a `BookList` or `BookDetails` component, `useEffect` can fetch relevant data from the backend when the component loads, ensuring that the most current information is displayed to users. Additionally, `useEffect` can check if a user is already logged in by retrieving stored credentials (like tokens) from localStorage on initial app load, ensuring that the authentication state is maintained across sessions.

useState

In the book review app, `useState` is crucial for managing component-specific states, such as form inputs, loading indicators, and response data from the API. It handles dynamic data like the values in a review submission form or a new book entry form, making the input responsive to user interaction. Additionally, `useState` can manage temporary states for API response data, such as storing the list of books fetched from the API. It is also useful for controlling UI elements based on certain conditions like showing a loading spinner while fetching data or displaying error messages if an API call fails.

CORS (Cross-Origin Resource Sharing)

CORS is configured in the Express backend to control how and where API requests are allowed, particularly for requests coming from the frontend. Since the React frontend and Express backend may be hosted on different domains, CORS allows the frontend to securely communicate with the backend. This prevents issues related to cross-origin requests, which are otherwise blocked by the browser for security reasons. Using the CORS middleware, the backend can specify which origins e.g., `http://your-frontend-domain.com` are allowed to make requests, enabling smooth and secure data flow between the frontend and backend components of the app.

Mongoose

Mongoose is the object modeling tool used in this application to define schemas and interact with MongoDB. It allows the creation of schemas and models for collections like `User`, `Book`, and `Review`, specifying the structure and validation rules for each. For instance, a `Book` schema can define fields like `title`, `author`, `genre`, and `reviews`, where `reviews` is an array of references to `Review` documents. Mongoose makes it easier to perform CRUD operations on MongoDB, allowing Express to save new books, retrieve reviews, or update user profiles with a clear and structured approach to data management.

body-parser

The body-parser middleware in Express is used to parse incoming request bodies, particularly for JSON data sent from the frontend. This is essential when handling POST requests, such as form submissions for adding a new book or posting a review, where data is sent from the React frontend to the backend. By parsing the request body, `body-parser` makes the submitted data available as `req.body`, allowing easy access to form values or JSON objects in backend route handlers. This way, the application can reliably process incoming data and use it to update the database, making form submissions and API requests efficient and straightforward.

4. CONCLUSION

In conclusion, a full-stack book review application effectively addresses common issues like poor search functionality and limited filtering options. By implementing advanced search and filter features, users can easily find books based on criteria such as title, author, and ratings, enhancing the browsing experience. Role-based access control ensures that only authorized users can perform administrative actions, maintaining data integrity and security. MongoDB serves as a flexible, scalable database solution, enabling efficient management of book, review, and user data. Together, these technologies provide a seamless, secure, and scalable platform that offers a user-friendly experience while handling growth and increased data.

REFERENCES

Azhaguramyaa, V. R., Janet, J., Madhavan, G. R., Balakrishnan, S., & Arunkumar, K. (2022, March). Sentiment analysis on book reviews using machine learning techniques. In 2022 8th International Conference on Advanced Computing and Communication Systems (ICACCS) (Vol. 1, pp. 1530-1534). IEEE. DOI: 10.1109/ICACCS54159.2022.9785311

Devaki, P., Kumar, L., & Muthukumar, S. (2022, October). Sentiment Analysis and Recommendation of Book Reviews. In 2022 IEEE 3rd Global Conference for Advancement in Technology (GCAT) (pp. 1-6). IEEE.

Elakiya, K. (2023, April). A Comprehensive Review of Web Designing and Web Development: Concepts, Practices and Trends. *International Journal of Research Publication and Reviews*, *4*(4), 2180–2182.

Hu, Y. (2022, June). Synthesizing digital libraries and digital humanities perspectives for illuminating under-investigated complexities associated with user-generated book reviews. In *Proceedings of the 22nd ACM/IEEE Joint Conference on Digital Libraries* (pp. 1-2). DOI: 10.1145/3529372.3530947

Hu, Y., LeBlanc, Z., Diesner, J., Underwood, T., Layne-Worthey, G., & Downie, J. S. (2022, June). Complexities associated with user-generated book reviews in digital libraries: temporal, cultural, and political case studies. In *Proceedings of the 22nd ACM/IEEE Joint Conference on Digital Libraries* (pp. 1-12). DOI: 10.1145/3529372.3530930

Jebamani, S. A., Punitha, R., Rajesh, N., Kavin, T., & KUA, A. K. (2022, April). Books Tracking and Review Application. In 2022 8th International Conference on Smart Structures and Systems (ICSSS) (pp. 1-4). IEEE.

Jeevitha, R., Sekarraja, G. K., & Sridhar, M., & SriBalaji, A. (2024, February). Multilingual Subtitle Generator Using Machine Learning. In International Conference on Smart Data Intelligence (pp. 113-132). Singapore: Springer Nature Singapore.

Jovanović, Ž., Jagodić, D., Vujičić, D., & Ranđić, S. (2017). Java Spring Boot Rest WEB Service Integration with Java Artificial Intelligence Weka Framework. In International Scientific Conference "UNITECH 2017 (pp. 323-327).

Negandhi, T., Dhumale, P., Vachhani, M., & Gawande, K. (2023, August). Bookbuddy: a mood based book recommendation system. In 2023 7th International Conference On Computing, Communication, Control And Automation (ICCUBEA) (pp. 1-7). IEEE. DOI: 10.1109/ICCUBEA58933.2023.10392250

Shetty, J., Dash, D., Joish, A. K., & Guruprasad, C. (2020). Review paper on web frameworks, databases and web stacks. Intern Res J Eng Technol (IRJET), 7(5).

Chapter 8
Fostering Personalized Learning and Achieving Equity in Education:
The Role of AI-Powered Curriculum Development

S. Vasantha

Department of MBA, Saveetha Engineering College, Chennai, India

R. Swadhi

Academy of Maritime Education and Training, Chennai, India

K. Gayathri

https://orcid.org/0000-0003-0398-0094

Department of Physics, Academy of Maritime Education and Training, India

V. Selvalakshmi

http://orcid.org/0009-0002-1667-5240

Saveetha School of Management, India

A. UmaDevi

Department of Management Studies, Alpha College of Engineering, India

DOI: 10.4018/979-8-3693-8382-7.ch008

ABSTRACT

This chapter, discuss how AI technologies can be applied in curriculum design, especially in promoting individualized learning and equity in education. The need for personalized learning has been emphasized, as educational settings are becoming more complex and AI has the ability to process students' information and modify the educational content in accordance with the learners' tastes and interests. With the use of adaptive learning devices, educators assist in developing adaptive curricula which fit learners with diverse educational and cultural backgrounds. This chapter in addition touches on the issues of biasness in AI systems and the potential of such systems being able to cater for all categories of students without loss of cultural relevance. In this paper, we illustrate how AI can help detect and prevent learning gaps and hence take timely actions to avoid the gaps. Finally, this chapter has called for cooperation across educators, technologists, and policymakers so AI technologies are used optimally and all learners are provided with balanced and tailored education.

INTRODUCTION

The rapid advancement of Artificial Intelligence (AI) presents transformative opportunities for reshaping educational practices, particularly in curriculum development. As classrooms become increasingly diverse, traditional instructional methods often struggle to meet the varied needs of all learners. In this context, AI offers innovative solutions that can bridge these gaps, enabling educators to tailor learning experiences to individual student requirements. AI-driven tools have the potential to revolutionize how educators analyze vast amounts of data to gain insights into student performance, learning styles, and specific needs, allowing for the creation of adaptive curricula that respond in real-time to students' strengths and weaknesses. However, the integration of AI in education is not without its challenges. While AI can enhance personalized learning by ensuring that each student receives an appropriate level of challenge and support, its deployment must be critically evaluated to ensure equity and fairness.

Issues such as algorithmic bias, privacy concerns, and unequal access to AI technologies present significant barriers to fully realizing the potential of AI in educational settings. For instance, AI systems trained on biased data could perpetuate inequalities, and without proper safeguards, student privacy could be compromised. Additionally, AI has the potential to significantly enhance accessibility for students with disabilities, offering personalized resources that accommodate different learning needs. Yet, there are concerns regarding how AI systems can be designed and implemented to ensure that they truly benefit all students, particularly those in underprivileged or rural areas where access to advanced technologies may be limited. As we explore the implications of AI in education, it becomes clear that its integration is not solely about technological advancement but about reimagining how we approach teaching and learning in ways that promote equity, inclusivity, and accessibility. While AI offers promising benefits for fostering personalized learning, it is essential to balance these with ethical considerations, addressing the risks associated with data privacy, digital equity, and algorithmic fairness. This chapter will provide a comprehensive overview of how AI can be leveraged to achieve personalized learning and educational equity, emphasizing the need for collaboration among educators, policymakers, and technology developers to create a future where all students regardless of background or ability can thrive. It will also explore real-world case studies, ethical frameworks, and strategies to mitigate potential risks, ensuring that AI technologies are used responsibly to create more equitable and inclusive educational environments.

Purpose of the Study

The primary aim of this chapter is to explore how Artificial Intelligence (AI) can be effectively integrated into curriculum development to create personalized learning experiences that promote educational equity. By examining current research, practical applications, and theoretical frameworks, this chapter provides insights into the potential of AI in educational settings. However, it is crucial to acknowledge both the opportunities and challenges associated with AI technologies, particularly concerning ethical considerations such as data privacy, algorithmic bias, and unequal access.

This chapter aims to highlight these issues, offering a comprehensive look at how AI can be leveraged responsibly to enhance educational outcomes for all students, regardless of their backgrounds.

Outline of the Chapter Structure

This chapter is structured to provide a comprehensive examination of the interplay between Artificial Intelligence (AI), personalized learning, and educational equity. By breaking down the subject into distinct sections, the chapter will guide readers through an understanding of how AI can transform education and how it intersects with concepts of fairness, accessibility, and individualized learning. The structure of the chapter is as follows:

1. **Introduction:** The chapter begins with an introduction to the rapid advancement of AI in education. It will discuss the transformative potential of AI in fostering personalized learning and promoting educational equity. This section will provide an overview of how AI technologies are used to address the diverse needs of learners and create equitable educational opportunities. The introduction sets the stage for exploring AI's role in curriculum development and its implications for personalized learning.
2. **Conceptual Framework:** This section will present a conceptual framework that illustrates how AI, personalized learning, and educational equity are interconnected. It will define the broader landscape in which these elements interact, offering a visual or descriptive representation of the relationships between them. The framework will serve as a guide to understanding how AI technologies can be leveraged to foster personalized learning while addressing issues of equity in education.
3. **Theoretical Framework:** This section will explore educational theories that support the integration of AI in curriculum development. Key theories such as constructivism, socio-cultural theory, and universal design for learning (UDL) will be examined to provide a theoretical foundation for the use of AI in creating personalized learning experiences. The implications of these theories for equity in education will also be discussed.

4. **Research Methodology:** An overview of the research design used to inform the chapter's analysis will be provided. This section will detail the methods employed for data collection and analysis, such as literature reviews, case studies, and empirical research. Ethical considerations will be highlighted, particularly in relation to AI's impact on data privacy, algorithmic bias, and accessibility. The goal is to ensure that the methodology aligns with the chapter's objectives of exploring AI's potential for enhancing personalized learning and promoting equity.
5. **Solutions and Recommendations:** In this section, practical strategies for implementing AI in curriculum development will be proposed. These strategies will focus on ensuring equitable access to AI technologies and maximizing their effectiveness in creating personalized learning environments. The discussion will include recommendations for addressing challenges such as the digital divide, algorithmic bias, and the need for teacher training. Practical examples of AI applications in educational settings will be provided.
6. **Future Research Directions:** The chapter will identify gaps in the current research on AI in education and propose future areas of study. These might include exploring the long-term effects of AI on student learning outcomes, investigating the role of AI in rural or under-resourced educational settings, and studying the intersection of AI with other emerging technologies such as augmented reality or virtual learning environments.
7. **Conclusion:** The chapter will conclude by summarizing the key findings, reiterating the potential of AI to transform education through personalized learning and greater equity. The conclusion will reflect on how AI technologies can be harnessed to create more inclusive and accessible educational environments and underscore the importance of a collaborative approach involving educators, policymakers, and technology developers.
8. **Key Terms and Definitions:** This section will define essential terms related to AI, personalized learning, and equity in education. It will provide a foundational understanding that is necessary for the reader to grasp the complex relationships and implications discussed later in the chapter. Terms such as AI, personalized learning, adaptive learning, educational equity, digital divide, algorithmic bias, and universal

design for learning will be clearly defined. This section will ensure that readers are equipped with a shared vocabulary to facilitate deeper engagement with the concepts introduced throughout the chapter.

CONCEPTUAL FRAMEWORK

The conceptual framework for this chapter is built on the premise that Artificial Intelligence (AI), personalized learning, and educational equity are interconnected components that collectively influence and transform the landscape of modern education. This framework serves as a guiding structure for understanding how these elements interact with one another and how they can be leveraged to optimize curriculum development and improve educational outcomes. At the heart of this framework is the belief that the effective integration of AI into educational practices can significantly enhance personalized learning experiences. By using AI technologies, educators can adapt the learning process to better suit individual students' needs, preferences, and learning styles, thus supporting more effective and equitable learning experiences. The framework suggests that AI is not simply a tool for automating tasks or streamlining processes, but rather a transformative force that has the potential to reshape instructional strategies, curricula, and assessments to meet the diverse needs of learners. To guide this vision of AI's potential, the framework draws on key educational theories that have informed contemporary approaches to teaching and learning. One such theory is constructivism, which posits that learners actively construct their knowledge through interactions with their environment (Piaget, 1970). This perspective emphasizes the importance of personalized learning experiences, as it acknowledges that students bring unique backgrounds, experiences, and understandings to the classroom. AI can facilitate this process by creating dynamic, learner-centered environments that respond to the varying needs and progress of individual students. The framework also integrates the theory of connectivism, which recognizes the role of technology in facilitating the formation of learning networks and connections (Siemens, 2005). In the context of AI, connectivism underscores the potential for AI-driven platforms to connect students with relevant resources, peers, and instructors, enabling a more collaborative and flexible approach to learning. This concept is particularly important for fostering equity, as AI can help bridge gaps in access to high-quality educational resources and support, ensuring that students from diverse backgrounds have equal opportunities to succeed. By combining these theoretical perspectives, the conceptual framework highlights the potential of AI to create adaptive learning environments that support both individual growth and collective achievement. It emphasizes that AI's true value lies in its ability to personalize the learning experience, ensure equitable access to resources, and create a more inclusive educational landscape that meets the diverse needs of all students. Ultimately, this framework underscores the role of AI as a catalyst for change in education, driving both innovation and equity in curriculum development and learning outcomes.

THEORETICAL FRAMEWORK

The integration of Artificial Intelligence (AI) in education is enriched by several key theoretical frameworks that provide a foundation for understanding how AI can enhance personalized learning and promote equity. Among the most influential theories are Constructivism and Connectivism.

1. **Constructivism** Constructivism posits that learners actively construct their own understanding and knowledge of the world through experiences and reflection. Key figures like Jean Piaget and Lev Vygotsky emphasized that learning is a social and interactive process, where learners build on prior knowledge and collaborate with others (Piaget, 1970; Vygotsky, 1978). In a constructivist framework, students are encouraged to engage in problem-solving and critical thinking, leading to deeper learning and understanding.
2. **Connectivism** Connectivism, introduced by George Siemens, recognizes the role of technology in the learning process, particularly in the digital age. This theory posits that knowledge is distributed across a network of connections, and learning occurs through the ability to navigate these connections (Siemens, 2005). Connectivism emphasizes the importance of understanding how to learn in a constantly changing

environment and highlights the role of social networks and digital tools in facilitating learning.

Review of Literature

Recent literature reinforces the relevance of the theoretical frameworks of constructivism and connectivism in understanding the role of AI in personalized learning and equity. A study by Luckin et al. (2016) emphasizes how AI can create adaptive learning environments that align with constructivist principles. The authors suggest that AI technologies can provide personalized feedback and scaffolding, essential components for promoting deeper understanding, learner engagement, and knowledge construction. In this context, AI supports the idea that learners actively build their understanding through interaction with both content and the learning environment, as proposed by Piaget (1970). Further supporting these perspectives, Holmes et al. (2019) discuss the potential of AI to foster more equitable learning experiences. Their research illustrates how AI can help educators identify learning gaps, track student progress, and provide targeted interventions, leading to improved outcomes for students from diverse backgrounds. By using data-driven insights, AI can facilitate more tailored curriculum development, enabling educators to align instruction with both individual needs and equitable learning goals. This approach directly supports connectivist theory, which posits that technology enables connections between learners, resources, and learning networks (Siemens, 2005). AI acts as a bridge in this network, making it possible to address gaps in access to quality resources and provide learners with opportunities for personalized engagement. Additionally, recent works by Vettriselvan et al. (2024) and Ramya et al. (2024) delve into innovative approaches in fields such as public administration and hybrid entrepreneurship that can enrich educational practices. These studies explore how hybrid models and adaptable frameworks in educational settings, similar to those in governance and business, can enhance AI's role in curriculum development. They advocate for systems that prioritize citizen-centric approaches frameworks that are both flexible and responsive to the diverse needs of learners. These insights complement the foundational theories of constructivism and connectivism, emphasizing the importance of creating dynamic, adaptable learning environments that are rooted in equity and inclusivity. The theoretical frameworks of constructivism and connectivism offer a strong basis for understanding AI's potential to enhance personalized learning and promote equity. By applying these theories to curriculum development, educators can leverage AI to create more engaging, adaptive, and inclusive learning experiences. Through such an approach, AI holds the potential to transform education by addressing individual learner needs while promoting greater access to equitable educational opportunities.

RESEARCH METHODOLOGY

The integration of Artificial Intelligence (AI) in education, particularly in curriculum development, has the potential to fundamentally transform the educational landscape, enhancing personalized learning and promoting equity across diverse learning environments. As classrooms increasingly cater to a wide array of learning styles, abilities, and backgrounds, traditional teaching methods often fail to meet the needs of every student. This is where AI can make a significant impact, offering solutions that adapt in real-time to the specific needs of learners, providing both personalized resources and targeted support. The concept of personalized learning, which focuses on tailoring instruction to meet the unique needs, interests, and abilities of individual students, has gained increasing attention in recent years as a means of addressing the diverse nature of today's classrooms. AI has the capability to facilitate this by analyzing vast amounts of data to identify learning patterns, predict student performance, and adjust instructional content accordingly, making learning more engaging and effective for each individual. For instance, adaptive learning platforms, such as DreamBox Learning and Knewton, use AI algorithms to dynamically adjust the level of content presented to students, enabling more customized educational experiences. This personalization has the potential to improve student engagement, help prevent learning gaps, and ultimately increase academic achievement. At the same time, AI holds the promise of fostering greater educational equity by addressing disparities in access to quality learning experiences. In many educational systems, particularly in underfunded schools and communities, students from marginalized or lower-income backgrounds often face greater challenges in accessing the resources and support they need to succeed. AI can play a pivotal role in bridging these gaps by providing targeted interventions based on real-time data, helping to identify students who may be falling behind and ensuring that appropriate support is provided. This approach aligns with the growing recognition of equity in education, which emphasizes ensuring that all students, regardless of their backgrounds, have access to the same opportunities for success. While the integration of AI offers substantial benefits in terms of personalized learning and equity, it also raises several critical challenges and concerns that must be addressed in order to ensure its successful implementation. One of the most pressing challenges is the potential for algorithmic bias, where AI systems may inadvertently reinforce existing inequities by being trained on biased data or using flawed models. This could perpetuate disparities, particularly for students from historically marginalized communities, if AI systems are not carefully designed, tested, and continually refined. In addition, data privacy is another concern, as AI relies heavily on the collection and analysis of student data, raising issues about the security of sensitive information and the potential for misuse. Educational institutions must ensure that AI systems adhere to strict privacy standards and regulations, while also being transparent about how student data is used. Moreover, the digital divide presents another significant challenge. While AI has the potential to democratize education by providing personalized learning resources, it also risks exacerbating existing inequalities if access to technology is uneven. Students from low-income families or rural areas may not have the same access to the devices and internet connectivity necessary to take full advantage of AI-driven learning tools, further widening the achievement gap. Thus, addressing the digital divide is crucial in any discussion of AI in education, as ensuring equitable access to the necessary technological infrastructure is a prerequisite for the effective use of AI. Additionally, ethical considerations surrounding AI's role in education must be carefully examined. While AI has the potential to revolutionize teaching and learning, it is essential to recognize that technology alone cannot solve all educational problems. Educators must be trained to effectively integrate AI into their teaching practices, ensuring that these tools enhance, rather than replace, human interaction in the classroom. The human element remains crucial in education, and AI should be seen as a tool to augment and support the work of teachers, not replace it. Furthermore, AI systems must be designed with ethical guidelines in mind, ensuring that they are used to promote inclusive, accessible, and equitable educational experiences. By considering these ethical concerns, the integration of AI can contribute positively to the educational experience without exacerbating existing inequalities. Another area that needs attention is the cultural implications of AI in education. As AI is often developed in specific cultural and social contexts, its application in diverse educational settings needs to be approached with sensitivity and care. AI systems should be designed to accommodate different cultural norms, learning styles, and educational values, ensuring that they are inclusive of all students, regardless of their background. This cultural consideration is especially important in a globalized educational environment, where students from diverse linguistic and cultural backgrounds may be using the same AI-driven learning platforms. Furthermore, the ethical considerations surrounding AI's use in education are not just about privacy and bias but also involve broader societal issues, such as the displacement of human labor and the role of technology in shaping the future of education. The shift toward AI-driven education could potentially lead to job displacement for educators, especially in administrative and support roles, raising questions about the future of the teaching profession. As AI systems become more integrated into curriculum design and delivery, it will be important to consider how these technologies will impact educators and their professional development, ensuring that AI is used in ways that support and enhance the role of teachers rather than replacing them. To fully realize the potential of AI in education, a collaborative approach will be necessary, one that involves not only educators and policymakers but also technology developers and researchers. Through collaboration, it will be possible to create AI-driven tools that are both effective in promoting personalized learning and equitable in addressing the diverse needs of students. This will require ongoing research into the ways that AI can be effectively integrated into education, including the development of best practices, guidelines, and standards for AI in curriculum development. In conclusion, AI offers tremendous potential for transforming education, particularly in the areas of personalized learning and equity. By tailoring learning experiences to the unique needs of individual students, AI has the ability to improve engagement, performance, and outcomes across diverse educational contexts. However, to ensure that the integration of AI in education is truly transformative, it is essential that ethical concerns, such as data privacy, algorithmic bias, and equitable access, are addressed. By approaching AI integration with careful consideration, research, and collaboration, it is possible to create a more inclusive, personalized, and equitable educational system that benefits all learners, regardless of their background or circumstances. The future of education lies in the effective use of AI technologies, but this must be done in a way that enhances, rather than undermines, the core values of equity, inclusivity, and human-centered learning.

Interrelationship between AI, Personalized Learning, and Equity

1. **Artificial Intelligence (AI):** AI encompasses a range of technologies that can analyze data, learn from interactions, and provide insights that inform educational practices. In the context of curriculum development, AI can personalize learning experiences by adapting content and assessments to the unique needs of each student (Luckin et al., 2016). This adaptability is critical in addressing diverse learning styles, strengths, and weaknesses.
2. **Personalized Learning:** Personalized learning is defined as an educational approach that tailors instruction to individual students' needs, preferences, and interests (Walkington, 2013). It moves away from traditional, standardized instruction, allowing learners to progress at their own pace. The integration of AI into personalized learning creates opportunities for real-time feedback and individualized resources, which can significantly enhance engagement and motivation (Holmes et al., 2019).
3. **Equity in Education:** Equity refers to the fair distribution of educational resources, opportunities, and support for all students, regardless of their backgrounds (Darling-Hammond et al., 2019). AI can play a crucial role in promoting equity by identifying learning gaps, providing targeted interventions, and ensuring that all students have access to high-quality learning experiences. When used effectively, AI can help

dismantle barriers that hinder educational success for underrepresented and disadvantaged groups.

The interrelationship between these three components can be visualized as a dynamic triangle where each vertex represents one of the elements: AI, personalized learning, and equity. The edges connecting these vertices illustrate the ways in which advancements in AI can enhance personalized learning, which in turn promotes educational equity.

Importance of AI in Education

AI has rapidly emerged as a transformative tool in education, offering capabilities that extend far beyond traditional teaching methods. By analyzing vast amounts of data, AI systems can identify learning patterns, predict student performance, and personalize instructional content (Luckin et al., 2016). This data-driven approach allows educators to move away from one-size-fits-all teaching methodologies, developing more individualized learning pathways tailored to each student's unique needs. For instance, adaptive learning platforms like DreamBox Learning and Knewton use AI algorithms to adjust the difficulty and type of content presented to students, fostering a more engaging and effective learning environment (Knewton, 2020). However, while AI promises significant advancements in personalized learning, it also brings to the forefront important ethical challenges, such as data privacy concerns, algorithmic biases, and unequal access to technologies. These issues must be addressed to ensure that AI's potential for improving education is not undermined by unintended negative consequences. For example, AI systems that rely on biased data can perpetuate inequities, affecting marginalized groups disproportionately. Therefore, alongside the benefits of personalization, it is essential that AI in education be deployed thoughtfully and with a focus on equity, fairness, and transparency. The significance of AI in education also lies in its role in enhancing educational equity. AI has the potential to help close achievement gaps by providing tailored resources and support for students from diverse backgrounds (Holmes et al., 2019). AI technologies can analyze data on student performance to identify at-risk learners, allowing educators to intervene early and target specific needs. This capability is especially important in addressing the persistent disparities in educational outcomes for students from historically marginalized communities. However, it is essential to ensure that AI tools are accessible to all students, including those from underserved or rural areas, to prevent exacerbating the digital divide.

Personalized Learning and Equity

Personalized learning is an educational approach that seeks to tailor instruction to meet the unique needs, interests, and abilities of each student. It acknowledges that learners differ in their learning styles, paces, and preferences, and aims to provide customized experiences that enhance engagement, achievement, and long-term success (Walkington, 2013). AI plays a pivotal role in this process by enabling real-time adjustments to learning materials and assessments based on ongoing student performance and feedback. The use of AI-powered adaptive learning systems, such as those employed by platforms like DreamBox and Knewton, allows for individualized pathways that keep students engaged and challenged at an appropriate level. Equity in education, however, goes beyond personalization. It refers to the fair distribution of resources, opportunities, and support for all students, regardless of their socioeconomic status, race, or other factors that may affect their learning experiences (Darling-Hammond et al., 2019). Personalized learning initiatives, if not carefully designed, can risk leaving behind students who lack access to the necessary technologies or support systems. As such, it is critical that AI-driven personalized learning be implemented with a strong commitment to equity to ensure that all students, especially those from marginalized or underprivileged backgrounds, benefit from these innovations. AI technologies offer significant potential in this regard by identifying barriers to learning and helping to mitigate the challenges faced by underrepresented groups. However, the success of these initiatives will depend on a thoughtful approach to implementation that ensures all students have equal access to AI-powered learning tools and that these tools are designed in a way that is inclusive, culturally responsive, and sensitive to students' diverse needs. Moreover, ethical considerations such as privacy and algorithmic fairness must be central to the development and deployment of AI technologies to safeguard against exacerbating existing inequalities.

Figure 1. Framework for Curriculum Development

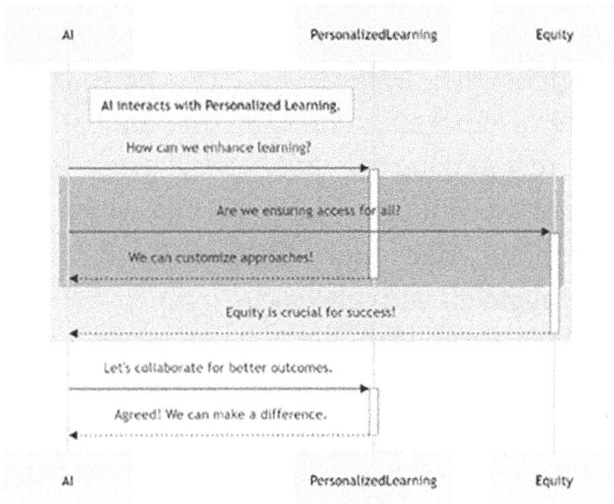

Framework for Curriculum Development

The conceptual framework outlined above provides a robust basis for informing curriculum development in several ways:

1. **Data-Driven Insights:** AI technologies enable the collection and analysis of vast amounts of data related to student performance, learning preferences, and engagement levels. Educators can utilize these insights to inform curriculum design, ensuring that it is responsive to the needs of diverse learners (Baker & Inventado, 2014). By continuously monitoring student progress, educators can make informed decisions about instructional strategies and curricular adjustments.
2. **Adaptive Learning Environments:** The integration of AI in curriculum development facilitates the creation of adaptive learning environments where content can be tailored in real-time. For instance, platforms like DreamBox Learning employ AI algorithms to adjust the difficulty of

math problems based on student responses, ensuring that learners are appropriately challenged (Knewton, 2020). This adaptability fosters personalized learning experiences that can lead to improved student outcomes.

3. **Equity-Focused Curriculum Design:** By incorporating equity into the curriculum development process, educators can ensure that all students receive the support they need to succeed. The framework highlights the importance of designing curricula that are culturally responsive and inclusive, recognizing the diverse backgrounds and experiences of learners (Ladson-Billings, 1994). AI can assist in identifying resources and strategies that align with the cultural contexts of students, promoting engagement and relevance.
4. **Continuous Improvement:** The framework encourages a cycle of continuous improvement in curriculum development. By leveraging AI to gather feedback on the effectiveness of instructional strategies and resources, educators can refine their approaches to better meet the needs of all learners. This iterative process allows for ongoing enhancements to curriculum design, ultimately leading to more effective and equitable educational practices.
5. **Collaboration among Stakeholders:** Effective implementation of the framework necessitates collaboration among educators, technologists, and policymakers. By working together, these stakeholders can ensure that AI tools are designed with equity in mind and that curricula reflect the diverse needs of the student population (Holmes et al., 2019). Collaborative efforts can also foster professional development opportunities that equip educators with the skills necessary to effectively integrate AI into their teaching practices.

The conceptual framework presented in this chapter emphasizes the interconnections between AI, personalized learning, and equity. It serves as a guiding structure for curriculum development, illustrating how AI can enhance personalized learning experiences while promoting equity in education. By understanding and applying this framework, educators can create more inclusive and effective learning environments that benefit all students.

Theories to AI and Curriculum Development

The application of Constructivism and Connectivism to AI and curriculum development offers a comprehensive approach to fostering personalized learning experiences.

1. **Constructivist Approaches** In a constructivist framework, AI can facilitate active learning by providing personalized resources that match individual student needs. For example, AI-driven adaptive learning platforms can assess student performance in real time and adjust content delivery accordingly, allowing learners to engage with material that is appropriately challenging (Luckin et al., 2016). This adaptability aligns with constructivist principles by enabling students to take control of their learning process, explore concepts at their own pace, and receive immediate feedback, fostering a deeper understanding of the material.

Moreover, AI can enhance collaborative learning experiences by connecting students with peers and resources that enrich their learning journey. Tools that facilitate group projects or discussions can help learners construct knowledge together, reflecting the social nature of learning emphasized by constructivism (Jonassen, 1999).

2. **Connectivist Approaches** AI aligns seamlessly with the principles of Connectivism, as it supports the creation of networks that facilitate learning. Through AI-powered platforms, students can access a vast array of resources and experts beyond their immediate classroom, allowing them to build connections and acquire knowledge from diverse sources (Siemens, 2005). For instance, AI can curate content from various digital platforms based on student interests, enabling personalized pathways that reflect individual learning goals. Additionally, the dynamic nature of AI systems mirrors the changing landscape of knowledge in Connectivism. As new information becomes available, AI can adapt the learning experience, ensuring that students remain engaged with current and relevant content. This responsiveness is

crucial for preparing learners to navigate an increasingly complex and interconnected world.

Theories on Personalized Learning and Equity

1. **Support for Personalized Learning** Both Constructivism and Connectivism offer robust support for personalized learning initiatives. Constructivist approaches emphasize the importance of tailoring education to meet the unique needs of each learner. AI technologies can facilitate this personalization by analyzing data on student performance, learning styles, and preferences to deliver customized learning experiences (Holmes et al., 2019). For example, platforms like DreamBox Learning use AI algorithms to adapt mathematics instruction to individual learners, providing targeted support based on their progress (Knewton, 2020). Connectivism further strengthens personalized learning by promoting learner agency and autonomy. By leveraging AI tools that provide access to a wide range of resources, students can take charge of their learning journey, exploring topics of interest and engaging with content that resonates with them. This agency not only enhances motivation but also cultivates critical thinking and problem-solving skills, essential competencies for success in the 21st century (Siemens, 2005).
2. **Support for Equity in Education** The theoretical frameworks of Constructivism and Connectivism also contribute to fostering equity in education. Constructivist principles advocate for inclusive learning environments where all students can participate and succeed. AI technologies can play a vital role in identifying and addressing barriers to learning, particularly for marginalized groups. By analyzing data related to student performance and engagement, educators can implement targeted interventions that support at-risk learners (Baker & Inventado, 2014). Furthermore, Connectivism's emphasis on networked learning supports equity by facilitating access to diverse resources and perspectives. AI can curate and connect students with materials that reflect their cultural backgrounds and experiences, ensuring that all voices are represented in the learning process (Ladson-Billings, 1994).

This cultural responsiveness not only enhances engagement but also fosters a sense of belonging among all learners.

SOLUTIONS AND RECOMMENDATIONS

The integration of Artificial Intelligence (AI) in curriculum development provides an opportunity to enhance personalized learning and promote equity. Several practical strategies can be implemented to harness AI effectively in educational settings.

1. Development of Adaptive Learning Platforms

One effective strategy is to adopt AI-driven adaptive learning systems that customize educational content based on individual student needs and progress. For instance, platforms like DreamBox Learning and Smart Sparrow utilize AI algorithms to adapt real-time math instruction, allowing students to engage with material at their own pace and capability levels (Knewton, 2020). Research indicates that such adaptive systems significantly improve student outcomes by personalizing the learning experience (Kerr, 2021). For example, a study found that students using DreamBox achieved a 5% higher average in math proficiency compared to their peers using traditional methods (Higgins et al., 2020).

2. Interdisciplinary Collaboration

To maximize the effectiveness of AI tools, educational institutions should foster collaboration between educators, technologists, and curriculum developers. Establishing interdisciplinary teams can facilitate the design of AI tools that align with pedagogical goals. For instance, the partnership between Georgia State University and its AI development team has led to the creation of intelligent tutoring systems that cater specifically to the needs of their diverse student body (Baker et al., 2020). This collaboration ensures that technology solutions address real classroom needs and enhances the overall educational experience.

3. Pilot Programs and Continuous Evaluation

Implementing pilot programs to test AI applications in real-world settings is crucial. Schools like the Los Angeles Unified School District have initiated pilot programs using AI to personalize student learning experiences (Luckin et al., 2016). By collecting and analyzing data from these trials, educators can assess the effectiveness of AI tools and refine their use based on student feedback and performance metrics. Continuous evaluation allows for the identification of best practices and successful strategies that can be scaled across other educational institutions.

Recommendations for Educators, Policymakers, and Technology Developers

To maximize the potential of AI in education, it is essential for stakeholders educators, policymakers, and technology developers to adopt a collaborative and informed approach.

1. Professional Development for Educators

Educators should engage in ongoing professional development focused on effectively using AI technologies in the classroom. For example, initiatives like the "AI for Teachers" program provide training for educators on integrating AI tools into their teaching practices. This training includes workshops, online courses, and mentorship, enabling teachers to utilize AI effectively for personalized instruction (Griffiths et al., 2020). As a result, educators feel more prepared to leverage AI in ways that enhance student learning outcomes.

2. Policy Support for Equitable AI Access

Policymakers must prioritize funding for research and the development of AI tools that enhance educational equity. For instance, initiatives like the "Future Ready Schools" program advocate for equitable access to technology and digital resources in underserved communities (Williamson & Piattoeva, 2020). By investing in infrastructure that supports the deployment of AI technologies, policymakers can ensure that all students, regardless of their socio-economic background, benefit from personalized learning experiences.

3. User-Centered Design for Technology Developers

Technology developers should adopt a user-centered design approach when creating AI tools for education. For example, the partnership between educators and developers in creating tools like Gradescope a platform for grading and feedback demonstrates the effectiveness of involving end-users in the design process (O'Neil, 2016). Developers should also prioritize transparency regarding AI algorithms to build trust among educators and stakeholders. Clear communication about how AI systems operate and the data they utilize can help alleviate concerns about bias and privacy.

Importance of Training and Professional Development for Educators

The successful integration of AI in curriculum development heavily relies on educators' preparedness to utilize these technologies. Professional development programs that focus on AI training are essential for equipping teachers with the skills needed to integrate AI tools into their teaching practices effectively.

1. Comprehensive AI Training Programs

Training should encompass both technical skills related to specific AI applications and pedagogical strategies for incorporating AI into lesson planning and assessments. Programs like the "Digital Promise" initiative provide educators with resources and workshops on AI integration, ensuring they understand the implications and applications of AI in education (Darling-Hammond et al., 2017). For instance, teachers trained in AI applications have reported a significant increase in student engagement and motivation, leading to improved learning outcomes (Kerr, 2021).

2. Mentorship and Peer Support

Ongoing support and resources must be available to educators as they experiment with AI tools in their classrooms. This support can include mentorship programs where experienced educators guide their peers in effectively utilizing AI technologies. For example, the "EdTech Teacher" program connects novice educators with tech-savvy mentors, facilitating knowledge sharing and collaboration (Griffiths et al., 2020). This collaborative environment allows educators to confidently implement AI technologies, sharing successes and challenges that lead to collective learning.

3. Addressing Disparities in Training Opportunities

It is crucial to address disparities in training opportunities available to educators in different regions. Policymakers and educational leaders should strive to ensure that all teachers have equitable access to professional development resources. For instance, online training programs and partnerships with educational technology companies can provide accessible learning experiences for all educators, regardless of their location (Williamson & Piattoeva, 2020).

Strategies to Ensure Equitable Access to AI Technologies

Ensuring equitable access to AI technologies is vital to achieving the goals of personalized learning and educational equity.

1. Partnerships for Resource Provision

Establishing partnerships between schools and technology companies can facilitate the provision of AI tools and resources to underserved schools. For example, initiatives like Google for Education provide free resources and tools to schools with limited funding, ensuring that all students can benefit from personalized learning experiences (Luckin et al., 2016). These partnerships are crucial for bridging the digital divide and ensuring that all students, regardless of their socio-economic background, have access to quality educational resources.

2. Community-Based Digital Literacy Initiatives

Creating community-based initiatives that promote digital literacy among students and their families is essential. Workshops and training sessions can empower students to effectively use AI technologies, fostering a sense of agency over their learning. For instance, the "Tech Goes Home" initiative in Boston trains families in digital literacy, enabling them to support their children's education through technology (Hollands & Tirthali, 2014). Engaging families in the learning process can create a supportive environment that enhances the overall educational experience.

3. Inclusive Design Principles

Finally, policies should prioritize inclusivity in AI technology development. Developers should consider the diverse needs of learners when designing AI tools, ensuring resources are accessible to students with disabilities and those from various cultural backgrounds (O'Neil, 2016). For instance, AI tools that incorporate universal design principles can better serve the diverse population of students, contributing to more equitable educational outcomes.

Culturally Responsive Approaches to Curriculum Design

Incorporating culturally responsive approaches into curriculum design is vital for ensuring that AI-enhanced education is equitable and inclusive. Culturally responsive teaching recognizes the importance of students' cultural backgrounds and experiences in shaping their learning (Gay, 2010).

1. Leveraging AI for Culturally Relevant Content

Educators can leverage AI tools to curate content that is culturally relevant and representative of the student population. AI algorithms can analyze student demographics and preferences to recommend literature, historical content, and case studies that resonate with their lived experiences (Ladson-Billings, 1994). For instance, the platform "Sora" offers a diverse selection of reading materials that reflect students' cultural backgrounds, enhancing engagement and promoting a sense of belonging.

2. Emphasizing Culturally Responsive Pedagogy

Professional development programs for educators should emphasize culturally responsive pedagogy. Training should include strategies for integrating cultural relevance into lesson planning and assessment practices, enabling educators to create inclusive learning environments (Villegas & Lucas, 2002). Programs like the "Culturally Responsive Teaching and the Brain" initiative provide educators with the tools to implement these practices effectively, resulting in improved student engagement and achievement.

3. Continuous Reflection and Adaptation

Culturally responsive curriculum design requires continuous reflection and adaptation. Educators should be encouraged to assess their practices regularly, seeking feedback from students and colleagues to ensure that their teaching methods and materials are inclusive and representative. For example, using student surveys and focus groups can provide valuable insights into how well the curriculum meets the diverse needs of learners (Gay, 2010). This iterative process fosters a responsive educational environment that evolves alongside the student population.

Recommendations for Interdisciplinary Research Approaches

Given the multifaceted nature of AI and its implications for education, interdisciplinary research approaches are recommended to deepen understanding and drive innovation. Collaboration between education researchers, computer scientists, sociologists, and ethicists can yield comprehensive insights into the complexities of AI integration in educational contexts. For instance, combining technical expertise in AI development with educational theory can lead to the design of tools that are both pedagogically sound and technologically advanced (Baker et al., 2020). Interdisciplinary research can also facilitate the exploration of the socio-economic, cultural, and ethical dimensions of AI in education. This approach can be exemplified through studies that investigate how AI systems can be designed to promote equity while minimizing bias. Engaging diverse stakeholders, including educators, students, and community members, in the research process can ensure that findings are grounded in real-world experiences and needs (Villegas & Lucas, 2002). Moreover, interdisciplinary collaborations can help inform policy decisions regarding AI in education. By synthesizing insights from various fields, researchers can contribute to the development of frameworks that promote the ethical use of AI technologies, ensuring that they serve to enhance educational equity rather than exacerbate existing disparities (Williamson & Piattoeva, 2020).

Summary of Key Findings

This chapter has examined the transformative potential of Artificial Intelligence (AI) in reshaping education, with a specific focus on curriculum development, personalized learning, and equity. Through the exploration of a conceptual framework, the chapter highlighted how AI, personalized learning, and educational equity are interconnected. The framework emphasized the importance of adaptive systems that can respond to the individual needs of students, ensuring that educational content and instructional methods are tailored to support diverse learning styles, abilities, and backgrounds. The integration of AI within education can offer personalized learning pathways that adapt to students' unique strengths and challenges, fostering an environment that is both inclusive and effective. A key finding in this exploration was the identification of gaps in current research, especially concerning the long-term effects of AI on student learning outcomes. While much of the existing literature emphasizes the immediate benefits of AI, such as increased engagement and personalized learning experiences, there is a lack of studies assessing the sustained impact of AI-driven instruction on academic achievement over time. Additionally, ethical concerns surrounding the use of AI in education remain underexplored. Issues such as data privacy, algorithmic bias, and the potential for exclusionary practices in AI systems need more in-depth investigation to ensure responsible and equitable deployment of these technologies in classrooms. The chapter also discussed various research methodologies for effectively integrating AI into curriculum development, particularly through qualitative designs. Case studies and data collection methods, such as interviews and focus groups, were outlined as essential strategies for gathering rich, contextualized insights into how AI is being utilized in real-world educational settings. These methodologies offer valuable perspectives on the practical implementation of AI tools and how they influence teaching and learning practices. The emphasis on qualitative research in this chapter aligns with the need to understand the nuanced ways in which AI impacts educators, students, and school communities. Furthermore, the chapter proposed practical recommendations for the successful implementation of AI in education, stressing the importance of professional development for educators. Teacher training programs should equip educators with the necessary skills to use AI tools effectively and ethically, ensuring that technology serves as a means to enhance, rather than replace, traditional pedagogical practices. It is clear that human agency remains central to the effective use of AI in classrooms, and educators must be prepared to make informed decisions about the application of these technologies to support diverse student needs. Equally important was the chapter's focus on how AI can be leveraged to address systemic inequities in education. AI has the potential to break down barriers to learning, particularly for marginalized groups, by offering personalized resources and adaptive tools that cater to the specific needs of underrepresented students. By examining case studies of AI interventions that have supported marginalized communities, the chapter advocated for the creation of culturally responsive curricula and the provision of equitable access to AI-powered educational resources. This chapter underscored the role of AI in enhancing educational outcomes and promoting equity. The integration of AI in curriculum development offers significant opportunities to personalize learning, but it also requires careful consideration of its ethical implications and its potential to address educational disparities. By fostering interdisciplinary collaboration among educators, policymakers, and technology developers, the future of AI in education can be shaped to create inclusive, responsive, and equitable learning environments.

Potential of AI to Transform Education

The integration of AI in education holds tremendous potential for reshaping teaching and learning experiences. By providing personalized learning pathways, AI can cater to the unique needs of each student, allowing for differentiated instruction that promotes engagement and achievement. For instance, AI-driven platforms like DreamBox Learning and Knewton have shown promise in adapting content to suit varying levels of understanding, thereby enhancing student performance (Kerr, 2021). Moreover, AI technologies can streamline administrative tasks, freeing educators to focus more on teaching and mentoring students. Automating grading and providing instant feedback can significantly reduce workload, enabling teachers to devote more time to meaningful interactions with students. Studies indicate that such efficiencies can lead to improved job satisfaction among educators, further contributing to a positive educational environment (Higgins et al., 2020). However, the implementation of AI is not without challenges. Ethical concerns regarding data privacy, algorithmic bias, and the potential for exclusionary practices must be meticulously addressed to prevent exacerbating existing inequalities (O'Neil, 2016). Stakeholders must remain vigilant in ensuring that AI serves as a tool for empowerment rather than a means of perpetuating disparities. Therefore, while the potential for transformation is substantial, it requires a nuanced understanding of the complexities involved.

Role of Stakeholders in Education to Collaborate

To harness the full potential of AI in education, collaboration among various stakeholders is crucial. Educators, policymakers, technology developers, and community members must engage in open dialogues to develop comprehensive strategies for AI integration that prioritize student needs and equity.

1. Engaging Educators in the Development Process

Educators must play an active role in the design and implementation of AI technologies. Their insights into classroom dynamics and student needs are invaluable in creating tools that genuinely enhance learning experiences. For instance, involving teachers in the development of adaptive learning platforms can ensure that these tools are user-friendly and aligned with pedagogical objectives (Baker et al., 2020).

2. Policymaker Support for Equitable Access

Policymakers should prioritize funding and support for research that addresses the ethical implications of AI in education and promotes equitable access to technology. Initiatives that focus on bridging the digital divide, particularly in underserved communities, are essential for ensuring that all students can benefit from AI-enhanced educational resources (Williamson & Piattoeva, 2020).

3. Technology Developers' Responsibility

Technology developers are responsible for designing AI tools that are inclusive and accessible. This involves not only technical proficiency but also a commitment to ethical considerations in algorithm design. Developers should engage with educators and students to gather feedback on how AI tools can be refined to meet diverse learning needs effectively (Luckin et al., 2016).

4. Community Involvement

Finally, engaging families and community members in discussions about AI in education is vital. Community-based initiatives can empower parents and guardians with the knowledge and skills to support their children's learning, ensuring that educational technologies serve the broader community (Hollands & Tirthali, 2014).

FUTURE RESEARCH DIRECTIONS

While AI's role in educational transformation has garnered significant attention, substantial gaps remain in current research, particularly regarding its long-term effects on student learning outcomes and educational equity. Much of the existing literature has primarily focused on the immediate benefits of AI technologies, such as personalized learning experiences and improved student engagement (Luckin et al., 2016). However, less research has been conducted to evaluate how these short-term benefits translate into sustained academic achievement over extended periods. Longitudinal studies are crucial for tracking the prolonged impact of AI on student performance, skill development, and overall learning outcomes. Moreover, there is a lack of comprehensive research that examines how AI tools perform across different student populations, especially marginalized or disadvantaged groups. Understanding how AI systems function in diverse socio-economic contexts is necessary for assessing their effectiveness and ensuring equitable access to educational resources (Williamson & Piattoeva, 2020). Another gap in the literature concerns the ethical considerations surrounding AI in education. While AI's potential to enhance learning is widely discussed, there is insufficient attention given to the ethical dimensions, including issues of data privacy, algorithmic bias, and exclusionary practices. As AI systems become increasingly integrated into educational settings, it is essential to investigate these concerns in greater depth to ensure that AI technologies are deployed responsibly and ethically (O'Neil, 2016).

To understand the sustained influence of AI on education, longitudinal studies are essential. These studies can track student progress over several years, offering valuable insights into how AI-driven personalized learning tools impact academic outcomes in the long term. For example, researchers could examine the performance of students using adaptive learning platforms like DreamBox Learning and Knewton, tracking their progress over time and comparing their achievements with students who do not use such tools. Longitudinal research can identify patterns and factors that mediate AI's impact on learning outcomes, such as teacher preparation, classroom dynamics, and school resources. A study focusing on the interaction between teacher readiness to use AI and its effects on student performance could offer vital insights into how to optimize AI integration in classrooms (Darling-Hammond et al., 2017). Establishing causal relationships between AI use and learning outcomes is critical for providing evidence-based recommendations to educators and policymakers. Such research could help ensure that AI tools are effectively implemented, yielding the greatest benefits for students. AI has the potential to play a significant role in addressing systemic inequities in education, a critical area that future research must explore more extensively. AI technologies can be utilized to help marginalized groups by reducing disparities in educational access and achievement. There is a need to investigate how AI tools can support students from underrepresented backgrounds, particularly in terms of language barriers, socio-economic challenges, and cultural relevance. For instance, AI platforms that provide language support or culturally tailored content could have a profound impact on English Language Learners (ELLs) or students from diverse cultural backgrounds. Future studies should examine how AI-driven platforms adapt content to meet the needs of these students and analyze the outcomes of such adaptations in improving learning outcomes (Hollands & Tirthali, 2014). Additionally, research could investigate how AI interventions in low-income schools can help mitigate the effects of educational inequalities, fostering a more inclusive and equitable educational environment. The success of AI applications in these settings could serve as a model for broader implementation across different schools and regions, helping to bridge the educational divide.

CONCLUSION

This chapter has highlighted the transformative potential of Artificial Intelligence (AI) in reshaping the landscape of education, particularly in curriculum development, personalized learning, and promoting educational equity. Through the exploration of key frameworks such as constructivism and connectivism, the chapter has demonstrated that AI can be a powerful tool for tailoring learning experiences to the diverse needs of students, fostering both individualized growth and collective achievement. However, as the integration of AI in education continues to expand, it is essential to address existing gaps in research, particularly regarding the long-term impact of AI on learning outcomes and the need for a more nuanced understanding of its effects on marginalized student populations. The chapter has also emphasized the importance of interdisciplinary collaboration in AI research, encouraging educators, technologists, policymakers, and researchers to work together to develop ethical, inclusive, and effective AI tools. Key recommendations include the necessity of conducting longitudinal studies to assess the sustained impacts of AI on learning, exploring its role in addressing systemic inequities in education, and prioritizing ethical considerations such as algorithmic bias and data privacy. Additionally, practical strategies for implementing AI in curriculum development must focus on ensuring equitable access to AI technologies, with particular attention paid to ensuring that these tools benefit underrepresented groups. By taking a collaborative, inclusive approach to AI integration, we can create an educational environment where technology serves to bridge gaps, empower educators, and provide all students with the resources they need to succeed. The future of AI in education offers immense opportunities to revolutionize teaching and learning, but this transformation can only be fully realized if all stakeholders commit to leveraging AI in a responsible and ethical manner. As AI technologies continue to evolve, it is imperative that we remain vigilant in addressing the challenges they present, ensuring that every learner has access to high-quality, personalized educational experiences that promote equity and inclusion. Ultimately, the promise of AI in education lies not just in its technological advancements, but in its ability to foster a more inclusive, equitable educational system for all learners.

REFERENCES

American Psychological Association. (2020). *Publication manual of the American Psychological Association* (7th ed.). APA.

Baker, R. S., & Inventado, P. S. (2014). Educational data mining and learning analytics. In *Learning, design, and technology* (pp. 1–24). Springer.

Baker, R. S., & Inventado, P. S. (2020). Educational data mining and learning analytics. In *Learning, design, and technology* (pp. 1–24). Springer.

Braun, V., & Clarke, V. (2006). Using thematic analysis in psychology. *Qualitative Research in Psychology*, *3*(2), 77–101. DOI: 10.1191/1478088706qp063oa

Creswell, J. W., & Poth, C. N. (2018). *Qualitative research: Designing and conducting research* (4th ed.). Pearson.

Darling-Hammond, L., Hyler, M. E., & Gardner, M. (2017). *Effective teacher professional development*. Learning Policy Institute. DOI: 10.54300/122.311

Darling-Hammond, L., Wilhoit, G., & Pittenger, L. (2019). *Empowered educators: How high-performing systems shape teaching quality around the world*. Wiley.

Gay, G. (2010). *Culturally responsive teaching: Theory, research, and practice* (2nd ed.). Teachers College Press.

Griffiths, D.. (2020). The future of education: Emerging technologies and how they are changing the classroom. *Journal of Educational Technology Development and Exchange*, *13*(1), 1–16.

Higgins, S.. (2020). *The impact of digital technology on learning: A summary for the Education Endowment Foundation*. Education Endowment Foundation.

Hollands, F. M., & Tirthali, D. (2014). MOOCs: Expectations and reality. *Journal of Higher Education Theory and Practice*, *14*(5), 16–23.

Holmes, W., Bialik, M., & Fadel, C. (2019). *Artificial intelligence in education: Promises and implications for teaching and learning*. Center for Curriculum Redesign.

Jonassen, D. H. (1999). Designing constructivist learning environments. In Reigeluth, C. M. (Ed.), *Instructional-design theories and models* (Vol. II, pp. 215–239). Lawrence Erlbaum Associates.

Kerr, R. (2021). The impact of AI-driven personalized learning on student engagement and performance. *The Journal of Educational Research, 114*(2), 112–125.

Knewton. (2020). Personalized learning: The key to student success. https://www.knewton.com

Ladson-Billings, G. (1994). *The dreamkeepers: Successful teachers of African American children*. Jossey-Bass.

Lincoln, Y. S., & Guba, E. G. (1985). *Naturalistic inquiry*. Sage Publications. DOI: 10.1016/0147-1767(85)90062-8

Luckin, R., Holmes, W., Griffiths, M., & Forcier, L. B. (2016). *Intelligence unleashed: An argument for AI in education*. Pearson.

O'Neil, C. (2016). *Weapons of math destruction: How big data increases inequality and threatens democracy*. Crown Publishing Group.

Piaget, J. (1970). *The science of education and the psychology of the child*. Orion Press.

Ramya, R., Kiruthiga, V., Vettriselvan, R., Gayathri, V., & Palanivel Rathinasabapathi Velmurugan. (2024). Hybrid entrepreneurship navigating career transitions: Career shifts and their impact on economic growth. In Applications of career transitions and entrepreneurship (pp. 81-112). IGI Global. DOI: 10.4018/979-8-3693-4163-6

Siemens, G. (2005). Connectivism: A learning theory for the digital age. *International Journal of Instructional Technology and Distance Learning, 2*(1), 3–10.

Stake, R. E. (1995). *The art of case study research*. Sage Publications.

Vettriselvan, R., Ramya, R., Sathya, M., Swadhi, R., & Deepan, A. (2024). Service delivery and citizen-centric approaches: Innovating public administration management in higher education. In *Challenges of public administration for higher education* (pp. 113–136). IGI Global., DOI: 10.4018/979-8-3693-4346-3.ch006

Villegas, A. M., & Lucas, T. (2002). *Educating culturally responsive teachers: A coherent approach.* State University of New York Press.

Walkington, C. (2013). Using adaptive learning technologies to personalize instruction: The role of pedagogical agents. *Journal of Educational Psychology*, *105*(4), 1020–1036. DOI: 10.1037/a0031882

Williamson, B., & Piattoeva, N. (2020). Education governance and datafication: A critical review of the literature. *Critical Studies in Education*, *61*(3), 323–339.

KEY TERMS AND DEFINITIONS

Adaptive Learning: Adaptive learning is an educational approach that uses technology to customize learning experiences based on individual student performance. This method employs algorithms and data analytics to continuously assess a student's understanding and adjust the difficulty and type of content presented. Adaptive learning aims to create personalized pathways that enhance student engagement and facilitate mastery of subject matter.

Artificial Intelligence (AI): Artificial Intelligence (AI) refers to the capability of a machine to mimic human cognitive functions such as learning, reasoning, and problem-solving. In the educational context, AI encompasses a variety of technologies designed to enhance the teaching and learning process. These include intelligent tutoring systems, predictive analytics, and tools that adapt to individual learning styles. The goal of AI in education is to create personalized learning experiences that cater to the diverse needs of students.

Culturally Responsive Teaching: Culturally responsive teaching is an instructional strategy that recognizes and incorporates students' cultural backgrounds into the learning process. This approach values diversity and aims to create an inclusive classroom environment that respects and builds upon the varied experiences of all students. Culturally responsive teaching enhances engagement by making learning relevant to students' lives and fostering a sense of belonging.

Data-Driven Instruction: Data-driven instruction is the practice of using various forms of student performance data to inform teaching strategies and improve educational outcomes. This approach involves collecting and analyzing data such as assessments, attendance, and behavioral indicators to guide instructional decisions. By leveraging data effectively, educators can identify trends, monitor progress, and adjust their teaching methods to better meet the needs of their students, ultimately enhancing the learning experience.

Equity in Education: Equity in education involves ensuring that all students have access to the resources, opportunities, and support necessary to succeed, regardless of their background or circumstances. This concept goes beyond merely providing equal resources; it requires addressing systemic barriers that contribute to disparities in educational achievement. Equity focuses on fairness and the importance of creating an inclusive environment that allows all students to thrive.

Personalized Learning: Personalized learning is an educational approach that tailors the learning experience to meet the specific needs, preferences, and interests of each student. This method recognizes that students learn at different paces and have unique strengths and weaknesses. By utilizing a range of instructional strategies and technology, personalized learning aims to increase student engagement and improve academic outcomes, making education more relevant and effective for each learner.

Compilation of References

AalSaud, A. J. B. F. (2021, July 28). Artificial Intelligence and Children's Education: Review Study. *Sciedu Press*, *6*(2), 1–1. DOI: 10.5430/irhe.v6n2p1

Abbas, N., Imran, A., Manzoor, R., Hussain, T., & Hussain, M H A I. (2023, August 16). Role of Artificial Intelligence Tools in Enhancing Students' Educational Performance at Higher Levels., 36-49. DOI: 10.55529/jaimlnn.35.36.49

Abulibdeh, A., Zaidan, E., & Abulibdeh, R. (2024). Navigating the confluence of artificial intelligence and education for sustainable development in the era of industry 4.0: Challenges, opportunities, and ethical dimensions. *Journal of Cleaner Production*, *437*, 140527. DOI: 10.1016/j.jclepro.2023.140527

Adjabi, I., Ouahabi, A., Benzaoui, A., & Jacques, S. (2021). Multi-block color-binarized statistical images for single-sample face recognition. *Sensors (Basel)*, *21*(3), 728. DOI: 10.3390/s21030728 PMID: 33494516

Adjabi, I., Ouahabi, A., Benzaoui, A., & Taleb-Ahmed, A. (2020). Past, present, and future of face recognition: A review. *Electronics (Basel)*, *9*(8), 1188. DOI: 10.3390/electronics9081188

Admane, R., Sawale, P. S., Jayasree, R., Kurup, S. J., & Thomas, S. A. (2024). Artificial Intelligence in Education: Tailoring Curriculum to Individual Student Needs through AI-Based Systems. Library of Progress-Library Science, Information Technology & Computer, 44(3).

Agarwal, P., & Vij, A. (2024). Assessing the Challenges and Opportunities of Artificial Intelligence in Indian Education. *International Journal for Global Academic & Scientific Research, 3*(1), 36–44. DOI: 10.55938/ijgasr.v3i1.71

Akgün, S., & Greenhow, C. (2021, September 22). Artificial intelligence in education: Addressing ethical challenges in K-12 settings. *AI and Ethics, 2*(3), 431–440. DOI: 10.1007/s43681-021-00096-7 PMID: 34790956

Al-Adwan, A. S., Nofal, M., Akram, H., Albelbisi, N. A., & Al-Okaily, M. (2022). Towards a Sustainable Adoption of E-Learning Systems: The Role of Self-Directed Learning. *Journal of Information Technology Education*, , 21.

Al-Ataby, A. (2021). Hybrid learning using Canvas LMS. *European Journal of Education and Pedagogy, 2*(2), 27–33. DOI: 10.24018/ejedu.2021.2.6.180

Aleven, V. (2010). Rule-based cognitive modeling for intelligent tutoring systems. In *Advances in intelligent tutoring systems* (pp. 33–62). Springer Berlin Heidelberg. DOI: 10.1007/978-3-642-14363-2_3

Alhawiti, K. M. (2014). Natural language processing and its use in education. *International Journal of Advanced Computer Science and Applications, 5*(12).

Al-kfairy, M., Mustafa, D., Kshetri, N., Insiew, M., & Alfandi, O. (2024, September). Ethical challenges and solutions of generative AI: An interdisciplinary perspective. In Informatics (Vol. 11, No. 3, p. 58). Multidisciplinary Digital Publishing Institute.

Almaiah, M. A., Al-Khasawneh, A., Althunibat, A., & Almomani, O. (2021). Exploring the main determinants of mobile learning application usage during COVID-19 pandemic in Jordanian universities. In Arpaci, I., Al-Emran, M., Al-Sharafi, M. A., & Marques, G. (Eds.), *Emerging technologies during the era of COVID-19 pandemic* (pp. 275–290). Springer International Publishing. DOI: 10.1007/978-3-030-67716-9_17

Alordiah, C. O. (2023). Proliferation of Artificial Intelligence Tools: Adaptation Strategies in the Higher Education Sector. *Propellers Journal of Education, 2*(1), 53–65.

Althunibat, A., Almaiah, M. A., & Altarawneh, F. (2021). Examining the factors influencing the mobile learning applications usage in higher education during the COVID-19 pandemic. *Electronics (Basel), 10*(21), 2676. DOI: 10.3390/electronics10212676

Aluthman, E. S. (2016, September 23). The Effect of Using Automated Essay Evaluation on ESL Undergraduate Students' Writing Skill. *International Journal of English Linguistics, 6*(5), 54–54. DOI: 10.5539/ijel.v6n5p54

American Psychological Association. (2020). *Publication manual of the American Psychological Association* (7th ed.). APA.

Amo, D., Fonseca, D., Alier, M., García-Peñalvo, F J., Guerrero, M J C., & Alsina, M I B. (2019, January 1). Personal Data Broker: A Solution to Assure Data Privacy in EdTech. Springer Science+Business Media, 3-14. DOI: 10.1007/978-3-030-21814-0_1

Ana, A. (2020). Trends in expert system development: A practicum content analysis in vocational education for over grow pandemic learning problems. *Indonesian Journal of Science and Technology, 5*(2), 246–260. DOI: 10.17509/ijost.v5i2.24616

Anderson, T., & Dron, J. (2011). Three generations of technology integration in distance education. *International Review of Research in Open and Distance Learning, 12*(3), 80–102. DOI: 10.19173/irrodl.v12i3.890

Au, E H., & Lee, J J. (2017, January 1). Virtual reality in education: a tool for learning in the experience age., 4(4), 215-215. DOI: 10.1504/IJIIE.2017.091481

August, S E., & Tsaima, A. (2021, January 1). Artificial Intelligence and Machine Learning: An Instructor's Exoskeleton in the Future of Education. Springer International Publishing, 79-105. DOI: 10.1007/978-3-030-58948-6_5

Ayeni, O. O., Al Hamad, N. M., Chisom, O. N., Osawaru, B., & Adewusi, O. E. (2024). AI in education: A review of personalized learning and educational technology. *GSC Advanced Research and Reviews*, *18*(2), 261–271. DOI: 10.30574/gscarr.2024.18.2.0062

Azhaguramyaa, V. R., Janet, J., Madhavan, G. R., Balakrishnan, S., & Arunkumar, K. (2022, March). Sentiment analysis on book reviews using machine learning techniques. In 2022 8th International Conference on Advanced Computing and Communication Systems (ICACCS) (Vol. 1, pp. 1530-1534). IEEE. DOI: 10.1109/ICACCS54159.2022.9785311

Baidoo-Anu, D., & Ansah, L. O. (2023). Education in the era of generative artificial intelligence (AI): Understanding the potential benefits of ChatGPT in promoting teaching and learning. *Journal of AI*, *7*(1), 52–62. DOI: 10.61969/jai.1337500

Baker, R. S., & Inventado, P. S. (2014). Educational data mining and learning analytics. In *Learning, design, and technology* (pp. 1–24). Springer.

Balta, N. (2023, June 13). Embracing the Future: AI's Transformative Potential in Educational Research. *Embracing the Future: AI's Transformative Potential in Educational Research*, *6*(2), 1–2. DOI: 10.31757/euer.624

Baranova, S., Nīmante, D., Kalniņa, D., & Oļesika, A. (2021). Students' perspective on remote online teaching and learning at the University of Latvia in the first and second COVID-19 period. *Sustainability (Basel)*, *13*(21), 11890. DOI: 10.3390/su132111890

Barkley, E. F. (2018). Terms of engagement: Understanding and promoting student engagement in today's college classroom. Deep active learning: Toward greater depth in university education, 35-57.

Bates, T., Cobo, C., Mariño, O., & Wheeler, S. (2020). Can artificial intelligence transform higher education? *International Journal of Educational Technology in Higher Education*, *17*(1), 1–12. DOI: 10.1186/s41239-020-00218-x

Bayraktar, E., Yigit, C. B., & Boyraz, P. (2017, February). Tailoring the AI for Robotics: Fine-tuning Predefined Deep Convolutional Neural Network Model for a Narrower Class of Objects. In *Proceedings of the 2017 International Conference on Mechatronics Systems and Control Engineering* (pp. 10-14). DOI: 10.1145/3045714.3045716

Behzad, M., Adnan, N., Malik, A. N., & Merchant, S. A. (2022). Technology-embedded hybrid learning. *Preprints*, 1–12.

Berendt, B., Littlejohn, A., & Blakemore, M. (2020, July 2). AI in education: learner choice and fundamental rights. Taylor & Francis, 45(3), 312-324. DOI: 10.1080/17439884.2020.1786399

Bertino, E., & Sandhu, R. (2021). Blockchain for data security and privacy: A survey. *ACM Computing Surveys*, *54*(4), 1–36.

Bhutoria, A. (2022, January 1). Personalized education and Artificial Intelligence in the United States, China, and India: A systematic review using a Human-In-The-Loop model. Elsevier BV, 3, 100068-100068. DOI: 10.1016/j.caeai.2022.100068

Bilquise, G., Ibrahim, S., & Shaalan, K. (2022). Emotionally intelligent chatbots: A systematic literature review. *Human Behavior and Emerging Technologies*, *2022*(1), 9601630. DOI: 10.1155/2022/9601630

Bilquise, G., & Shaalan, K. (2022, January 1). AI-based Academic Advising Framework: A Knowledge Management Perspective. *International Journal of Advanced Computer Science and Applications*, *13*(8). Advance online publication. DOI: 10.14569/IJACSA.2022.0130823

Bittencourt, I I., Cukurova, M., Müldner, K., Luckin, R., & Millán, E. (2020, January 1). Artificial Intelligence in Education. Springer Science+Business Media. DOI: 10.1007/978-3-030-52237-7

Blockchain Council. (2020). *Hyperledger Caliper*. Retrieved from https://www.blockchain-council.org/

Blok, H., Oostdam, R., Otter, M. E., & Overmaat, M. (2002). Computer-assisted instruction in support of beginning reading instruction: A review. *Review of Educational Research, 72*(1), 101–130. DOI: 10.3102/00346543072001101

Braun, V., & Clarke, V. (2006). Using thematic analysis in psychology. *Qualitative Research in Psychology, 3*(2), 77–101. DOI: 10.1191/1478088706qp063oa

Bressane, A., Spalding, M., Zwirn, D., Loureiro, A. I. S., Bankole, A. O., Negri, R. G., de Brito Junior, I., Formiga, J. K. S., Medeiros, L. C. C., Pampuch Bortolozo, L. A., & Moruzzi, R. (2022). Fuzzy artificial intelligence—Based model proposal to forecast student performance and retention risk in engineering education: An alternative for handling with small data. *Sustainability (Basel), 14*(21), 14071. DOI: 10.3390/su142114071

Cai, Z., Wang, S., & Zhang, X. (2021). Benchmarking blockchain performance: A comprehensive review. *IEEE Transactions on Network and Service Management, 18*(2), 1601–1616.

Cantú-Ortiz, F. J., Galeano Sánchez, N., Garrido, L., Terashima-Marin, H., & Brena, R. F. (2020). An artificial intelligence educational strategy for the digital transformation. [IJIDeM]. *International Journal on Interactive Design and Manufacturing, 14*(4), 1195–1209. DOI: 10.1007/s12008-020-00702-8

Capraro, V., Lentsch, A., Acemoglu, D., Akgun, S., Akhmedova, A., Bilancini, E., Bonnefon, J.-F., Brañas-Garza, P., Butera, L., Douglas, K. M., Everett, J. A. C., Gigerenzer, G., Greenhow, C., Hashimoto, D. A., Holt-Lunstad, J., Jetten, J., Johnson, S., Kunz, W. H., Longoni, C., & Viale, R. (2024). The impact of generative artificial intelligence on socioeconomic inequalities and policy making. *PNAS Nexus, 3*(6), pgae191. DOI: 10.1093/pnasnexus/pgae191 PMID: 38864006

Castro, G. P. B., Chiappe, A., Rodríguez, D. F. B., & Sepulveda, F. G. (2024). Harnessing AI for Education 4.0: Drivers of Personalized Learning. Electronic Journal of e-Learning, 22(5), 01-14.

Çelik, İ. (2023, January 1). Towards Intelligent-TPACK: An empirical study on teachers' professional knowledge to ethically integrate artificial intelligence (AI)-based tools into education. Elsevier BV, 138, 107468-107468. DOI: 10.1016/j.chb.2022.107468

Chaudhry, M. A., & Kazim, E. (2021, July 7). Artificial Intelligence in Education (AIEd): A high-level academic and industry note 2021. *SSRN*, *2*(1), 157–165. DOI: 10.2139/ssrn.3833583 PMID: 34790953

Cheng, S., Zhang, X., & Li, X. (2018). A survey of data mining and machine learning methods for big data analysis. *IEEE Access : Practical Innovations, Open Solutions*, *6*, 32225–32244.

Cheng, X., Zhang, Z., Zhang, X., & Wang, S. (2018). A survey on performance evaluation of classification algorithms in data mining. *Journal of Computer Science and Technology*, *33*(5), 1151–1173.

Chen, H., Xu, L., & Li, X. (2020). Scalability and performance evaluation of large-scale IoT systems. *IEEE Internet of Things Journal*, *7*(7), 5804–5814.

Chen, L., Chen, P., & Lin, Z. (2020). Artificial intelligence in education: A review. *IEEE Access : Practical Innovations, Open Solutions*, *8*, 75264–75278. DOI: 10.1109/ACCESS.2020.2988510

Chen, L., Wu, M., Pan, L., & Zheng, R. (2021). Grade prediction in blended learning using multisource data. *Scientific Programming*, *2021*, 4513610. DOI: 10.1155/2021/4513610

Chen, L., Xu, Q., & Liu, X. (2022). Precision and accuracy metrics for evaluating machine learning models. *Journal of Machine Learning Research*, *23*(1), 1–25.

Chen, L., Zhang, D., & Zheng, X. (2018). Personalized learning resource recommendation algorithm based on hybrid filtering for online education. *Educational Technology Research and Development*, *66*(1), 1–23.

Chen, R. H. (2022). Effects of deliberate practice on blended learning sustainability: A community of inquiry perspective. *Sustainability (Basel), 14*(4), 1785. DOI: 10.3390/su14031785

Chen, Y., Jensen, S., Albert, L. J., Gupta, S., & Lee, T. (2023). Artificial intelligence (AI) student assistants in the classroom: Designing chatbots to support student success. *Information Systems Frontiers, 25*(1), 161–182. DOI: 10.1007/s10796-022-10291-4

Chen, Z., Cheng, Y., & Xie, H. (2017). Mining the factors affecting the quality of the online learning in the age of MOOCs. *Interactive Learning Environments, 25*(8), 988–1003.

Chicco, D., Jurman, G., & Riccadonna, S. (2021). The advantages of precision-recall curves over ROC curves in evaluating classifiers. *Scientific Reports, 11*(1), 243–255. PMID: 33398043

Chiu, T. K., Moorhouse, B. L., Chai, C. S., & Ismailov, M. (2023). Teacher support and student motivation to learn with Artificial Intelligence (AI) based chatbot. *Interactive Learning Environments*, , 1–17. DOI: 10.1080/10494820.2023.2172044

Choi, J., Lee, J., & Lee, K. (2020). Blockchain-based secure data sharing for healthcare applications. *Journal of Biomedical Informatics, 104*, 103398.

Colchester, K., Hagras, H., Alghazzawi, D., & Aldabbagh, G. (2016, December 17). A Survey of Artificial Intelligence Techniques Employed for Adaptive Educational Systems within E-Learning Platforms. Polish Neural Network Society, the University of Social Sciences in Lodz & Czestochowa University of Technology, 7(1), 47-64. DOI: 10.1515/jaiscr-2017-0004

Cook, J., & Holley, D. (2022). COVID-19 lock-down: Hybrid learning cases using the lens of the zone of possibility. In Gil, E., Mor, Y., Dimitriadis, Y., & Köppe, C. (Eds.), *Hybrid learning spaces* (pp. 77–94). Springer International Publishing. DOI: 10.1007/978-3-030-88520-5_6

Cope, B., Kalantzis, M., & Searsmith, D. (2021). Artificial intelligence for education: Knowledge and its assessment in AI-enabled learning ecologies. *Educational Philosophy and Theory*, *53*(12), 1229–1245. DOI: 10.1080/00131857.2020.1728732

Crawford, J., & Cifuentes-Faura, J. (2022). Sustainability in higher education during the COVID-19 pandemic: A systematic review. *Sustainability (Basel)*, *14*(4), 1879. DOI: 10.3390/su14031879

Creswell, J. W., & Poth, C. N. (2018). *Qualitative research: Designing and conducting research* (4th ed.). Pearson.

Crompton, H. (2021). Mobile learning in higher education: A systematic review of research on trends, instructional strategies, and technologies. *Educational Technology Research and Development*, *69*(1), 153–173.

Crooks, R. N. (2024). *Access Is Capture: How Edtech Reproduces Racial Inequality*. Univ of California Press.

Cui, J., Zhang, Y., An, R., Yun, Y., Dai, H., & Shang, X. (2021). Identifying key features in student grade prediction. In *Proceedings of the 2021 IEEE International Conference on Progress in Informatics and Computing (PIC)* (pp. 519–523). Shanghai, China. DOI: 10.1109/PIC53636.2021.9687042

Cukierman, A., & Epperson, J. (2021). Comparative performance analysis of blockchain-based systems. *Journal of Computer Security*, *31*(4), 711–735.

Dagman, A., & Wärmefjord, K. (2022). An evidence-based study on teaching computer-aided design in higher education during the COVID-19 pandemic. *Education Sciences*, *12*(1), 29. DOI: 10.3390/educsci12010029

Darling-Hammond, L., Hyler, M. E., & Gardner, M. (2017). *Effective teacher professional development*. Learning Policy Institute. DOI: 10.54300/122.311

Darling-Hammond, L., Wilhoit, G., & Pittenger, L. (2019). *Empowered educators: How high-performing systems shape teaching quality around the world*. Wiley.

Dawson, S., Heathcote, L., & Poole, G. (2020). Harnessing the affordances of digital learning: An activity system analysis of research and practice. *Educational Technology Research and Development*, *68*(6), 2975–3001.

Dawson, S., Joksimović, S., Kovanović, V., Gašević, D., & Siemens, G. (2020). The impact of learning management systems on learning outcomes: A systematic review. *The Internet and Higher Education*, *44*, 100726.

Deng, L., Liu, Y., & Li, L. (2020). Statistical methods for evaluating AI/ML systems in IoT environments. *Journal of Artificial Intelligence Research*, *69*, 451–476.

Devaki, P., Kumar, L., & Muthukumar, S. (2022, October). Sentiment Analysis and Recommendation of Book Reviews. In 2022 IEEE 3rd Global Conference for Advancement in Technology (GCAT) (pp. 1-6). IEEE.

Ejjami, R. (2024). AI-driven justice: Evaluating the impact of artificial intelligence on legal systems. *Int. J. Multidiscip. Res*, *6*(3), 1–29.

Ekowo, M., & Tait, M. (2020). *Creating conditions for equity in schools: Technology, culture, and power*. New America.

El Morabit, S., Rivenq, A., Zighem, M.-E., Hadid, A., Ouahabi, A., & Taleb-Ahmed, A. (2021). Automatic pain estimation from facial expressions: A comparative analysis using off-the-shelf CNN architectures. *Electronics (Basel)*, *10*(16), 1926. DOI: 10.3390/electronics10161926

Elakiya, K. (2023, April). A Comprehensive Review of Web Designing and Web Development: Concepts, Practices and Trends. *International Journal of Research Publication and Reviews*, *4*(4), 2180–2182.

Ellikkal, A., & Rajamohan, S. (2024). *AI-enabled personalized learning: empowering management students for improving engagement and academic performance*. Vilakshan-XIMB Journal of Management.

Fagbohun, O., Iduwe, N. P., Abdullahi, M., Ifaturoti, A., & Nwanna, O. M. (2024). Beyond traditional assessment: Exploring the impact of large language models on grading practices. *Journal of Artifical Intelligence and Machine Learning & Data Science*, *2*(1), 1–8. DOI: 10.51219/JAIMLD/oluwole-fagbohun/19

Fahad Mon, B., Wasfi, A., Hayajneh, M., Slim, A., & Abu Ali, N. (2023, September). Reinforcement Learning in Education: A Literature Review. In Informatics (Vol. 10, No. 3, p. 74). MDPI. DOI: 10.3390/informatics10030074

Familoni, B. T., & Onyebuchi, N. C. (2024). Advancements and challenges in AI integration for technical literacy: A systematic review. *Engineering Science & Technology Journal*, *5*(4), 1415–1430. DOI: 10.51594/estj.v5i4.1042

Fawcett, T. (2006). An introduction to ROC analysis. *Pattern Recognition Letters*, *27*(8), 861–874. DOI: 10.1016/j.patrec.2005.10.010

Feijóo, C., Kwon, Y., Bauer, J. M., Bohlin, E., Howell, B., Jain, R., Potgieter, P., Vu, K., Whalley, J., & Xia, J. (2020). Harnessing artificial intelligence (AI) to increase wellbeing for all: The case for a new technology diplomacy. *Telecommunications Policy*, *44*(6), 101988. DOI: 10.1016/j.telpol.2020.101988 PMID: 32377031

Fitria, T. N. (2021, December). Artificial intelligence (AI) in education: Using AI tools for teaching and learning process. In Prosiding Seminar Nasional & Call for Paper STIE AAS (Vol. 4, No. 1, pp. 134-147).

Fletcher-Flinn, C. M., & Gravatt, B. (1995). The efficacy of computer assisted instruction (CAI): A meta-analysis. *Journal of Educational Computing Research*, *12*(3), 219–241. DOI: 10.2190/51D4-F6L3-JQHU-9M31

Frey, N., Fisher, D., & Smith, D. (2019). *All learning is social and emotional: Helping students develop essential skills for the classroom and beyond*. Ascd.

Fuchs, K. (2023, May). Exploring the opportunities and challenges of NLP models in higher education: Is Chat GPT a blessing or a curse? *Frontiers in Education*, *8*, 1166682. DOI: 10.3389/feduc.2023.1166682

Galés, N. L., & Gallon, R. (2020). Sharing personalized learning to cultivate creativity. In *Pedagogies of Digital Learning in Higher Education* (pp. 61–87). Routledge. DOI: 10.4324/9781003019466-4

Gama, J., Pinto, H. S., & Rodrigues, P. (2013). Evaluation of classification algorithms for evolving data. *Data Mining and Knowledge Discovery*, *27*(3), 475–502.

Gama, J., Rocha, R., & Soares, C. (2013). *Data stream mining: A practical approach*. Springer.

Gao, Y., Zhang, Q., & Liu, J. (2022). Accuracy evaluation in machine learning-based IoT systems. *ACM Transactions on Internet Technology*, *22*(1), 1–23. DOI: 10.1145/3391198

García-Martínez, I., Batanero, J. M. F., Cerero, J. F., & León, S. P. (2023, January 1). Analysing the Impact of Artificial Intelligence and Computational Sciences on Student Performance: Systematic Review and Meta-analysis. *University of Alicante*, *12*(1), 171–171. DOI: 10.7821/naer.2023.1.1240

Garrett, N., Beard, N., & Fiesler, C. (2020, February). More than" If Time Allows" the role of ethics in AI education. In Proceedings of the AAAI/ACM Conference on AI, Ethics, and Society (pp. 272-278).

Gay, G. (2010). *Culturally responsive teaching: Theory, research, and practice* (2nd ed.). Teachers College Press.

George, A. S. (2023). Preparing students for an AI-driven world: Rethinking curriculum and pedagogy in the age of artificial intelligence. *Partners Universal Innovative Research Publication*, *1*(2), 112–136.

Gerard, L., Matuk, C., McElhaney, K W., & Linn, M C. (2015, May 2). Automated, adaptive guidance for K-12 education. Elsevier BV, 15, 41-58. DOI: 10.1016/j.edurev.2015.04.001

Ge, Z., & Hu, Y. (2020, April 1). Innovative Application of Artificial Intelligence (AI) in the Management of Higher Education and Teaching. *Journal of Physics: Conference Series*, *1533*(3), 032089–032089. DOI: 10.1088/1742-6596/1533/3/032089

Gianfrancesco, M. A., Tamang, S., Yazdany, J., & Schmajuk, G. (2018). Potential biases in machine learning algorithms using electronic health record data. *JAMA Internal Medicine*, *178*(11), 1544–1547. DOI: 10.1001/jamainternmed.2018.3763 PMID: 30128552

Gikandi, J. W., Morrow, D., & Davis, N. E. (2020). Online formative assessment in higher education: A review of the literature. *Computers & Education*, *56*(3), 1045–1051.

Gil, P. D., da Cruz Martins, S., Moro, S., & Costa, J. M. (2021). A data-driven approach to predict first-year students' academic success in higher education institutions. *Education and Information Technologies*, *26*(2), 2165–2190. DOI: 10.1007/s10639-020-10346-6

Gleason, N. W. (2018). Singapore's higher education systems in the era of the fourth industrial revolution: Preparing lifelong learners. Higher education in the era of the fourth industrial revolution, 145-169.

Gligorea, I., Cioca, M., Oancea, R., Gorski, A. T., Gorski, H., & Tudorache, P. (2023). Adaptive learning using artificial intelligence in e-learning: A literature review. *Education Sciences*, *13*(12), 1216. DOI: 10.3390/educsci13121216

González-Calatayud, V., Prendes-Espinosa, P., & Roig-Vila, R. (2021). Artificial intelligence for student assessment: A systematic review. *Applied Sciences (Basel, Switzerland)*, *11*(12), 5467. DOI: 10.3390/app11125467

Graf, S., & Liu, T. C., & Kinshuk. (2009). Analysis of learners' navigational behaviour and their learning styles in an online course. *Journal of Computer Assisted Learning*, *25*(2), 140–156.

Greenland, S., Senn, S. J., Rothman, K. J., Carlin, J. B., Poole, C., Goodman, S. N., & Altman, D. G. (2016). Statistical tests, p values, confidence intervals, and power: A guide to misinterpretations. *European Journal of Epidemiology, 31*(4), 337–350. DOI: 10.1007/s10654-016-0149-3 PMID: 27209009

Grieve, R., Woodley, J., Hunt, S E., & McKay, A B. (2021, July 15). Student fears of oral presentations and public speaking in higher education: a qualitative survey. Routledge, 45(9), 1281-1293. DOI: 10.1080/0309877X.2021.1948509

Griffiths, D.. (2020). The future of education: Emerging technologies and how they are changing the classroom. *Journal of Educational Technology Development and Exchange, 13*(1), 1–16.

Guan, C., Mou, J., & Jiang, Z. (2020). Artificial intelligence innovation in education: A twenty-year data-driven historical analysis. *International Journal of Innovation Studies, 4*(4), 134–147. DOI: 10.1016/j.ijis.2020.09.001

Halagatti, M., Gadag, S., Mahantshetti, S., Hiremath, C. V., Tharkude, D., & Banakar, V. (2023). Artificial intelligence: the new tool of disruption in educational performance assessment. In *Smart Analytics, Artificial Intelligence and Sustainable Performance Management in a Global Digitalised Economy* (pp. 261–287). Emerald Publishing Limited. DOI: 10.1108/S1569-37592023000110A014

Haldar, S. K. (2024, August). Privacy and security in AI education for gender studies. In Artificial Intelligence in Education (p. 39).

Hämäläinen, R., & Vähäsantanen, K. (2022). Adaptive learning in higher education: A systematic review of research literature. *Computers & Education, 175*, 104319.

Handayani, T., Kalengkongan, J., Marini, A., & Sumantri, M. S. (2021). Developing hybrid learning models platform based on user experience. *IOP Conference Series. Materials Science and Engineering, 1098*(3), 032018. DOI: 10.1088/1757-899X/1098/3/032018

Haneche, H., Boudraa, B., & Ouahabi, A. (2020). A new way to enhance speech signal based on compressed sensing. *Measurement, 151*, 107117. DOI: 10.1016/j.measurement.2019.107117

Harry, A. (2023). Role of AI in Education. *Interdiciplinary Journal and Hummanity*, *2*(3), 260–268.

Henkel, O., Horne-Robinson, H., Kozhakhmetova, N., & Lee, A. (2024, February 15). Effective and Scalable Math Support: Evidence on the Impact of an AI- Tutor on Math Achievement in Ghana. Cornell University. https://doi.org//arxiv.2402.09809DOI: 10.48550

Higgins, S.. (2020). *The impact of digital technology on learning: A summary for the Education Endowment Foundation.* Education Endowment Foundation.

Hodges, C., & McCullough, H. (2021). The adjacent possible for higher education: The digital transformation of faculty. EDUCAUSE Review. Retrieved from https://er.educause.edu/articles/2021/9/the-adjacent-possible-for-higher-education-the-digital-transformation-of-faculty

Hollands, F. M., & Tirthali, D. (2014). MOOCs: Expectations and reality. *Journal of Higher Education Theory and Practice*, *14*(5), 16–23.

Holmes, W., Porayska-Pomsta, K., Holstein, K., Sutherland, E., Baker, T T., Shum, S B., Santos, O C., Rodrigo, M M T., Cukurova, M., Bittencourt, I I., & Koedinger, K R. (2021, April 9). Ethics of AI in Education: Towards a Community-Wide Framework. Springer Science+Business Media, 32(3), 504-526. DOI: 10.1007/s40593-021-00239-1

Holmes, W., Bialik, M., & Fadel, C. (2019). *Artificial intelligence in education: Promises and implications for teaching and learning.* Center for Curriculum Redesign.

Holmes, W., & Tuomi, I. (2022). State of the art and practice in AI in education. *European Journal of Education*, *57*(4), 542–570. DOI: 10.1111/ejed.12533

Holstein, K., Aleven, V., & Rummel, N. (2020, January 1). A Conceptual Framework for Human–AI Hybrid Adaptivity in Education. Springer Science+Business Media, 240-254. DOI: 10.1007/978-3-030-52237-7_20

Hooda, M., Rana, C., Dahiya, O., Rizwan, A., & Hossain, M. S. (2022). Artificial intelligence for assessment and feedback to enhance student success in higher education. *Mathematical Problems in Engineering*, *2022*(1), 5215722. DOI: 10.1155/2022/5215722

Huang, L. (2023, June 30). Ethics of Artificial Intelligence in Education. *Student Privacy and Data Protection.*, *16*(2), 2577–2587. DOI: 10.15354/sief.23.re202

Hu, Y. (2022, June). Synthesizing digital libraries and digital humanities perspectives for illuminating under-investigated complexities associated with user-generated book reviews. In *Proceedings of the 22nd ACM/IEEE Joint Conference on Digital Libraries* (pp. 1-2). DOI: 10.1145/3529372.3530947

Hu, Y., LeBlanc, Z., Diesner, J., Underwood, T., Layne-Worthey, G., & Downie, J. S. (2022, June). Complexities associated with user-generated book reviews in digital libraries: temporal, cultural, and political case studies. In *Proceedings of the 22nd ACM/IEEE Joint Conference on Digital Libraries* (pp. 1-12). DOI: 10.1145/3529372.3530930

Ifenthaler, D. (2022, January 1). Automated Essay Scoring Systems., 1-15. DOI: 10.1007/978-981-19-0351-9_59-1

ISO/IEC. (2020). *ISO/IEC 30141:2018 Internet of Things (IoT) - Reference Architecture*. International Organization for Standardization.

Jacques, S., Ouahabi, A., & Lequeu, T. (2020). Remote knowledge acquisition and assessment during the COVID-19 pandemic. [iJEP]. *International Journal of Engineering Pedagogy*, *10*(6), 120–138. DOI: 10.3991/ijep.v10i6.16205

Jamalova, M., & Bálint, C. (2022). Modelling students' adoption of e-learning during the COVID-19 pandemic: Hungarian perspective. [iJET]. *International Journal of Emerging Technologies in Learning*, *17*(14), 275–292. DOI: 10.3991/ijet.v17i07.29243

Jebamani, S. A., Punitha, R., Rajesh, N., Kavin, T., & KUA, A. K. (2022, April). Books Tracking and Review Application. In 2022 8th International Conference on Smart Structures and Systems (ICSSS) (pp. 1-4). IEEE.

Jeevitha, R., Sekarraja, G. K., & Sridhar, M., & SriBalaji, A. (2024, February). Multilingual Subtitle Generator Using Machine Learning. In International Conference on Smart Data Intelligence (pp. 113-132). Singapore: Springer Nature Singapore.

Jia, K., Wang, P., Li, Y., Chen, Z., Jiang, X., Lin, C., & Chin, T. (2022, February 16). Research Landscape of Artificial Intelligence and e-Learning: A Bibliometric Research. *Frontiers of Medicine*, *13*, 795039. Advance online publication. DOI: 10.3389/fpsyg.2022.795039 PMID: 35250730

Jiang, C., Li, J., & Wang, Y. (2021). Reliability and availability metrics for IoT systems. *IEEE Transactions on Network and Service Management*, *18*(2), 345–357.

Jiang, R. (2022, November 16). How does artificial intelligence empower EFL teaching and learning nowadays? A review on artificial intelligence in the EFL context. *Frontiers of Medicine*, *13*, 1049401. Advance online publication. DOI: 10.3389/fpsyg.2022.1049401 PMID: 36467167

Johnson, W. L., Lester, J. C., & Ritter, S. (2013). Face-to-face interaction with pedagogical agents, twenty years later. *International Journal of Artificial Intelligence in Education*, *23*(4), 412–430.

Jonassen, D. H. (1999). Designing constructivist learning environments. In Reigeluth, C. M. (Ed.), *Instructional-design theories and models* (Vol. II, pp. 215–239). Lawrence Erlbaum Associates.

Jones, K. M., Asher, A., Goben, A., Perry, M. R., Salo, D., Briney, K. A., & Robertshaw, M. B. (2020). "We're being tracked at all times": Student perspectives of their privacy in relation to learning analytics in higher education. *Journal of the Association for Information Science and Technology*, *71*(9), 1044–1059. DOI: 10.1002/asi.24358

Jones, S., Fox, C., Gillam, S. L., & Gillam, R. B. (2019, October 31). An exploration of automated narrative analysis via machine learning. *PLoS One*, *14*(10), e0224634–e0224634. DOI: 10.1371/journal.pone.0224634 PMID: 31671140

Joshi, S., Rambola, R. K., & Churi, P. (2021, January 1). Evaluating Artificial Intelligence in Education for Next Generation. *Journal of Physics: Conference Series*, *1714*(1), 012039–012039. DOI: 10.1088/1742-6596/1714/1/012039

Jovanović, Ž., Jagodić, D., Vujičić, D., & Ranđić, S. (2017). Java Spring Boot Rest WEB Service Integration with Java Artificial Intelligence Weka Framework. In International Scientific Conference "UNITECH 2017 (pp. 323-327).

Kamalov, F., Calonge, D. S., & Gurrib, I. (2023, August 16). New Era of Artificial Intelligence in Education: Towards a Sustainable Multifaceted Revolution. *Sustainability (Basel)*, *15*(16), 12451–12451. DOI: 10.3390/su151612451

Kanchon, M. K. H., Sadman, M., Nabila, K. F., Tarannum, R., & Khan, R. (2024). Enhancing personalized learning: AI-driven identification of learning styles and content modification strategies. *International Journal of Cognitive Computing in Engineering*, *5*, 269–278. DOI: 10.1016/j.ijcce.2024.06.002

Kanetaki, Z., Stergiou, C., Bekas, G., Troussas, C., & Sgouropoulou, C. (2021). Analysis of engineering student data in online higher education during the COVID-19 pandemic. [iJEP]. *International Journal of Engineering Pedagogy*, *11*(5), 27–49. DOI: 10.3991/ijep.v11i6.23259

Kanetaki, Z., Stergiou, C., Bekas, G., Troussas, C., & Sgouropoulou, C. (2022). A hybrid machine learning model for grade prediction in online engineering education. [iJEP]. *International Journal of Engineering Pedagogy*, *12*(3), 4–24. DOI: 10.3991/ijep.v12i3.23873

Kanetaki, Z., Stergiou, C., Bekas, G., Troussas, C., & Sgouropoulou, C. (2022). Evaluating remote task assignment of an online engineering module through data mining in a virtual communication platform environment. *Electronics (Basel), 11*(1), 158. DOI: 10.3390/electronics11010158

Kaur, S., Tandon, N., & Matharou, G. S. (2020). Contemporary trends in education transformation using artificial intelligence. In *Transforming Management Using Artificial Intelligence Techniques* (pp. 89–103). CRC Press. DOI: 10.1201/9781003032410-7

Kayyali, M. (2024). Global Perspectives on Personalized Learning: Case Studies and Best Practices. In Transforming Education for Personalized Learning (pp. 66-84). IGI Global.

Kayyali, M. (2024). Future possibilities and challenges of AI in education. In *Transforming education with generative AI: Prompt engineering and synthetic content creation* (pp. 118–137). IGI Global. DOI: 10.4018/979-8-3693-1351-0.ch006

Kerr, R. (2021). The impact of AI-driven personalized learning on student engagement and performance. *The Journal of Educational Research, 114*(2), 112–125.

Khaldi, Y., Benzaoui, A., Ouahabi, A., Jacques, S., & Taleb-Ahmed, A. (2021). Ear recognition based on deep unsupervised active learning. *IEEE Sensors Journal, 21*(18), 20704–20713. DOI: 10.1109/JSEN.2021.3100151

Khan, M. A., Kamal, T., Illiyan, A., & Asif, M. (2021). School students' perception and challenges towards online classes during COVID-19 pandemic in India: An econometric analysis. *Sustainability (Basel), 13*(9), 4786. DOI: 10.3390/su13094786

Khanna, S., Kaushik, A., & Barnela, M. (2010, March). Expert systems advances in education. In Proceedings of the National Conference on Computational Instrumentation NCCI-2010. CSIO (pp. 109-112).

Khosravi, H., Shum, S. B., Chen, G., Conati, C., Tsai, Y. S., Kay, J., & Gašević, D. (2022). Explainable artificial intelligence in education. *Computers and Education: Artificial Intelligence, 3*, 100074.

Kim, J., Lee, H., & Cho, Y H. (2022, January 28). Learning design to support student-AI collaboration: perspectives of leading teachers for AI in education. Springer Science+Business Media, 27(5), 6069-6104. DOI: 10.1007/s10639-021-10831-6

Kim, D., Han, J., & Yoo, S. (2021). Evaluating the performance of IoT systems in smart cities. *IEEE Internet of Things Journal*, *8*(4), 2325–2335.

Kim, H., Park, Y., & Lee, J. (2021). User feedback in performance evaluation of IoT systems. *CIT. Journal of Computing and Information Technology*, *29*(3), 179–192.

Kim, J. (2024). Leading teachers' perspective on teacher-AI collaboration in education. *Education and Information Technologies*, *29*(7), 8693–8724. DOI: 10.1007/s10639-023-12109-5

Kizilcec, R F. (2023, June 9). To Advance AI Use in Education, Focus on Understanding Educators. Springer Science+Business Media, 34(1), 12-19. DOI: 10.1007/s40593-023-00351-4

Knewton. (2020). Personalized learning: The key to student success. https://www.knewton.com

Kotsiantis, S., Pierrakeas, C., & Pintelas, P. (2004). Predicting students' performance in distance learning using machine learning techniques. *Applied Artificial Intelligence*, *18*(5), 411–426. DOI: 10.1080/08839510490442058

Kučak, D., Juričić, V., & Đambić, G. (2018). Machine learning in education-A survey of current research trends. Annals of DAAAM & Proceedings, 29.

Kuleto, V., Ilić, M., Dumangiu, M., Ranković, M., Martins, O. M., Păun, D., & Mihoreanu, L. (2021). Exploring opportunities and challenges of artificial intelligence and machine learning in higher education institutions. *Sustainability (Basel)*, *13*(18), 10424. DOI: 10.3390/su131810424

Kwan, R., Fong, J., Kwok, L.-F., & Lam, J. (Eds.). (2011). *Hybrid learning:4th International Conference, ICHL 2011,Hong Kong, China,August 10–12, 2011, Proceedings*. Springer Science & Business Media.

Ladson-Billings, G. (1994). *The dreamkeepers: Successful teachers of African American children*. Jossey-Bass.

Lainjo, B., & Tsmouche, H. (2023). The impact of artificial intelligence on higher learning institutions. *International Journal of Education, Teaching, and Social Sciences*, *3*(2), 96–113. DOI: 10.47747/ijets.v3i2.1028

Leddo, J., & Garg, K. (2021). Comparing the effectiveness of AI-powered educational software to human teachers. *International Journal of Social Science and Economic Research*, *6*(3), 953–963. DOI: 10.46609/IJSSER.2021.v06i03.015

Lew, M. J. (2020). A reckless guide to p-values. In Bespalov, A., Michel, M. C., & Steckler, T. (Eds.), *Good research practice in non-clinical pharmacology and biomedicine* (pp. 223–256). Springer International Publishing.

Li, J. (2020, June 8). Research on the Application of AI Intelligent Adaptation System in Primary and Secondary School Learning Process. Destech Publications. DOI: 10.12783/dtssehs/icesd2020/34447

Li, C., Yang, Y., & Liu, J. (2022). Handling noisy data in precision evaluation of AI systems. *IEEE Transactions on Neural Networks and Learning Systems*, *33*(2), 450–462.

Li, M., Wang, S., & Zhang, T. (2021). Benchmarking techniques for evaluating IoT systems. *Journal of Computer Networks and Communications*, *2021*, 1–15. DOI: 10.1155/2021/9290853

Lincoln, Y. S., & Guba, E. G. (1985). *Naturalistic inquiry*. Sage Publications. DOI: 10.1016/0147-1767(85)90062-8

Li, Y., Yang, J., & Wang, X. (2021). Performance evaluation of blockchain-based data management systems. *IEEE Transactions on Network and Service Management*, *18*(2), 321–334.

Lowry, O. H., Rosebrough, N. J., Farr, A. L., & Randall, R. J. (1951). Protein measurement with the Folin phenol reagent.

Luan, H., Géczy, P., Lai, H., Gobert, J. D., Yang, S. J., Ogata, H., Baltes, J., Guerra, R. D. S., Li, P., & Tsai, C. (2020, October 19). Challenges and Future Directions of Big Data and Artificial Intelligence in Education. *Frontiers of Medicine*, *11*, 580820. Advance online publication. DOI: 10.3389/fpsyg.2020.580820 PMID: 33192896

Luckin, R.. (2016). *Intelligence Unleashed: An Argument for AI in Education*. Pearson Education.

Luckin, R., Holmes, W., Griffiths, M., & Forcier, L. B. (2016). *Intelligence unleashed: An argument for AI in education*. Pearson.

Ma, X., & Jiang, C. (2023, May 30). On the Ethical Risks of Artificial Intelligence Applications in Education and Its Avoidance Strategies., 14, 354-359. DOI: 10.54097/ehss.v14i.8868

Mahdaoui, A. E., Ouahabi, A., & Moulay, M. S. (2022). Image denoising using a compressive sensing approach based on regularization constraints. *Sensors (Basel)*, *22*(6), 2199. DOI: 10.3390/s22062199 PMID: 35336367

Makransky, G., & Petersen, G B. (2021, January 6). The Cognitive Affective Model of Immersive Learning (CAMIL): a Theoretical Research-Based Model of Learning in Immersive Virtual Reality. Springer Science+Business Media, 33(3), 937-958. DOI: 10.1007/s10648-020-09586-2

Malik, G., Tayal, D K., & Vij, S. (2018, November 3). An Analysis of the Role of Artificial Intelligence in Education and Teaching. Springer Nature, 407-417. DOI: 10.1007/978-981-10-8639-7_42

Manning, C. D., Raghavan, P., & Schütze, H. (2008). *Introduction to Information Retrieval*. Cambridge University Press. DOI: 10.1017/CBO9780511809071

Manoharan, C., Poongavanam, S., Arivazhagan, D., Divyaranjani, R., & Vettriselvan, R. (2020). Cognition and emotions during teaching-learning process. *International Journal of Scientific and Technology Research*, *9*(2), 267–269.

Markowitz, D. M., Laha, R., Perone, B., Pea, R., & Bailenson, J. N. (2018, November 30). Immersive Virtual Reality Field Trips Facilitate Learning About Climate Change. *Frontiers of Medicine*, *9*, 2364. Advance online publication. DOI: 10.3389/fpsyg.2018.02364 PMID: 30555387

McKnight, K., O'Malley, K., Ruzic, R., Horsley, M. K., Franey, J. J., & Bassett, K. (2016). TEACHING IN A DIGITAL AGE: How educators use technology to improve student learning. *Journal of Research on Technology in Education*, *74*(3), 36–42. DOI: 10.1080/15391523.2016.1175856

McNamara, D S., Crossley, S A., Roscoe, R D., Allen, L K., & Dai, J. (2014, November 11). A hierarchical classification approach to automated essay scoring. Elsevier BV, 23, 35-59. DOI: 10.1016/j.asw.2014.09.002

Means, B., Bakia, M., & Murphy, R. (2020). *Learning online: What research tells us about whether, when and how*. Routledge.

Mehendale, P. (2023). Personalization in Education through AI. *European Journal of Advances in Engineering and Technology*, *10*(3), 60–65.

Meyer, J., Jansen, T., Schiller, R., Liebenow, L W., Steinbach, M., Horbach, A., & Fleckenstein, J. (2023, December 29). Using LLMs to bring evidence-based feedback into the classroom: AI-generated feedback increases secondary students' text revision, motivation, and positive emotions. Elsevier BV, 6, 100199-100199. DOI: 10.1016/j.caeai.2023.100199

Miller, A., O'Neill, B., & Anderson, K. (2019). Benchmarking techniques for evaluating AI/ML systems. *Journal of Computer Science and Technology*, *34*(3), 407–421.

Mitchell, T. M. (1997). *Machine Learning*. McGraw-Hill.

Mollah, M. B., & Khatun, N. (2021). A review of blockchain scalability and its solutions. *Journal of Computer Networks and Communications*, *2021*, 6696470.

Mollah, M. B., & Khatun, S. (2021). Blockchain-based secure data management for IoT applications. *Journal of King Saud University. Computer and Information Sciences*.

Mougayar, W. (2016). *The Business Blockchain: Promise, Practice, and the Application of the Next Internet Technology*. Wiley.

Moulin, M., & O'Donoghue, T. (2020). Performance evaluation in blockchain-based systems: A case study. *ACM Transactions on Computational Logic*, *21*(1), 1–20.

Mukhallafi, T. R. A. (2020, August 17). Using Artificial Intelligence for Developing English Language Teaching/Learning: An Analytical Study from University Students' Perspective. *International Journal of English Linguistics*, *10*(6), 40–40. DOI: 10.5539/ijel.v10n6p40

Murumba, J., & Micheni, E. (2017). Big data analytics in higher education: A review. *The International Journal of Engineering and Science*, *6*(06), 14–21. DOI: 10.9790/1813-0606021421

Nafea, I. (2018, September 19). Machine Learning in Educational Technology. DOI: 10.5772/intechopen.72906

Nair, M., Svedberg, P., Larsson, I., & Nygren, J. M. (2024). A comprehensive overview of barriers and strategies for AI implementation in healthcare: Mixed-method design. *PLoS One*, *19*(8), e0305949. DOI: 10.1371/journal.pone.0305949 PMID: 39121051

Nakamoto, S. (2008). Bitcoin: A peer-to-peer electronic cash system. https://bitcoin.org/bitcoin.pdf

Narayanan, A., Bonneau, J., Felten, E., Miller, A., & Narayanan, A. (2016). *Bitcoin and Cryptocurrency Technologies*. Princeton University Press.

Narayanan, K. S., & Kumaravel, A. (2024). Hybrid Gamification and AI Tutoring Framework using Machine Learning and Adaptive Neuro-Fuzzy Inference System. *Journal of Advanced Research in Applied Sciences and Engineering Technology*, *42*(2), 221–233. DOI: 10.37934/araset.42.2.221233

Negandhi, T., Dhumale, P., Vachhani, M., & Gawande, K. (2023, August). Bookbuddy: a mood based book recommendation system. In 2023 7th International Conference On Computing, Communication, Control And Automation (ICCUBEA) (pp. 1-7). IEEE. DOI: 10.1109/ICCUBEA58933.2023.10392250

Ng, D T K., Leung, J K L., Su, J., Ng, C W., & Chu, S K W. (2023, February 1). Teachers' AI digital competencies and twenty-first century skills in the post-pandemic world. Springer Science+Business Media, 71(1), 137-161. DOI: 10.1007/s11423-023-10203-6

Nguyen, A., Ngo, H N., Hong, Y., Dang, B., & Nguyen, B T. (2022, October 13). Ethical principles for artificial intelligence in education. Springer Science+Business Media, 28(4), 4221-4241. DOI: 10.1007/s10639-022-11316-w

Nguyen-Duc, A., & Abrahamsson, P. (2020, November). Continuous experimentation on artificial intelligence software: a research agenda. In *Proceedings of the 28th ACM Joint Meeting on European Software Engineering Conference and Symposium on the Foundations of Software Engineering* (pp. 1513-1516). DOI: 10.1145/3368089.3417039

Ning, H., Zhang, L., & Wu, J. (2022). Security metrics for IoT systems: A survey. *IEEE Access : Practical Innovations, Open Solutions*, *10*, 20943–20956.

Nye, B D. (2014, October 7). Intelligent Tutoring Systems by and for the Developing World: A Review of Trends and Approaches for Educational Technology in a Global Context. Springer Science+Business Media, 25(2), 177-203. DOI: 10.1007/s40593-014-0028-6

O'Neil, C. (2016). *Weapons of math destruction: How big data increases inequality and threatens democracy*. Crown Publishing Group.

Orlovskyi, D., & Yuskovych-Zhukovska, V. (2023). Interactive learning platform with gamification elements. Automation of Technological and Business Processes, 15(1), 11-11.

Owoc, M L., Sawicka, A., & Weichbroth, P. (2021, January 1). Artificial Intelligence Technologies in Education: Benefits, Challenges and Strategies of Implementation. Springer Science+Business Media, 37-58. DOI: 10.1007/978-3-030-85001-2_4

Owoc, M. L., Sawicka, A., & Weichbroth, P. (2019, August). Artificial intelligence technologies in education: benefits, challenges and strategies of implementation. In *IFIP International Workshop on Artificial Intelligence for Knowledge Management* (pp. 37-58). Cham: Springer International Publishing.

Pane, J. F., Steiner, E. D., Baird, M. D., & Hamilton, L. S. (2017). *Informing Progress: Insights on Personalized Learning Implementation and Effects*. RAND Corporation. DOI: 10.7249/RR2042

Papanastasiou, G., Drigas, A., Skianis, C., Lytras, M., & Papanastasiou, E. (2019). Virtual and augmented reality effects on K-12, higher and tertiary education students' twenty-first century skills. *Virtual Reality (Waltham Cross)*, *23*(4), 425–436. DOI: 10.1007/s10055-018-0363-2

Park, S., & Kim, Y. (2021). A systematic review of research trends in mobile learning studies in Korea: A social network analysis. *Interactive Learning Environments*, *29*(1), 109–125.

Pedro, F., Subosa, M., Rivas, A., & Valverde, P. (2019). Artificial intelligence in education: Challenges and opportunities for sustainable development.

Pedro, F., Subosa, M., Rivas, A., & Valverde, P. (2019). Artificial intelligence in education: Challenges and opportunities for sustainable development. Academic Press.

Petousi, V., & Sifaki, E. (2020). Contextualizing harm in the framework of research misconduct: Findings from discourse analysis of scientific publications. *International Journal of Sustainable Development*, *23*(3–4), 149. DOI: 10.1504/IJSD.2020.115206

Piaget, J. (1970). *The science of education and the psychology of the child*. Orion Press.

Pollock, J. E., & Tolone, L. J. (2020). *Improving student learning one teacher at a time*. ASCD.

Polonetsky, J., & Jerome, J. T. J. (2014, January 1). Student Data: Trust, Transparency, and the Role of Consent. RELX Group (Netherlands). DOI: 10.2139/ssrn.2628877

Postholm, M. B. (2018). Teachers' professional development in school: A review study. *Cogent Education*, *5*(1), 1522781. DOI: 10.1080/2331186X.2018.1522781

Ramya, R., Kiruthiga, V., Vettriselvan, R., Gayathri, V., & Palanivel Rathinasabapathi Velmurugan. (2024). Hybrid entrepreneurship navigating career transitions: Career shifts and their impact on economic growth. In Applications of career transitions and entrepreneurship (pp. 81-112). IGI Global. DOI: 10.4018/979-8-3693-4163-6

Ray, S., & Sikdar, D. P. (2024). AI-Driven Flipped Classroom: Revolutionizing Education Through Digital Pedagogy. *Br. J. Educ. Learn. Dev. Psychol*, *7*, 169–179. DOI: 10.52589/BJELDP-LTDJFLIH

Razinkina, E., Pankova, L., Trostinskaya, I., Pozdeeva, E., Evseeva, L., & Tanova, A. (2018). Student satisfaction as an element of education quality monitoring in innovative higher education institution. In *E3S web of conferences* (Vol. 33, p. 03043). EDP Sciences. DOI: 10.1051/e3sconf/20183303043

Rekha, K., Gopal, K., Satheeskumar, D., Anand, U. A., Doss, D. S. S., & Elayaperumal, S. (2024, May). Ai-Powered Personalized Learning System Design: Student Engagement and Performance Tracking System. In 2024 4th International Conference on Advance Computing and Innovative Technologies in Engineering (ICACITE) (pp. 1125-1130). IEEE.

Rhoades, A. (2020). Big tech makes big data out of your child: The FERPA loophole edtech exploits to monetize student data. *Am. U. Bus. L. Rev.*, *9*, 445.

Robertson, S. (2023). *Designing for Reliability in Algorithmic Systems*. University of California.

Rodway, P., & Schepman, A. (2023). The impact of adopting AI educational technologies on projected course satisfaction in university students. *Computers and Education: Artificial Intelligence*, *5*, 100150. DOI: 10.1016/j.caeai.2023.100150

Rotherham, A. J., & Willingham, D. T. (2010). "21st-century" skills: Not new, but a worthy challenge. *American Educator*, *34*(1), 17–20.

Royakkers, L., Timmer, J., Kool, L., & Van Est, R. (2018). Societal and ethical issues of digitization. *Ethics and Information Technology*, *20*(2), 127–142. DOI: 10.1007/s10676-018-9452-x

Rožman, M., Tominc, P., & Vrečko, I. (2023). Building skills for the future of work: Students' perspectives on emerging jobs in the Data and AI Cluster through artificial intelligence in education. Environment and Social Psychology, 8(2).

Russell, S., & Norvig, P. (2021). *Artificial intelligence: A modern approach*. Pearson.

Sajja, R., Sermet, Y., Cikmaz, M., Cwiertny, D., & Demir, I. (2024). Artificial intelligence-enabled intelligent assistant for personalized and adaptive learning in higher education. *Information (Basel)*, *15*(10), 596. DOI: 10.3390/info15100596

Schneider, J., Abraham, R., Meske, C., & Brocke, J V. (2022, June 20). Artificial Intelligence Governance For Businesses. Taylor & Francis, 40(3), 229-249. DOI: 10.1080/10580530.2022.2085825

Seo, K., Tang, J., Roll, I., Fels, S., & Yoon, D. (2021). The impact of artificial intelligence on learner–instructor interaction in online learning. *International Journal of Educational Technology in Higher Education*, *18*(1), 1–23. DOI: 10.1186/s41239-021-00292-9 PMID: 34778540

Sha, R. (2023, August). Data Science and Engineering, University of New South Wales, Sydney 2052 NSW, Australia z5384544@ ad. unsw. edu. au. In Proceedings of the 2023 2nd International Conference on Urban Planning and Regional Economy (UPRE 2023) (Vol. 253, p. 43). Springer Nature. DOI: 10.2991/978-94-6463-218-7_7

Shemwell, J. T., Chase, C. C., & Schwartz, D. L. (2015). Seeking the general explanation: A test of inductive activities for learning and transfer. *Journal of Research in Science Teaching*, *52*(1), 58–83. DOI: 10.1002/tea.21185

Shetty, J., Dash, D., Joish, A. K., & Guruprasad, C. (2020). Review paper on web frameworks, databases and web stacks. Intern Res J Eng Technol (IRJET), 7(5).

Siemens, G. (2005). Connectivism: A learning theory for the digital age. *International Journal of Instructional Technology and Distance Learning*, *2*(1), 3–10.

Siemens, G. (2013). *Learning Analytics: The Emergence of a New Era for Education*. Educational Technology Magazine.

Siemens, G. (2020). Automation in education: Future prospects. *Education and Information Technologies*, *25*(6), 4853–4865.

Sil, P., Chaudhuri, P., & Raman, B. (2024, January 1). Can AI Assistance Aid in the Grading of Handwritten Answer Sheets?. Springer Science+Business Media, 291-298. DOI: 10.1007/978-3-031-64312-5_35

Srinivasan, V., & Murthy, H. (2021, January 1). Improving reading and comprehension in K-12: Evidence from a large-scale AI technology intervention in India. Elsevier BV, 2, 100019-100019. DOI: 10.1016/j.caeai.2021.100019

Stake, R. E. (1995). *The art of case study research*. Sage Publications.

Steiss, J., Tate, T., Graham, S., Cruz, J., Hébert, M., Wang, J., Moon, Y., Tseng, W., Warschauer, M., & Olson, C B. (2024, June 1). Comparing the quality of human and ChatGPT feedback of students' writing. Elsevier BV, 91, 101894-101894. DOI: 10.1016/j.learninstruc.2024.101894

Strayhorn, T. L. (2018). *College students' sense of belonging: A key to educational success for all students*. Routledge. DOI: 10.4324/9781315297293

Suresh Babu, C. V., Anniyappa, C. S., & Sastha, B. D. (2024). Unraveling the Inner Workings of Massive Language Models: Architecture, Training, and Linguistic Capacities. In B. Gupta (Ed.), Challenges in Large Language Model Development and AI Ethics (pp. 239-279). IGI Global. DOI: 10.4018/979-8-3693-3860-5.ch008

Suresh Babu, C. V. (2023). *Artificial Intelligence and Expert Systems*. Anniyappa Publicaitons.

Suresh Babu, C. V., & Adhithya, S. (2023). ChatGPT and Other Generative AI Tools in Education: Transformative Potential and Ethical Considerations. In Keengwe, J. (Ed.), *Creative AI Tools and Ethical Implications in Teaching and Learning* (pp. 135–152). IGI Global. DOI: 10.4018/979-8-3693-0205-7.ch007

Suresh Babu, C. V., & Rohan, B. (2023). Evaluation and Quality Assurance for Rapid E-Learning and Development of Digital Learning Resources. In Santally, M., Rajabalee, Y., & Rajputh, R. (Eds.), *Implementing Rapid E-Learning Through Interactive Materials Development* (pp. 139–170). IGI Global. DOI: 10.4018/978-1-6684-4940-0.ch008

Suresh Babu, S., & Dhakshina Moorthy, A. (2024). Application of artificial intelligence in adaptation of gamification in education: A literature review. *Computer Applications in Engineering Education*, *32*(1), e22683. DOI: 10.1002/cae.22683

Swan, M. (2015). *Blockchain: Blueprint for a New Economy*. O'Reilly Media.

Sweeney, M., Lester, J., & Rangwala, H. (2015). Next-term student grade prediction. In *Proceedings of the 2015 IEEE International Conference on Big Data (Big Data)* (pp. 970–975). IEEE. DOI: 10.1109/BigData.2015.7363847

Swiecki, Z., Khosravi, H., Chen, G., Martínez-Maldonado, R., Lodge, J M., Milligan, S., Selwyn, N., & Gašević, D. (2022, January 1). Assessment in the age of artificial intelligence. Elsevier BV, 3, 100075-100075. DOI: 10.1016/j.caeai.2022.100075

Taber, K. S. (2018). The use of Cronbach's alpha when developing and reporting research instruments in science education. *Research in Science Education, 48*(6), 1273–1296. DOI: 10.1007/s11165-016-9602-2

Tapalova, O., & Zhiyenbayeva, N. (2022). Artificial intelligence in education: AIEd for personalised learning pathways. *Electronic Journal of e-Learning, 20*(5), 639–653. DOI: 10.34190/ejel.20.5.2597

Taylor, D., Yeung, M., & Bashet, A Z. (2021, January 1). Personalized and Adaptive Learning. Springer International Publishing, 17-34. DOI: 10.1007/978-3-030-58948-6_2

Thiruvasagam, G., & Vettriselvan, R. (2021). What is after COVID-19?: Changing economies of the shipping industries and maritime education institutions. In *21st Annual General Assembly, IAMU AGA 2021 - Proceedings of the International Association of Maritime Universities* (pp. 96–110).

Thornhill-Miller, B., Camarda, A., Mercier, M., Burkhardt, J. M., Morisseau, T., Bourgeois-Bougrine, S., Vinchon, F., El Hayek, S., Augereau-Landais, M., Mourey, F., Feybesse, C., Sundquist, D., & Lubart, T. (2023). Creativity, critical thinking, communication, and collaboration: Assessment, certification, and promotion of 21st century skills for the future of work and education. *Journal of Intelligence, 11*(3), 54. DOI: 10.3390/jintelligence11030054 PMID: 36976147

USA. Making the grade - privacy considerations for AI in the education sector. (2024, February 23). https://www.dataguidance.com/opinion/usa-making-grade-privacy-considerations-ai-education

Van den Berg, G., & Du Plessis, E. (2023). ChatGPT and generative AI: Possibilities for its contribution to lesson planning, critical thinking and openness in teacher education. *Education Sciences, 13*(10), 998. DOI: 10.3390/educsci13100998

Vettriselvan, R., Ramya, R., Sathya, M., Swadhi, R., & Deepan, A. (2024). Service delivery and citizen-centric approaches: Innovating public administration management in higher education. In *Challenges of public administration for higher education* (pp. 113–136). IGI Global., DOI: 10.4018/979-8-3693-4346-3.ch006

Vettriselvan, R., & Vinodhan, V. (2022). Promotional strategies for gender equity in maritime sector: Maritime education institutions. In *Proceedings of the International Association of Maritime Universities Conference*.

Villegas, A. M., & Lucas, T. (2002). *Educating culturally responsive teachers: A coherent approach*. State University of New York Press.

Vojak, C., Kline, S., Cope, B., McCarthey, S J., & Kalantzis, M. (2011, May 25). New Spaces and Old Places: An Analysis of Writing Assessment Software. Elsevier BV, 28(2), 97-111. DOI: 10.1016/j.compcom.2011.04.004

Walkington, C. (2013). Using adaptive learning technologies to personalize instruction: The role of pedagogical agents. *Journal of Educational Psychology*, *105*(4), 1020–1036. DOI: 10.1037/a0031882

Wang, N., & Lester, J C. (2023, June 1). K-12 Education in the Age of AI: A Call to Action for K-12 AI Literacy. Springer Science+Business Media, 33(2), 228-232. DOI: 10.1007/s40593-023-00358-x

Wang, Y. (2020, March 18). When artificial intelligence meets educational leaders' data-informed decision-making: A cautionary tale. Elsevier BV, 69, 100872-100872. DOI: 10.1016/j.stueduc.2020.100872

Wang, Y. (2021). RETRACTED: Educational management system of colleges and universities based on embedded system and artificial intelligence.

Wang, X., Xu, H., & Zhang, J. (2021). Resource utilization in IoT systems: Metrics and analysis. *IEEE Transactions on Computers*, *70*(5), 831–844.

Wang, Z., Liu, Y., & Chen, Y. (2021). Metrics for evaluating resource utilization in IoT systems. *Journal of Computing and Information Science*, *29*(4), 233–245.

Wan, J., Li, X., Dai, H. N., Kusiak, A., Martinez-Garcia, M., & Li, D. (2020). Artificial-intelligence-driven customized manufacturing factory: Key technologies, applications, and challenges. *Proceedings of the IEEE*, *109*(4), 377–398. DOI: 10.1109/JPROC.2020.3034808

Williamson, B., & Piattoeva, N. (2020). Education governance and datafication: A critical review of the literature. *Critical Studies in Education*, *61*(3), 323–339.

Winkler, R., & Söllner, M. (2018). Unleashing the potential of chatbots in education: A state-of-the-art analysis. Academy of Management Annual Meeting Proceedings, 2018(1), 11058. DOI: 10.5465/AMBPP.2018.15903abstract

Wirtz, B. W., Weyerer, J. C., & Sturm, B. J. (2020). The dark sides of artificial intelligence: An integrated AI governance framework for public administration. *International Journal of Public Administration*, *43*(9), 818–829. DOI: 10.1080/01900692.2020.1749851

Wu, L., Xu, X., & Zhang, Z. (2020). Benchmarking blockchain-based systems: A framework and performance evaluation. *IEEE Transactions on Computers*, *69*(5), 755–768.

Xia, Q., Chiu, T. K., Lee, M., Sanusi, I. T., Dai, Y., & Chai, C. S. (2022). A self-determination theory (SDT) design approach for inclusive and diverse artificial intelligence (AI) education. *Computers & Education*, *189*, 104582. DOI: 10.1016/j.compedu.2022.104582

Xie, H., Chu, H., Hwang, G., & Wang, C. (2019, June 6). Trends and development in technology-enhanced adaptive/personalized learning: A systematic review of journal publications from 2007 to 2017. Elsevier BV, 140, 103599-103599. DOI: 10.1016/j.compedu.2019.103599

Xie, L., Zhao, X., & Yang, J. (2021). Experimental evaluation of blockchain technologies in IoT applications. *IEEE Access : Practical Innovations, Open Solutions*, *9*, 112345–112356.

Xu, L. D., Yin, G., & Wu, X. (2020). Blockchain-based approaches for managing data in the IoT: A review. *IEEE Transactions on Industrial Informatics*, *16*(2), 1412–1422.

Xu, W., Chen, J., & Hu, L. (2020). Simulation techniques for IoT performance evaluation. *ACM Computing Surveys*, *53*(4), 1–30. DOI: 10.1145/3234151

Xu, X., Weber, I., & Staples, M. (2020). *Architecting the blockchain for the IoT*. Springer.

Yang, D., Sinha, T., Adamson, D., & Rosé, C. P. (2018). Turn on, tune in, drop out: Anticipating student dropouts in Massive Open Online Courses. Proceedings of the 2013 NIPS Data-driven education workshop, 11(15), 14.

Yao, P. (2009). Integrating generalized linear auto-regression and artificial neural networks for coal demand forecasting. In Yu, W., He, H., & Zhang, N. (Eds.), *Advances in neural networks—ISNN 2009* (pp. 993–1001). Springer. DOI: 10.1007/978-3-642-01507-6_112

Yilmaz, R., & Yilmaz, F. G. K. (2023). The effect of generative artificial intelligence (AI)-based tool use on students' computational thinking skills, programming self-efficacy and motivation. *Computers and Education: Artificial Intelligence*, *4*, 100147. DOI: 10.1016/j.caeai.2023.100147

Young, W., Allen, L., & Warfield, K. (2016). Developing online/hybrid learning models for higher education programs. *Alabama Journal of Educational Leadership*, *3*, 47–56.

Yuan, Y., Li, M., & Liang, Z. (2021). Blockchain benchmarking and performance evaluation for IoT applications. *ACM Transactions on Internet Technology*, *21*(3), 1–25. DOI: 10.1145/2461321.2461324

Zaranis, N., & Exarchakos, G. M. (2018). The use of ICT and the realistic mathematics education for understanding simple and advanced stereometry shapes among university students. In Mikropoulos, T. A. (Ed.), *Research on e-learning and ICT in education: Technological, pedagogical and instructional perspectives* (pp. 135–152). Springer International Publishing. DOI: 10.1007/978-3-319-95059-4_8

Zawacki-Richter, O., Marín, V. I., Bond, M., & Gouverneur, F. (2019). Systematic review of research on artificial intelligence applications in higher education–where are the educators? *Educational Technology Research and Development*, *67*(4), 2071–2099.

Zhai. (2021). A Review of Artificial Intelligence (AI) in Education from 2010 to 2020. Complexity, 1, 8812542.

Zhai, X., Chu, X., Chai, C. S., Jong, M. S., Starčič, A. I., Spector, M., Li, J., Jing, Y., & Li, Y. (2021, April 20). A Review of Artificial Intelligence (AI) in Education from 2010 to 2020. *Complexity*, *2021*(1), 1–18. DOI: 10.1155/2021/8812542

Zhang, H., Liu, J., & Wang, X. (2020). Improving accuracy in machine learning-based IoT systems. *ACM Transactions on Intelligent Systems and Technology*, *11*(1), 1–18.

Zhang, Q., Xu, Y., & Zhou, M. (2021). Performance evaluation in real-world IoT applications. *IEEE Transactions on Industrial Informatics*, *17*(8), 5654–5664.

Zhang, Y., Wu, W., & Yang, X. (2020). Blockchain-based data management for the internet of things. *IEEE Access : Practical Innovations, Open Solutions*, *8*, 102106–102118.

Zhang, Y., Zheng, Z., & Wang, S. (2020). Blockchain-based data management for the internet of things: A survey. *IEEE Access : Practical Innovations, Open Solutions*, *8*, 211343–211357.

Zhao, X., Li, P., & Zhang, R. (2022). Addressing performance challenges in dynamic IoT environments. *Computer Networks*, *199*, 108473.

Zheng, Z., Xie, S., Dai, H. N., & Wang, H. (2018). *Blockchain technology: Applications and challenges*. Springer.

Zhou, L., & Brown, D. (2015). The ethical challenges of ubiquitous personalized learning of environments in higher education: A constructivist perspective. *Ethics and Information Technology*, *17*(4), 283–293.

Zulkarnain, N. N., & Yunus, M. M. (2023, May 23). Teachers'. *Perceptions and Continuance Usage Intention of Artificial Intelligence Technology in Tesl.*, *06*(05). Advance online publication. DOI: 10.47191/ijmra/v6-i5-34

About the Contributors

Houssem Chemingui, is an Assistant Professor in Information Systems at Brest Business School. With a PhD in Computer Science from Paris 1 Panthéon Sorbonne University, his research focuses on streamlining product line configuration processes. He's published extensively on topics like Artificial Intelligence, Data Analytics, and Software Configuration. Beyond academia, he's contributed to development projects and consultancy initiatives, showcasing his commitment to advancing technology and education.

Munir Ahmad is a seasoned professional in the realm of Spatial Data Infrastructure (SDI), Geo-Information Productions, Information Systems, and Information Governance, boasting over 25 years of dedicated experience in the field. With a PhD in Computer Science, Dr. Ahmad's expertise spans Spatial Data Production, Management, Processing, Analysis, Visualization, and Quality Control. Throughout his career, Dr. Ahmad has been deeply involved in the development and deployment of SDI systems specially in the context of Pakistan, leveraging his proficiency in Spatial Database Design, Web, Mobile & Desktop GIS, and Geo Web Services Architecture. His contributions to Volunteered Geographic Information (VGI) and Open Source Geoportal & Metadata Portal have significantly enriched the geospatial community. As a trainer and researcher, Dr. Ahmad has authored over 50 publications, advancing the industry's knowledge base and fostering innovation in Geo-Tech, Data Governance, and Information Infrastructure, and Emerging Technologies.

His commitment to Research and Development (R&D) is evident in his role as a dedicated educator and mentor in the field.

***

Umadevi A. is an Assistant Professor in Department of Management Studies at AlphaCollege of Engineering, Chennai. She is MBA with Finance & HR specialisation with UGC Net qualification. She is pursuing Ph.D in the stream of Finance at AnnaUniversity. Has a 16 years of experience in handling Finance, HR and Operations Management classes. She too possess few years of corporate experience as Process executive with International exposure. She is a qualified trainer on "Entrepreneurship Development Programme" (Learn-Wise course) by EDII. She has completed IIC's training program and been certified as Innovation Ambassador. She is a Life Member of "Indian Society for Technical Education (ISTE)". Has wide contributions to profession through many research journals and hold patents on Supply Chain area and Information system field. She is currently exploring research on Artificial Intelligence in Management field. She has received fund for a research project on farming community from Tamilnadu State Council for Science and Technology under Student Project Scheme during 2024. To her Credit, she has published Indian patents titled, "Programming The Supply Chain Network for Customers with Uncertain Demand" and "Block Chain-Based Shoppingcart" and received Grant for Australian patent titled, "Block Chain Basedriceatm". She is been recognized as NPTEL discipline star during the year 2024 for her continuous learning of courses in the field of management.

| **Andi Asrifan**, S.Pd, M.Pd, a distinguished figure in the realm of education, particularly in English Language Education, has made significant contributions through his extensive research, teaching, and leadership roles. As the Head of the Institute for Cooperation and International Affairs at Universitas Muhammadiyah Sidenreng Rappang, Dr. Asrifan's academic journey is marked by a rich tapestry of achievements, including a Doctor of Education in English Language Education. His work spans various facets of education, language, and technology, reflecting the

diverse topics covered in his publications and research endeavors. These include, but are not limited to, the impact of the COVID-19 pandemic on educational practices, methodologies in English as a Foreign Language (EFL) classrooms, and the integration of technology in teaching and learning processes. Dr. Asrifan's commitment to advancing educational standards and practices is further evidenced by his active participation in international conferences, webinars, and workshops across countries like India, the Philippines, and Pakistan. These events, organized by various institutions and associations, underscore his role as a global educator and thought leader. His dedication to professional development is also highlighted through his involvement in numerous courses and certifications in personal branding, public speaking, and literacy teaching. Moreover, Dr. Asrifan's leadership extends beyond academia into organizational and educational development, where he has served in various capacities, including as an external examiner for Ph.D. dissertations and a reviewer for scientific journals. His accolades, memberships in professional organizations, and roles as an ambassador for international associations speak volumes of his influence and commitment to fostering educational excellence and sustainable development goals globally.

Catherene Julie Aarthy C is an Assistant Professor (Senior Grade) with over 23 years of experience in the education industry. Her expertise spans curriculum design, academic intervention, and integrated instruction. She has published 27 research articles in Scopus, WOS, ABDC, and other peer-reviewed journals, with a citation count of 140. Dr. Catherene holds a Ph.D. in Management from Hindustan Institute of Technology and Science, India, and a prestigious Data Science for Business Analytics (DSBA) certification from the McCombs School of Business, University of Texas at Austin. Her research interests include marketing management, business analytics, strategic management, Hospitality Management and Health care Management. She has guided several projects and presented her research works at national and international conferences.

Gayathri K, Associate Professor & Deputy Head of the Department, Department of Physics at Academy of Maritime Education and Training, Chennai.

K. Madusudanan is an Assistant Professor at the School of Computer Science and Applications, REVA University. With hands full years of teaching experience, he specializes in Semantic Web technologies. His academic interests include E-Learning Technology, Computer Networks, Software Engineering, and Data Mining. Prof. Madusudanan has guided UG and PG projects and published 4 research articles in refereed journals. His area of interest is in the field of Semantic Web and E-Learning technologies. He has attended several FDP's to enrich the knowledge.

Mustafa Kayyali, I am an ardent advocate for excellence in higher education, driven by a relentless pursuit of quality, recognition, and innovation. My journey in academia started with a Master's in Quality Management and Evaluation in Higher Education from Universitat Oberta de Catalunya, followed by a Ph.D. in Quality Management from Azteca University. These academic pursuits have laid a strong foundation for my expertise in Accreditation, Quality Assurance, and Higher Education Rankings. As an entrepreneur, researcher, translator, and publisher, I am deeply involved in various facets of the academic world. My diverse interests encompass Management, Translation, Interpretation, and Academic consulting, contributing to a well-rounded understanding of the industry. Throughout my career, I have made significant contributions to academic literature, with more than 20 published papers and 7 book chapters to my name. Additionally, I take pride in having translated 5 books, bridging language gaps, and promoting knowledge exchange on a global scale. I am committed to fostering positive change in higher education and contributing to its continuous improvement.

Maemuna Muhayyang, M.Pd. is a distinguished academic and lecturer at Universitas Negeri Makassar, where she holds the position of Lektor Kepala (Associate Professor). She was born in Ma'rang on July 5, 1974, and has built a solid educational foundation with degrees in English education, educational theory, and communication culture from reputable institutions in Indonesia. Over the years, she has developed expertise in teaching courses such as Phonology, Bilingualism, Educational Psychology, and Research in English Language Teaching (ELT). Her research spans various aspects of language learning, including enhancing vocabulary skills in students through innovative methods and exploring the effectiveness of corrective feedback in English writing instruction. She has actively contributed to community development programs by providing training for teachers in interpersonal communication and academic writing. Dr. Muhayyang has published numerous articles in both national and international journals, focusing on blended learning, students' perceptions of weekly quizzes, and teachers' professional competencies in English language education. Her work also extends to presenting at several international conferences, where she has discussed issues like the role of English as a foreign language (EFL) teachers in classroom management and factors influencing student learning. In addition to her academic articles, Dr. Muhayyang has authored books, including a collection of hybrid learning poems and a guidebook on educational research fundamentals. Her dedication to advancing English education in Indonesia is reflected in her extensive research, publications, and community engagement efforts.

R. Swadhi, Research Scholar, Department of Physics, Academy of Maritime Education and Training, Chennai, India Specialized in Nano Bio materials. Served as Assistant Professor in Nirmala College, Coimbatore, Lecturers & Exam coordinator in DMI-St.Eugene University Zambia and Additional Examination Coordinator, Saraswathi Institute of Medical Sciences, Hapur published 15 articles in peer reviewed journals and edited book chapters.

S. Vasantha, Ph.D., is a distinguished academic with 30 years of teaching experience. A Professor at Saveetha Engineering College, she has published over 133 scopus indexed articles, authored 10 books, and guided 25 Ph.D. scholars. Her expertise spans Finance, supply chain management, microfinance, and technology-enabled education.

I**J. Arockia Venice**, B.Sc., M.Sc., Ph.D., working as Assistant Director and Associate Professor, Institute of Virtual and Distance Learning (IVDL), DMI-St. Eugene University, Lusaka, Zambia. Served as Registrar from January 2013 to May 2022 and Head of the department & Asst. Lecturer in Dept. Of ICT from Feb 2008 – Dec 2011 DMI, St.Eugene University, Lusaka, Zambia, Africa and Asst. Registrar DMI-St.John the

Baptist University, Mangochi, Malawi, Africa from Jan 2012 – Dec 2012. Specialized in Data Science and DBMS.

Like Raskova Octaberliana, M.Ed, stands out as a distinguished educational figure, particularly in English language teaching. With an impressive educational background that includes a Master's degree from Monash University, Australia, and a Doctorate from the State University of Malang, Indonesia, she brings a wealth of knowledge and expertise to her profession. Prof. Like Raskova Octaberliana is recognized for her academic achievements and dynamic involvement in various capacities, such as a speaker, trainer, and keynote speaker at national and international platforms. Her contributions extend to numerous conferences, workshops, and seminars, where she shares her insights on English language teaching, education, and motivation training. Her professional journey is marked by a strong foundation in English linguistics, literature, and language teaching methodologies, complemented by her publications in several esteemed journals. Prof. Like Raskova Octaberliana's dedication to the field is further evidenced by her active participation in international conferences and research projects and her commitment to teaching English. As a member of various professional organizations, she has enriched her experience by working across different educational institutions, fostering an environment of learning and growth. Moreover, Prof. Like Raskova Octaberliana's expertise is not limited to language teaching; she is also highly skilled in public speaking, human resource development, and personality character building. Her motivational training sessions are particularly noteworthy, as she has earned numerous awards and scholarships. This recognition is a testament to her impactful contributions to education and her ability to inspire and cultivate the minds of learners and educators alike. Prof. Dr. Like Raskova Octaberliana, M.Ed, embodies the essence of a dedicated educator and mentor whose work continues to influence English language teaching and beyond.

Sadaruddin was born in Bone on June 15, 1980. He is a dedicated lecturer in the Early Childhood Education Teacher Training Program at the Faculty of Teacher Training and Education, Universitas Islam Makassar. He also serves as a tutor at the Open University (UPBJJT) and as an adjunct lecturer at Universitas Negeri Makassar and Universitas

Islam Negeri Alauddin Makassar. Sadaruddin holds a Bachelor's degree in Automotive Engineering Education from Universitas Negeri Makassar, a Master's degree in Early Childhood Education Administration from the same university, and a Doctorate in Educational Sciences. His professional experience includes roles such as Head of Administration at the Regional Distribution Center of the Ministry of Trade and Industry, Business Development Manager at Kospermindo, and local consultant for various international projects. He has actively contributed to the academic community as an assessor for the National Accreditation Board for Early Childhood and Non-Formal Education, and as a member of the editorial boards for several journals. His research focuses on early childhood education, and he has published numerous articles and presented at national and international conferences. Sadaruddin's dedication to education and his extensive experience in teaching, research, and administration highlight his commitment to advancing the field of early childhood education.

| **SyamsuardiSaodi** was born in Bulu, Lappariaja District, on February 10, 1983. He is the second child of H. Saodi Nuntung and Hj. Haneria Haddaning. He began his elementary education at State Elementary School 146 Bengo and continued to SLTP Negeri 2 Lappariaja and SMA Negeri 1 Lappariaja. He earned his bachelor's degree from the State University of Makassar in Automotive Engineering Education in 2000 and completed his master's degree in Language Studies with a concentration in Early Childhood Education at the same university in 2006. Dr. Syamsuardi completed his Ph.D. in Educational Sciences at the State University of Makassar in 2021. Dr. Syamsuardi is a permanent lecturer in the Early Childhood Teacher Education Study Program at the Faculty of Education, State University of Makassar. He has held various significant positions, including Head of the Early Childhood Teacher Education Study Program (2014-2018), Coordinator of the Center for Cooperation and Innovation Development in Education (2021-2022), and Head of the Curriculum and Entrepreneurship Module Center at the Institute for Innovation and Entrepreneurship Development (LIPK) from 2021 to 2025.

C.V. Suresh Babu is a pioneer in content development. A true entrepreneur, he founded Anniyappa Publications, a company that is highly active in publishing books related to Computer Science and

Management. Dr. C.V. Suresh Babu has also ventured into SB Institute, a center for knowledge transfer. He holds a Ph.D. in Engineering Education from the National Institute of Technical Teachers Training & Research in Chennai, along with seven master's degrees in various disciplines such as Engineering, Computer Applications, Management, Commerce, Economics, Psychology, Law, and Education. Additionally, he has UGC-NET/SET qualifications in the fields of Computer Science, Management, Commerce, and Education. Currently, Dr. C.V. Suresh Babu is a Professor in the Department of Information Technology at the School of Computing Science, Hindustan Institute of Technology and Science (Hindustan University) in Padur, Chennai, Tamil Nadu, India.

Shaleen Jain is an Associate Professor in the Department of Surgery at Saraswati Institute of Medical Sciences. He brings valuable clinical and academic experience to his role, focusing on imparting surgical knowledge and skills to undergraduate and postgraduate students. Dr. Jain previously served as a Junior Resident Doctor at Muzaffarnagar Medical College & Hospital, where he gained hands-on experience in various surgical procedures and patient care. His dedication to medical education and clinical excellence ensures quality learning and healthcare delivery. He is committed to advancing surgical practices and mentoring the next generation of healthcare professionals.

V. Selvalakshmi is an academician, educator, researcher, and mentor currently serving Professor Saveetha School of Management, Chennai. With more than two decades of rich experience, her experience and interest likes in the fields of research, incubation, entrepreneurship and have published more than 30 research papers and 5 books. I have served as one of the Expert Committee member for course development at NAHEP – IPD, Dapoli.

R. Vettriselvan, an Associate Professor, AMET University, specialised in HRM and Marketing. He is acting as Mentor, Saraswathi Institute of Medical Sciences, Hapur. He served as Review Board member, National Council for Higher Education, Malawi, Head of the Department, School of Commerce and Management Studies, St. Eugene University, Zambia, and Director, Research and Publication, St. John the Baptist University,

Malawi. He has published 25 books and 95 articles in peer reviewed journals and edited book chapters. Under his guidance two have completed and five are pursuing their PhD.

Index

A

B

C

D

E

G

M

N

P

R

S

W

X

www.ingramcontent.com/pod-product-compliance
Ingram Content Group UK Ltd.
Pitfield, Milton Keynes, MK11 3LW, UK
UKHW050946290926
15470UKWH00005B/1660

9 798369 383827